Trespassers?

Trespassers?

ASIAN AMERICANS AND THE BATTLE FOR SUBURBIA

Willow S. Lung-Amam

UNIVERSITY OF CALIFORNIA PRESS

University of California Press, one of the most distinguished university presses in the United States, enriches lives around the world by advancing scholarship in the humanities, social sciences, and natural sciences. Its activities are supported by the UC Press Foundation and by philanthropic contributions from individuals and institutions. For more information, visit www.ucpress.edu.

University of California Press
Oakland, California

Library of Congress Cataloging-in-Publication Data

Names: Lung-Amam, Willow S., author.
Title: Trespassers? : Asian Americans and the battle for suburbia / Willow S. Lung-Amam.
Description: Oakland, California : University of California Press, [2017] | Includes bibliographical references and index.
Identifiers: LCCN 2016050509 (print) | LCCN 2016052202 (ebook) | ISBN 9780520293892 (cloth : alk. paper) | ISBN 9780520293908 (pbk. : alk. paper) | ISBN 9780520967229 (ebook)
Subjects: LCSH: Asian Americans—California—Santa Clara Valley (Santa Clara County) | Suburbs—California—Santa Clara Valley (Santa Clara County)
Classification: LCC E184.A75 L86 2017 (print) | LCC E184.A75 (ebook) | DDC 305.895/073079473—dc23
LC record available at https://lccn.loc.gov/2016050509

25   24   23   22   21   20   19   18   17   16
10   9   8   7   6   5   4   3   2   1

For Mom

CONTENTS

ACKNOWLEDGMENTS

Writing can sometimes be a lonely process, but completing a book is not. It takes the time, effort, and resources of many people. My deepest regards go out to the many colleagues, mentors, funders, students, editors, friends, family members, and firm believers who have supported this project from the beginning. This book has been a long time in the making, and I have benefited in countless ways from their support and encouragement.

I am grateful for my closest readers and advisers. Randy Hester taught me what it means to be an activist-scholar and to measure my work by its impact on the world. Margaret Crawford first introduced me to the suburbs as an interesting place of study and has remained a steadfast enthusiast of great ideas and always pushed me to think bigger. Louise Mozingo grounded me in both the worlds of theory and practice, taught me to never hold my tongue, and always made time for me, even in the midst of completing two books of her own. Paul Groth taught me how to read and interpret ordinary landscapes and be a meticulous writer and scholar. Mai Nguyen kept close eyes on me and never failed to remind me about the grace and grit required to break down barriers. There is no one who put more wind in my sails during the final stages of this project than Carol Stack. A gifted writer and compassionate soul, Carol saw things in these pages and in me that I did not know or trust were there. I called on her for big things and small but mostly to hear her perpetually cheery voice and glimpses into the life of a true public intellectual.

This book has traveled with me across the country and through several institutions. To colleagues and friends at the University of California at Berkeley, the University of North Carolina at Chapel Hill, and the University of Maryland at College Park who have read drafts, given me feedback, and supported my scholarship in so many other ways—thank you. I could not have been luckier to find such remarkable mentors so early on in my career. I am especially indebted to my longtime colleague and friend Shenglin Elijah Chang, who has always taught me to work hard and enjoy the journey that is our life's work. Becky Nicolaides, Andrew Wiese, and John Archer, whose books all sat beside me and were copiously referenced, also provided me heavy doses of support and feedback along the way. Katrin Anacker, Tom Campanella, Wendy Cheng, David Freund, Bruce Haynes, Jeffrey Lowe, Marie Howland, Jim Cohen, Carol McKibben, Christopher Neidt, Herbert Ruffin, Alex Schafran, and Abel Valenzuela, you too have influenced this book in ways that you may not fully realize but are deeply appreciated.

I have been especially thankful to be a part of scholarly groups that have critically shaped how I think and write about issues of social justice. A special thanks goes to the Institute for the Study of Societal Issues at Berkeley, which provided not only financial support but also an intellectual home for a lonely social change scholar. Thanks especially to Christine, David, and Deborah for caring about the whole me, for your insightful and close reads, and for being among my best critics and cheerleaders. At the University of North Carolina, this role was taken up by my cohort of Carolina Postdoctoral Research Fellows. And at the University of Maryland, I have found a comfortable intellectual home in many places but most especially among the scholars and mentors I have connected with through their ADVANCE programs. Thanks especially to KerryAnn, Stephen, and Carol for never giving up or giving in. To my writing buddies both far and near—Andrew, Marisa, and Tonya—thank you for being there, do or die, and thanks to Kanisha for all the sweet potato fries and small victories that we have shared together along the way.

I have presented portions of this work at countless conferences, symposia, and invited talks. A hearty thanks is due to the Urban History Association and the Society of American City and Regional Planning Historians, whose conferences have been among my favorite places to present my work and, as I often tell my students, provide some of the best graduate student mentorship and writing support that I have found.

My thanks also go to funders at the University of California at Berkeley (the University of California Dissertation Year Fellowship, the Dean's Normative Time Fellowship, the Eugene Cota Robles Fellowship, the Department of Landscape Architecture and Environmental Planning, and the University of California child care system) that eased both the time and financial burdens of writing; the University of North Carolina's Carolina Postdoctoral Research Fellowship and Department of City and Regional

Planning; and the University of Maryland's School of Architecture, Planning, and Preservation, which has never wavered in its support of my scholarship.

To the staff and editors at the University of California Press. Naomi, you are everything that I wanted and did not know that I needed for a first book—a steady guide and a stanch ally. And to the many anonymous reviewers of the book and previous versions of chapters published elsewhere, your exhaustive feedback has been generous beyond measure.

Thanks go to the many departmental staff members and graduate students who have tirelessly and graciously given their time to this project and responded to more than their fair share of frantic e-mails and last-minute requests. I also thank my students, who inspire me every day in the classroom, asking all the right "wrong" questions that take me to task and push my thinking.

I am grateful for all the people in Fremont who opened their homes, businesses, hearts, and minds to this project and spoke frankly and reflectively about their experiences in ways that I never expected.

My gratitude also goes to my friends in the many places that I call home, some of whom have read and commented on my work but perhaps more important interrupted me for study breaks, a glass of wine, or a warm cup of tea. They celebrated all of my milestones along the way and reminded me that writing a book takes a lot more than willpower.

My family both near and far cheered me on from day one often without the faintest idea of what I was writing about unfailingly maintained that whatever it was, it was going to be brilliant simply because it was mine. The stories that my father told inspired my interest and connection in Fremont, and his simple truths about life and work kept me resolute during the hardest of times. My mother never forgot to tell me how proud she was and always helped me to keep things in perspective with stories about her latest gardening adventure and culinary experiments. She was a fighter in every way who taught me the unbending courage that it takes to speak your truth. This book is written in her memory.

No one deserves more thanks than my husband, who suffered none of my doubts yet quietly listened as I recounted my own misgivings. He forced me to write in "plain English" and not sweat the small things. His calm and confidence made my writing better and bolder. This book took a tremendous amount of time and resources, and he shouldered the load without a question or complaint. I also thank Ashay and Temani, who never let me forget why I do what I do, for interrupting at all the right times, for their patience with my impatience, and for their endless curiosity that continues to inspire my own.

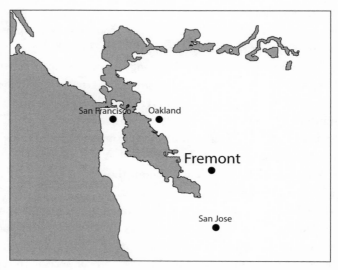

MAP 1. Fremont is located in the San Francisco Bay Area. It is widely considered a Silicon Valley suburb because of the large number of high tech companies and residents employed in high tech industries that have located there. Image by author.

Introduction

LANDSCAPES OF DIFFERENCE

What happens to a dream deferred?
  Does it dry up
  like a raisin in the sun?
  Or fester like a sore—
  And then run?
  Does it stink like rotten meat?
  Or crust and sugar over—
  like a syrupy sweet?

Maybe it just sags
  like a heavy load.

Or does it explode?

                     LANGSTON HUGHES, 1951

IT IS MIDDAY IN FREMONT, California, one of the many suburbs sandwiched along Interstate 880 in the 40-mile stretch between Oakland and San Jose. From the highway, Fremont appears no different than many other communities that line the eastern edge of Silicon Valley. Like San Leandro, Hayward, Union City, and Milpitas, the suburb sprawls over a vast terrain punctuated by strip malls, tract homes, office parks, and an endless sea of parking. But if one takes Exit 22 at Alvarado Boulevard and meanders through the neighborhoods, a different scene emerges.

Just off of Fremont's main artery stands the Islamic Society of the East Bay, a newly renovated mosque and school with gold and royal blue cupolas adorning traditional Islamic architecture. Less than a mile south 99 Ranch, the nation's largest Asian American supermarket chain, anchors Northgate

FIGURE I. Elders regularly gather beside Fremont's Lake Elizabeth in the early morning to practice tai chi and other martial arts. A regular visitor claimed that the lake's positive feng shui was a major reason for its popularity. Photo by author.

Shopping Center alongside an array of bakeries, banks, beauty salons, tea shops, and other mom-and-pop stores selling familiar products from many regions in Asia. Farther south, Sikh elders and multiethnic teens gather at Fremont Hub, a large shopping mall marking the heart of the city. Similar scenes can be found a few blocks away at Gateway Plaza, where Naz8 Cinema, the self-proclaimed first "multicultural entertainment megaplex in North America," shows Bollywood films on eight screens daily.[1]

From the Central District, it is a straight shot along Paseo Padre Boulevard to Central Park, where Chinese American elders crowd the banks of Lake Elizabeth in the early morning to practice fan dancing, tai chi, and other martial arts (Figure I).

Nearby in the historic neighborhood of Irvington, ethnic enterprises, an Indian wedding hall, and various Chinese and Korean Christian churches have revitalized aging storefronts and strip malls. Across from the local elementary school, cars spill out of Vedic Dharma Samaj, a Hindu temple carved from the remains of an old Methodist church.

In the background, cows graze the steep sides of the canyon that overlooks the bucolic Niles neighborhood, the once well-known backdrop of Charlie

FIGURE 2. Gurdwara Sahib, one of the largest and most influential Sikh temples in the world, was founded in Fremont in 1978. It serves as a symbol of the suburb's rise as a major gateway for new immigrants from all over the world, especially Asia. Photo by author.

Chaplin silent films. Today the scene includes the Gurdwara Sahib, said to be one of the most influential Sikh temples outside of India with over 9,000 members, as well as the Wat Buddhanusorn, a popular Thai Buddhist temple and monastery (Figure 2).[2]

Mirroring the Wat Buddhanusorn across Quarry Lake, the Purple Lotus Temple and Dharma Institute is under construction on a sweeping five-and-a-half-acre campus, soon to be marked by eight-foot prayer stupas and a perimeter wall decorated with the names of Buddha, Buddhist mantras, and auspicious signs to welcome its visitors.

Abutting Irvington is the plush hillside community of Mission San Jose, where feng shui and Vishnu principles have been used to reorient and redesign high-end houses and even entire subdivisions. Ornate iron fencing, grand fountains, columns, ornamental gardens, and Buddha and Krishna statues adorn the lawns of the neighborhood's many well-to-do homes.

Chinese and Indian American elders push strollers along its twisted streets and gather at local parks to exercise, gamble, or simply pass the time while attending to their grandchildren.

.   .   .

Fremont may seem to be an anomaly in an otherwise staid and predictable suburban American landscape. Images of *Ozzie and Harriet* suburbs populated by White middle-class residents, postwar tract homes packed on postage-stamp lots, and sterile shopping malls dominate the scholarly literature, popular media, and public perceptions of suburbia to this day. These images remain part of the dominant American narrative about who and what are suburban.

The reality, however, is much more diverse and complex than these stereotypes suggest. Over the past several decades while many urban downtowns have experienced a resurgence of energetic White millennials and affluent seniors, the suburbs of the largest U.S. metropolitan areas have quietly emerged as home to the majority of their racial and ethnic minority, immigrant, and poor residents.[3] For the past several decades, predominantly non-White and diverse suburbs have exploded, experiencing far faster population gains than central cities and majority White suburbs.[4]

The suburbs have, in fact, never really been the placid, homogeneous spaces that have so captivated the American imaginary. A growing body of scholarship shows that diversity has long defined the culture, landscape, and inhabitants of suburbia. Combating popular stereotypes and scholarly literature that tend to paint a uniform portrait of suburbia and exclude the contributions of non-White and non-middle-class groups, a host of cultural and historic studies attest to the diversity that has always comprised suburbia.[5] In the past several decades, scholarship on the suburban poor, new immigrants, and racial minorities, among others, has shown that social diversity has become more the suburban rule than the exception.[6]

How has the suburban landscape been reshaped by its changing demographic profile? How have these "other" suburbanites made home and built community among suburbia's parks, playgrounds, schools, shopping malls, office parks, and other everyday spaces? How have they remolded the landscape in ways that challenge stereotypes about suburbia's built environment and its residents? If mosques, Buddha lawn figurines, and Chinese fan dancers still appear out of place in suburbia, it is in part because scholarship has yet to sufficiently show how diverse suburban inhabitants have reshaped the look and feel of their chosen communities.

Trespassers? focuses on the processes of place making among Asian Americans, a group who have long existed on the suburban sidelines but are now at the center of its changing character. Asian Americans are the fastest growing of all racial minority groups in U.S. suburbs today. With 62% of all Asian Americans now residing in the suburbs of America's 100 largest metropolitan areas, they are nearly as suburban as White Americans.[7] This book examines the material products of Asian Americans' attempts to build suburban communities to fit their complex identities and aspirations and the politics of their place-making practices. It asks how Asian Americans made their home in Silicon Valley by reshaping and repurposing their given landscapes. What social and political conflicts have been fought over the physical changes that Asian American inspired? And how have these challenges affected the ways in which Asian Americans have been integrated into their communities and the benefits that suburbia once seemed to promise its residents?

Silicon Valley is a dynamic region that for nearly half a century has been at the cutting edge of technology as well as suburban change. In 2012, 18 of the 20 U.S. cities with the highest proportion of Asian American residents were suburbs. Among these, 7 were located in Silicon Valley—more than in any other region.[8] Since the 1970s, Asian Americans have tended to concentrate in what geographer Wei Li popularly termed "ethnoburbs"—multiethnic, largely immigrant suburbs such as Monterey Park in southern California's San Gabriel Valley.[9] Many early ethnoburbs emerged near traditional immigrant gateway cities such as New York and Los Angeles.[10] Increasingly, however, they can be found in places that have never before served as popular immigrant destinations: Research Triangle Park in North Carolina; Silicon Desert in Arizona; North Austin, Texas; Route 128 outside Boston; the Dulles and I-270 corridors outside Washington, D.C.; Route 1 in Middlesex County, New Jersey; and Silicon Valley.[11]

The common factor linking these regions is their thriving innovation economies. High-tech regions are diverse and fast-growing destinations for creative-class migrants and new immigrants, especially Asian Americans.[12] As Wei Li and Edward Park point out, these "techno-ethnoburbs" are distinct from other centers of suburban immigration, including "LA-type ethnoburbs" such as Monterey Park, in terms of the populations they attract, their geographies, and their economic base.[13] Through a deep investigation of Fremont, a suburb that is one of the most popular destinations for Asian Americans in Silicon Valley, this book highlights how high tech is shaping the dynamics of Asian American migration and community formation as well as the region's landscape and often heated politics of social and spatial change.

Most scholarship on Asian Americans in Silicon Valley and other high-tech areas is concerned with their role in fueling the economy as scientists, engineers, researchers, and entrepreneurs or as low-wage, low-skilled laborers.[14] *Trespassers?*, however, shows Asian Americans as community builders and place makers. It examines the ways in which Asian Americans in Fremont refashioned their surroundings to meet their desired lifestyles, paying particular attention to places through which they have marked and crafted their suburban sense of place.

Shut out of mainstream suburban social and economic life, Asian American migrants have long built "places of their own" in Silicon Valley suburbia.[15] Particularly in the last few decades as Asian Americans and particularly Chinese and Indian immigrants have become a more significant presence in the region and wealthier than previous generations, they have transformed the spatial landscape of the valley in distinct ways. They moved into high-end neighborhoods to give their children the best education they could afford, shifting the social and academic culture of schools toward a more competitive environment with a more rigorous focus on math and science. In ethnic shopping centers, they established vibrant community spaces that service many suburbanites' desires for Asian products and places that bridge the divide between their multiple geographies of home. And in several Silicon Valley neighborhoods, Asian Americans built homes that showcased their desires for modern spaces that fit their multigenerational households and aesthetic sensibilities.

These places mark a particular expression of the suburban American Dream for many Asian Americans in Silicon Valley. For generations of White Americans, white picket fences surrounding modest middle-class homes in racially homogeneous neighborhoods with good schools served as important markers of their success and prosperity. Among a generation of well-to-do, professional, and educated Asian Americans, however, their ability to move into racially diverse communities with high-performing schools, ethnic shopping centers, and large new homes are equally important markers of their achievements and desires.

Asian Americans' efforts to weave their dreams within the valley's existing spatial fabric have, however, been embattled. Over and over again, their efforts were met with skepticism, derision, and sometimes outright distain by established residents, city officials, planners, and others. Landscapes built by and for Asian Americans were portrayed as abnormal, undesirable, or simply "out of place."[16] The forms and uses of schools, shopping malls, and homes that Asian American newcomers inspired became markers of their seeming failure to integrate with and conform to their new environment. Further, these places, which I call *landscapes of difference,* became the focus of new city planning and design policies that tried to manage and mute their difference.

In the past, suburban inequality was marked and measured primarily by the exclusion of low-income residents, especially those of color, from suburbia's borders. Today, however, inequalities exist among communities with far more diverse demographics and subtle expressions of social privilege and power. It is not only exclusionary attitudes that inhibit the ability of new suburbanites to carve out their own meaningful spaces. The dominant norms and standards that govern the landscape and limit expressions of difference in suburbia also reinforce White Americans' privileged place within it. Together they comprise a normative framework in which certain spatial expressions are understood as acceptable, normal, or good, while others are not. Suburbia's creed upholds spatial homogeneity, conformity, order, and stability as critical tenets of form. Though largely invisible, this framework has powerfully shaped suburban policy making and planning for decades, and its results are visible everywhere. Reinforced by local land-use policy, such ideas buttress the power of older suburbanites, principally the White middle class, to serve as the standard-bearers.

This book counters claims that boast of the postindustrial economy as color-blind and high-tech centers as postracial meritocracies. It also combats the proposition of Asian Americans as the so-called new Whites, whose high rates of homeownership, income levels, degree of educational attainment, and integration into White communities, particularly in the suburbs, suggest that they now enjoy the same privileges and benefits once reserved for White Americans.[17] It is true that by all traditional measures, Asian Americans in Silicon Valley have, as a group, made it to the middle class. They are among the region's most numerous and highly educated groups, have high incomes and high rates of homeownership, and are employed in large numbers in all ranks of high-tech employment. And yet, the landscapes they occupy, desire, and build are often read and regulated through the lens of racial and cultural difference. The constant challenges to their places of everyday life illustrate that not only class exclusion but also White cultural hegemony continue to push minorities to the suburban margins.

Importantly, Asian Americans in Silicon Valley have not been the passive recipients of such disregard. They have been highly vocal and politically active, commanding the attention of politicians, planners, and their neighbors. As Asian Americans cross the historically hardened boundaries of middle- and upper-class suburbs, they are no longer contesting exclusionary practices from the sidelines. They are fighting *within* suburbia for respect for the ways they use, occupy, and conceive of space and for a sense of place, belonging, and identity in their homes and communities. Their insurgent practices have claimed new spaces and challenged suburbia's prevailing wisdom.[18] They have drawn attention to Asian Americans' values and aspirations as place makers and to their unique sense of being suburban. In doing so, they underscore how suburban landscapes, which have been designed as spaces of exclusion, can serve as touchstones for debate over what it means to be part of a more global, diverse, and inclusive society. Moreover, they bring to light how planning and policy making can foster more equitable metropolitan landscapes that provide their diverse occupants with the opportunity to carve out their own American Dream.

. . .

Scholars have long understood that landscapes are not simply vessels of the many meanings, values, and ideas of their users but are also shaped by them. Spaces become places when their inhabitants invest their memories, labors, and dreams in them. In doing so, people craft an ethic of care and attachment to the places of their everyday lives. Repeated over time and across generations, place meanings sediment themselves, becoming the scripts through which places are read and recognized from the outside as well as from within.

These scripts change as new groups arrive with their own ideas and patterns of work, home, and play. Time and time again in American cities, the process has repeated itself for waves of new immigrants. As groups settle in a neighborhood, they make their mark. They start language schools and cultural institutions that help bridge the gap between their new and old homelands, launch small businesses to gain a foothold in the American economy, and establish community spaces where they can share their hardships and triumphs with others like themselves. In this way, urban landscapes accumulate rich layers, comprising a bricolage of people, ideas, and meanings. They become mosaics of their storied pasts that exert a constant force in shaping their futures—prisms that can be read from different vantage points to tell multiple stories.

These processes are not just at work in the inner city. They have transformed the landscapes of communities across the United States. In suburbia, scholars have documented the community garden practices of early African American suburbanites, the fences and soccer fields that mark the barrio suburbanism of predominantly Mexican American neighborhoods outside Los Angeles, the temples and language schools of suburban Sahibs in New Jersey's Middlesex County, and the garden apartments that served as social hotspots for seniors and young singles during the post-World War II period.[19] Though often overlooked, suburbia has long served as a reflection of the diverse lifestyles of its residents.

Inherit within processes of place making is a politics of landscape change. As new groups come in and lay their ideas upon the landscape, they subtly challenge or subvert those of former groups. Their news signs and symbols assert a kind of moral authority that is often viewed as a threat by established residents, be they White, Black, poor, or middle class. These tensions raise questions of entitlement and belonging: For whom is this place being built? Who belongs here, and who does not? These are questions not just about values but also about power. Who gets to decide who stays, who goes, and who feels welcome? Visible markers of neighborhood change are contested in part because of the invisible power they hold to assert a collective sense of belonging or, alternatively, marginality. Whether dog parks, bike lanes, and coffee shops in San Francisco or ethnic shopping centers, Buddhist temples, and Chinese schools in Fremont, landscapes of difference are often the focal points of conflict over neighborhood change.[20]

The urban landscape in which these battles are meted out is not an even playing field. Certain groups have more power than others to transform landscapes in accordance with their values and interests and shape the ways in which these landscapes are read and valued, socially as well as economically. Scholars have long understood that urban space sustains social inequities. Seminal works by Henri Lefebvre, Michel Foucault, and David Harvey provide a prism for understanding how systems of inequality are reproduced in and through the built environment of cities—our streets, sidewalks, and office buildings.[21] They show that the design, structure, and organization of urban places construct social identities and relationships of power, including those based on race and ethnicity.

Race is a social construction that requires the support of social, political, and economic institutions as well as spaces that mark social hierarchies and positionalities. As Michel Laguerre argues, "In order to have ethnic minorities, one must also have minoritized space."[22] Ghettos and barrios that were historically created by explicit policies of racial discrimination remain the subjects of uneven development and reinforce stereotypes about the incapacity or unwillingness of people of color to care for their communities and do what it takes to make it in America. In contrast, White neighborhoods, schools, and homes that have benefited from decades of discriminatory practices and policies are generally viewed as valued and valuable places that represent the fruits of White Americans' hard work and ability. The racialized American landscape is all around us. As geographer Richard Schein notes, "all American landscapes are racialized, and can and should be seen through the lens of race."[23]

For Asian Americans, the racialization of urban space was evident in the segregated Chinatowns, Japantowns, and Little Vietnams, whose borders were fiercely guarded by White vigilantes, urban planners, and city councils throughout much of the 19th and early 20th centuries. Yet these same places came to serve as evidence of Asian Americans' presumed inability to assimilate and their common depictions as "forever foreigners." These neighborhoods often lacked public and private investment in housing, commercial businesses, schools, infrastructure, and social services. Yet their widespread portrayals as seedy, dark havens of criminal activity came to reflect on Asian Americans as the source of contagion, blight, and vice.[24]

In the mid-20th century, the racialization of Asian American space was evident in the devaluation of many ethnic enclaves during the urban renewal era that allowed city governments and private developers to raze and redevelop them for profit and the benefit of White suburbanites. Today, the racialization of space remains robust in stories told about these neighborhoods that erase the hardships and inequalities that have gone into their making while upholding them as evidence of the virtues of hard work and the success of the American multicultural experiment. At the same time, economic development schemes court tourists to neighborhoods that aestheticize and exotify Asian American culture and market it for profit.[25] Discursively and materially, urban ethnic enclaves have helped to define Asianness in America.

The racialized landscape and its politics, however, does not respect city and suburban lines. Suburbia's form has long been used to construct ideas about Whiteness and reinforce White Americans' social and economic privilege and power.[26] Postwar suburban housing, neighborhoods, streets, and shopping centers idealized the White middle-class nuclear family. Its picturesque and pastoral landscapes were modeled on the estates of the European elite and sold by developers and "community builders" as a new, exclusive version of the American Dream.[27] Through practices such as racial steering, racially restrictive covenants, blockbusting, redlining, discriminatory Federal Housing Administration and Veterans Administration mortgage lending practices, and individual and collective acts of violence, this dream was denied to many lower-income residents, especially those of color.

As historians Becky Nicolaides and Andrew Wiese note, however, these spatial distinctions did not merely reify existing social hierarchies but also helped to shape ideas and understandings of them in ways that perpetuated them through time: "In building suburbia, Americans built inequality to last."[28] Contemporary suburban landscapes continue to naturalize ideas about who and what are rightly considered suburban. While all too often maintained by policies and practices such as common interest developments, gated communities, and exclusionary zoning that exclude poor and minority residents, suburban spaces often obscures the work that goes into maintaining their largely invisible though highly securitized borders as well as White Americans' privileged position within them.[29]

If the scholarship is clear that suburbia has served and continues to serve as a landscape that constructs Whiteness and helps White Americans maintain their dominant social and economic status, however, it is less clear how this dynamic is changing in the face of more diverse inhabitants. We have come to a largely unanticipated moment when the majority of minorities and immigrants now live *in* the suburbs of America's largest cities. Far more attention must be given to this side of the story. As several contemporary accounts of suburban minority and immigrant life have shown, neither discrimination against people of color nor the institutionalized barriers they face have been washed away by moving to the suburbs.[30] For Asian Americans, several notable works have documented their battles over issues of political representation, language accommodation, cultural celebrations, religious facilities, and others in suburbia.[31]

Trespassers? demonstrates that built landscapes and spatial uses that do not conform to the suburban trope often become points of negotiation for the terms of Asian American suburban inclusion. In this process, policy and planning prescriptions commonly reinforce dominant spatial norms and standards of suburban design and development. The spaces occupied primarily by Asian Americans frequently fall outside these norms, creating a sense of Asian

Americans as suburban trespassers—those who commit spatial acts that are not in accord with the dictates of the dominant rules. Governed by policies and processes that have long favored White Americans, suburbia's built environment continues to racialize Asian American space and produce subtle modes of social and spatial marginality, even among minorities of means.

Alternatively, in investigating the resistance and persistence of landscapes of difference amid the pressures to conform or adapt to hegemonic ideas of suburban acceptability, this book also demonstrates that attempts to govern or legislate the terms of Asian American inclusion within suburbia has been incomplete. These spaces obstruct rather than reify the suburban spatial order and Asian Americans presumed place within it. They beg questions about what it means to be included and how to promote a sense of multiracial and multiethnic belonging, justice, and equity in a landscape built upon exclusion and inequality.[32] This challenge requires looking at suburbia from the inside out. It demands an interrogation of the lived conditions and experiences of suburban newcomers and their struggles to build a sense of home and belonging. It also requires a recognition that simply living in suburbia or in diverse neighborhoods is not enough.[33] The power to shape the built environment as a reflection of their diverse identities and desires is a condition of suburban citizenship that Asian Americans and other marginalized groups have long been denied.

. . .

If every place has a story, so too does every book. Mine began not in Silicon Valley but instead in the hollows of West Virginia. My African American mother and Chinese immigrant father raised me deep in the Appalachian foothills. This strange pair of hippie homesteaders were social idealists tethered to a set of principles about racial equity, citizen activism, democratic decision making, and environmental stewardship.[34] Their vow to live principled, simplistic lifestyles led them and a few others to a small plot of land in my hometown, where they started a commune in the early 1970s. Like most, theirs did not last. Eventually the members dispersed into the backcountry of this rural region into which I was born.

As a product of this social experiment, my young life was governed by contradiction. I was raised to believe in social and racial equity, yet every day I felt the sting of discrimination and rural poverty around me. While I was taught to love and see my neighbors as equals, I was all too aware that many did not view me in the same light. My parents organized protests against the Ku Klux Klan, while some of our neighbors sat silently eyeing them with as much suspicion as the hooded shadows that paraded through my hometown.

Many of my summers were spent on the road with my father, who sold his handcrafted pottery at street fairs around the country. During these travels, I became fascinated by the possibilities of city life for fostering the kinds of communities that my parents had once imagined in which I might be raised—places not bound by color but held together by a commitment to diversity, democracy, and social justice. Here and there, I saw glimpses of the world my parents fought so hard for. In Chicago, New York, Ann Arbor, Minneapolis, and Cleveland, I was struck by how people of so many different colors and classes appeared to casually rub elbows on crowded urban streets. Eventually I also came to recognize the other side of this idyllic vision of city life—segregation, poverty, and the deep social inequalities that my parents had sought to escape.

These early experiences motivated my career as an urban planner and designer concerned with questions of urban social justice and inequality. As I learned about the forces that had shaped what Douglas Massey and Nancy Denton called "American Apartheid," I became convinced that in the right hands, urban policy, planning, and design could remake American cities into the vibrant, diverse, and hopeful places that I had once imagined them to be.[35]

My studies led me to explore many intentionally diverse communities such as those in Columbia, Maryland, and Shaker Heights, Ohio, that were largely a product of my parents' generation of progressive politics. But I found myself more concerned with the fundamental building blocks of cities—how the sidewalks, brick-and-mortar businesses, community centers, parks, and playgrounds supported diverse populations and improved people's life circumstances. During my doctoral studies at the University of California, Berkeley, I began to look for clues about how urban form could better support diversity by exploring communities in my own backyard.

Armed with maps of the San Francisco Bay Area's most ethnically diverse neighborhoods, I spent much of the summer of 2008 driving and walking through several low-income communities such as Pittsburg and Richmond as well as more middle-class communities such as Hercules, Vallejo, and Union City. To my surprise, my shoe-leather research brought me out of downtown Oakland and San Francisco into many low-density suburbs.

I was especially drawn to communities within Silicon Valley, where I sensed that there was something different happening. In contrast to the standard facades and manicured lawns I had seen in many suburbs, there I found custom-built homes, bustling ethnic businesses, and vibrant public spaces that appeared to be much richer expressions of difference. I wondered what had allowed these comparatively "messy" landscapes to emerge, how they supported the valley's diverse populations, and what they suggested about the ways that different groups were and were not sharing space and building community together.

In search of answers to my many questions, I began spending more time there—primarily in Fremont, the largest Silicon Valley suburb by land area and one of the region's most racially and ethnically diverse communities. On foot, by car, and lingering in many of Fremont's public and semipublic spaces, I started to "take the city apart."[36] I explored its many neighborhoods and learned by seeing signs of difference in the landscape and asking questions about the people and processes that produced them.[37] I sat down with business owners, residents, and city officials to hear their takes on the changing landscape I was witnessing firsthand. From old-timers, I heard what it was like to live through the valley's swift transformation from a spattering of small rural townships into a global gateway. Many of their stories carried a deep unease about the changing demographics of the region and its impact on places that had once seemed so familiar and stable. Some complained about their new neighbors' flashy oversized homes, Asian American parents pushing their kids too hard in schools, and the large number of new Asian-oriented shopping centers that were "taking over" the city. Asian Americans, especially recently arrived immigrants from China, Taiwan, and India, offered different perspectives. Their stories emphasized their struggles and successes in the valley. They spoke of the trials they underwent to establish themselves in the region and, with pride, at how far they had come. They showed off their large homes as signs of their success, boasted of their children's high grade point averages, and frequently noted how much easier their lives had become because of the growing number of Asian American-owned businesses in the region. In city council and planning commission meetings, I listened as heated debates over these issues went back and forth between long-term and new residents.

These conflicts led to me to consider the spaces at the center of these debates and their importance to Asian American newcomers. As I dug deeper, I began conducting in-depth interviews with the people most familiar with these spaces and the social conflicts that surrounded them. I spoke with students, parents, principals, teachers, and school board members; the mayor, council members, planning commission members, planners, and other city staff; mall developers, store owners, and shoppers; homeowners, architects, and designers—over 130 in all. I spent time observing the everyday life of these spaces—hanging out in ethnic shopping malls, quietly sitting in the back of high school classes, and wandering the streets of neighborhoods most affected by large home development. I tracked census figures and demographic and spatial data available from government offices; spent days engulfed in the archives of the city council, the school board, the planning department, and local libraries; and became an avid reader of local and regional news, both past and present.[38]

My research helped me to resolve my initial reluctance to write about Asian Americans in Silicon Valley from the perspective of some of the most economically privileged among them. I worried that focusing primarily on the stories of Chinese and Indian Americans, Fremont's largest Asian American groups, many of whom were highly educated, high-income professionals, would ignore the struggles of many who could not even afford entry into the valley's exclusive suburbs. Indeed, the class status of many of Fremont's Asian American residents has reinforced their efforts to carve out a place for themselves within this privileged suburb and many high-end neighborhoods within it. Further, their racialization as model minorities has led to their perceived exceptionalism compared with other groups that has further aided their integration and acceptance within White suburban communities.[39] Yet I also began to see that the desires of high-income professional Asian Americans to reshape their communities according to their own values were shared by many. Rich and poor, White and non-White, single parents, lesbians, gays, bisexuals, transgender people, teens, multigenerational households and other residents whose preferences do not conform to established suburban norms all struggle in various ways with a landscape that was simply not built with them in mind.[40]

.   .   .

Landscapes offer a way to tell stories about a place.[41] This book is organized around landscapes that recount Asian Americans' struggles to make their homes in Silicon Valley. Collectively, these places and their politics show a suburban region turned upside down by battles over growth and development during a period of rapid immigration and demographic change.

The book begins by tracing the forces that drove Asian Americans' multiple migrations to Silicon Valley. Chapter 1, "The New Gold Mountain," explores why the valley became such an important hub of racial and ethnic diversity, especially among recently arrived Asian immigrants in the latter half of the 20th century and the early 21st century. Beginning with a brief look back at the pathways forged by early Asian American pioneers, the chapter focuses on the sweeping changes that occurred in the region economically, spatially, and socially after World War II. This period was defined by the region's transformation from a largely rural economy to one driven by technological innovation and its simultaneous conversion from an agricultural landscape to one dominated by white-collar office parks and exclusive middle-class neighborhoods. After 1965, the valley's boom in high tech began to reshape the demographics of the region as successive waves of immigrants, particularly those from Asia, began arriving to fill both highly skilled and unskilled jobs in the region's burgeoning technology industries. The chapter shows how Asian Americans navigated their new terrain and put down roots in working- and middle-class neighborhoods. Some suburbs, such as Fremont, became particularly popular among middle-class Chinese and Indian Americans who made up the majority of the region's newcomers. Local factors such as good schools, new and relatively affordable homes, easy access to high-tech jobs, and an extant Asian American community contributed to Fremont's role as a popular meeting ground for Asian American migrants. The chapter underscores how this suburb's rapid growth and development were prefaced on the valley's booming innovation economy and Asian Americans' own suburban dreams.

The next three chapters focus on the ways in which Asian Americans reshaped the region's built form, social geography, and development politics. Chapter 2, "A Quality Education for Whom?," considers how migrants' educational priorities and practices reshaped Silicon Valley neighborhoods and schools. For many Asian American families, high-performing schools have been among the most important factors drawing them to particular communities around the region and to their imagined geography of "good" suburban neighborhoods. The academic culture and practices that Asian Americans introduced in Fremont schools, however, has been met with considerable resistance. A case study of the Mission San Jose neighborhood in Fremont shows that as large numbers of Asian American families moved into the community, primarily for access to its highly ranked schools, many established White families moved out. This pattern of so-called White flight was driven in part by tensions between Asian American and White students and parents over educational values, school culture, and academic competition. Although Asian Americans' new wealth bought them entrée into some of the region's best schools, their educational practices were widely criticized. Intense citywide battles erupted over school culture and curricula as parents and students asked whose values they represented and who they benefited most.

Chapter 3, "Mainstreaming the Asian Mall," investigates Asian American-oriented shopping centers that are an increasingly popular part of the Silicon Valley landscape. The chapter shows that these malls are central in the lives of Asian American suburbanites. For many, the malls serve their practical needs, support vital social networks, and foster their sense of place, community, and connection to the larger Asian diaspora. But these vibrant pseudopublic spaces are also deeply contested. In Fremont, many non-Asian American residents, policy makers, and planners have charged that these malls are socially exclusionary and questioned their deviance in form and norm from the conventions of suburban retail. The chapter shows how these debates have framed ethnic shopping malls as "problem spaces" that required greater regulation and scrutiny. Yet planners and city officials have also used their power to regulate and control these shopping centers to promote particular visions of multiculturalism that are more aligned with their projected image of a middle-class suburb.

Chapter 4, "That 'Monster House' Is My Home," examines controversies over the building of large homes, or what some derisively call "McMansions" or "monster homes," in established neighborhoods. Fremont's large home debates reveal the different norms and values for single-family suburban homes and neighborhoods held by many Asian American and White residents in Silicon Valley. The chapter shows that the planning processes, development standards, and design guidelines adopted to deal with these conflicts largely reflected the interests of established White residents while marginalizing those expressed by Asian Americans. The debate highlights how planning processes and seeming neutral regulations often employ dominant social and cultural norms about "good" and "appropriate" design that reinforce suburbia's established racial and class order.

Finally, Chapter 5, "Charting New Suburban Storylines," examines the lessons from this exploration of social and spatial change in Silicon Valley for suburban development, design, and community building. This case study challenges communities to examine the ways in which they are making space for minorities, immigrants, and other suburban newcomers. In an era characterized by global metropolitan diversity, the conditions that gave rise to development contests in Fremont are not unique. To welcome new suburban migrants, communities must wrestle with the standards and tools of regulation that govern their landscapes. They must shift their spatial norms from those that celebrate conformity, consensus, and stability to those that respect difference, contestation, and change. If the 21st-century migrant metropolis is to become more sustainable and more just, these principles must be central to efforts to regenerate and redesign suburbia.[42]

Suburbia is clearly not what it used to be. Scholars, residents, planners, and policy makers, however, have yet to develop shared vocabularies to describe what it is or is becoming. As Xavier de Sousa Briggs pointed out, suburbia offers an opportunity to think about old urban issues in new ways.[43] It is my hope that within these pages, readers will discover fresh ways of thinking about the challenges of inequality and social justice in the contemporary metropolis and new possibilities for improving our collective capacity to live at home together.

ONE

The New Gold Mountain

Dwelling is not primarily inhabiting but taking care of and creating that space within which something comes into its own and flourishes.... Dwelling is primarily saving, in the older sense of setting something free to become itself, what it essentially is.

MARTIN HEIDEGGER

THE CHANS MOVED TO SILICON VALLEY in the early 1980s when Dan, an engineer at Ford Aerospace in Detroit, received a job transfer to Palo Alto.[1] Dan and his wife Elaine had both emigrated from Taiwan in the 1960s and did their graduate work in the United States. Like most professional couples, they wanted the best home in the best neighborhood they could afford for their budding family. For them this was Mission San Jose, a neighborhood in the Fremont foothills with a mix of stately and modest single-family homes interspersed among vast stretches of rural farmland.

In their early days, the Chans were the only Asian American family they knew in Mission San Jose. While they never intended to be suburban pioneers, they also did not consider moving to denser urban neighborhoods in San Jose or San Francisco. They liked Mission San Jose's semirural appeal, accessibility to Dan's work, relatively affordable new homes, and up-and-coming schools. There they purchased a spacious three year-old home for $200,000—less than they would have paid for a row house in San Francisco or a smaller older home in Palo Alto. On a good day, Dan was able to get to his office in about 30 minutes. More important for them, Mission San Jose's schools, where their son would enroll in three years, were well regarded and getting better.

Soon after the Chans got settled, Mission San Jose and the larger region changed in ways that they had not anticipated. One by one their neighbors sold their homes to professional Chinese American and Indian American families. Residential development and home prices boomed. Dan and Elaine's success in their professions and the housing market allowed them to trade their first home for a much larger newer house in a more esteemed section of the neighborhood. By the late 2000s, their home value had increased nearly fivefold. And by the time their son graduated from Mission San Jose High School, it was a majority Asian American school in a majority Asian American neighborhood and was considered to be among the most competitive schools in the state.

These changes convinced Dan and Elaine that Silicon Valley was *the* place for educated middle-class Taiwanese American families like themselves. While back in the 1980s they questioned whether they had made the right move, 20 years later they could not imagine living anywhere else. "I don't know where we'd go," Dan told me. The Chans loved their home overlooking the San Francisco Bay—"great feng shui," Dan noted. Though over the years the neighborhood had lost some of its rural charm, it was still nothing like the crowded cities where they had grown up in Taiwan. Besides, Fremont's popularity among other Asian Americans was what allowed their most cherished amenities to flourish. Dan and Elaine now had a Chinese-language newspaper delivered to their front door, watched all the same television stations they had in Taiwan, ate out regularly in nearby Chinese restaurants, and shopped primarily at Asian supermarkets right down the street. Dan even retained his love of badminton, playing three times a week at the Fremont Community Center. The Chans had come to feel close to their culture and homeland in the valley. "We have all the conveniences we want and don't have to speak English," Dan explained, noting that Fremont's new-found amenities saved them from the regular trips they used to make to Oakland's Chinatown—a drive they had not made in over a decade.

The Chans' love for their Silicon Valley lifestyle was not rooted in nostalgia for their lives in Taiwan but rather in their belief that the region offered the best of both Asian and American cultures. Dan observed, with some pride, that Fremont was "not like Monterey Park," the suburb of Los Angeles that Timothy Fong dubbed "America's first suburban Chinatown."[2] Dan complained that "People tried to make [Monterey Park] exactly like Taiwan." Instead, he appreciated the small-town feel of Fremont's neighborhoods and the highly educated population they drew from all over the world. The Chans enjoyed the high-quality lifestyle that their privileged class status afforded them and, equally so, the diversity of faces and places that had become the norm in their well-to-do community.

Dan was not alone. Over the last half of the 20th century, Asian Americans emerged among Silicon Valley's largest and fastest-growing groups, largely consisting of well-educated, high-income, professional immigrants from Taiwan, China, and India. These newcomers were part of a population boom that changed many of the region's cauliflower fields, orange groves, and predominately White middle-class communities into Silicon Valley suburbs with Asian American majorities. Like the Chans, these newcomers not only settled on the land; they embedded themselves in it. They raised their families, built new businesses, got hired and fired, met lifelong friends, made their fortunes, and saw some of it decline during the dot-com bust and the Great Recession.

What drew the Chans and so many other middle-class Asian Americans to Silicon Valley and to suburbs such as Fremont in the latter half of the 20th century? And how did these suburban migrants establish a sense of place and community on unfamiliar turf? This chapter traces four decades of unprecedented growth, development, and demographic change in the valley, underscoring how these forces helped to shape Asian Americans' evolving suburban dreams.

Indeed, Asian Americans' pursuit of the suburban dream, replete with its material pleasures and personal freedoms, and their perception of Silicon Valley as a productive place in which to pursue it have been just as central to shaping the demographics of the region as larger structural forces. The valley's booming technology industry has often been described as a "New Gold Rush."[3] For many Asian Americans, the region's plentiful economic opportunities loosened the epicenter of their vision of the abundant riches of California's "Gold Mountain" from its roots in San Francisco. This shift refashioned the traditional narrative of immigrant success from one centered on small business entrepreneurship and tight kinship networks in relatively homogenous urban ethnic neighborhoods to one that relied on highly skilled workers and strong business ties within diverse suburban communities.

This version of the American Dream drew upon a prototype adopted by many middle-class Whites after World War II but was distinct.[4] It enmeshed the material accoutrements of modern suburban life with the premium that many Asian Americans placed on maintaining their ethnic communities, global ties, and everyday cultural practices. As Dan reflected, it was one that mixed the comforts and conveniences of suburban American life with the robust traditions of social and community life in Asia. As Dan also noted, this dream was not merely a suburban version of Chinatown; it was that of a more cosmopolitan community filled with cultured, educated, and professional people from all corners of the globe.

Asian Americans' paths to and within Silicon Valley were not paved—they were forged on often inhospitable grounds. Against tough odds, generation upon generation struggled to realize their own aspirations and those of the pioneers who had built the routes that they then followed. Each put another crack in suburbia's wall of intolerance, making it a more welcoming place for others like them. Their efforts reaffirmed their legitimacy and rights as suburbanites. Yet the terms of their inclusion have long remained open to question. Despite their increasingly robust populations in many valley communities, Asian Americans' ability to significantly reshape the landscape in accordance with their dreams has been limited.

Asian Americans' struggles to build their lives and livelihoods in Silicon Valley complicate the singular lens through which the region is often read. Despite nearly a half century of unrivaled immigration and demographic change, the valley is still largely referenced as a breeding ground for invention and entrepreneurship—home to America's creative class and the birthplace of the digital revolution.[5] Some scholars have given attention to Asian Americans' contributions to the valley's economy and culture of innovation, but they are all too often left out of the story.[6] Moreover, in a place so often measured by the number of startups and venture capitalists, attention to the diverse social and cultural life that Asian Americans have brought to Silicon Valley and the sometimes sobering realities behind their portrait of success have frequently gone unnoticed.

ON THE SUBURBAN SIDELINES (1945–1964)

Asian Americans have deep roots in Silicon Valley, laying claim to the land as early as the mid-1850s. But their claims were consistently challenged by White Californians who disputed Asian Americans' legal rights as citizens, property holders, and, later, suburbanites. Though sometimes skirting the law and social custom to take up residence in the valley's countryside and later its growing suburbs, the challenges of living on the social margins kept Asian Americans from enjoying the full benefits of their residence, largely reserved for Whites.

Prior to the 1970s, Silicon Valley was an agricultural region better known as the "Valley of the Heart's Delight." Sometimes called the "Prune Capital of the World," the region was a global headquarters for agricultural production in the early 20th century. Vast fields of apricots, cherries, almonds, peaches, pears, oranges, lemons, apples, cauliflower, grapes, and avocados covered the landscape as far as the eye could see, interrupted only by rolling foothills and San Francisco Bay. By the 1920s, Santa Clara County was the nation's leading exporter of dried and canned fruit.[7] In the 1930s the economy turned more to poultry, flowers, and nurseries, but the valley maintained its qualities as a rural region well into the 1970s.[8] Asian Americans were central to the region's agricultural industries. From the late 1800s, Chinese Americans, mostly from the seafaring province of Guangdong, toiled alongside many Japanese Americans to clear the chaparral for farmland and work in the canneries, packing sheds, and salt mines. Many were employed as laborers to build the San Jose–San Francisco Railway that connected to the transcontinental railroad and transported the valley's products across the country and around the world.

Prior to 1965, national quotas on Asian immigration, including the various exclusion laws passed between the 1880s and 1920s, prevented the establishment of any large Asian American settlements in Santa Clara Valley or elsewhere. The few Asians who were able to gain admission under the harsh immigration laws that favored European immigrants were largely men who could serve as low-skilled laborers and did not compete with White workers.[9] As late as 1960, Asian Americans, largely of Chinese, Japanese, and Filipino decent, constituted a mere 0.5% of the U.S. population and little more than 2% of that of Santa Clara County.[10]

Still, Asian Americans congregated in a few communities around the region. Most lived in San Jose's Chinatown and Japantown, which were the subject of repeated violence, arson, and displacement. Between the 1850s and 1930s, San Jose's Chinatown had to be rebuilt five times in different parts of the city.[11] Asian Americans also settled in a few communities beyond the San Jose border such as Alviso, which was home to various waves of new immigrants. These outlying communities, however, often lacked even the most basic municipal infrastructure systems such as streetlights and paved roads, which Alviso did not receive until the mid-1950s.[12] As the primary target of racial zoning and restrictive land tenure laws in the pre–World War II period, Asian Americans were generally limited to purchasing or renting homes within these areas. Those who did not comply with the formal and informal rules of segregation faced stiff legal penalties and sometimes lethal social consequences.[13] Given their legal status and the active threats to their bodies and pocketbooks, only a few settled among the various agricultural communities outside of San Jose.

One agricultural region that attracted a few early Asian American settlers was Washington Township. The township consisted of eight unincorporated communities in Alameda County just north of Santa Clara County—five of which would later come to form the City of Fremont. In the first half of the 1900s, Asian Americans in Washington Township largely worked as tenant farmers, seasonal laborers, and merchants, but few lived in the township permanently. Deed restrictions typically dictated that properties could not be sold to anyone who was not of the "Caucasian race." Further, alien land laws prevented nearly all Asian immigrants, who had been deemed ineligible for citizenship by federal naturalization policy, from owning land or holding long-term land leases in California until 1952.

Even still, by midcentury the township had a few prominent Japanese American landowning families. In California, such ownership was often made possible by a loophole in land tenure laws that allowed land to be held in the names of Nisei, or second-generation Japanese Americans who were eligible for American citizenship, rather than their Issei, or first-generation parents. In 1942 Japanese Americans families were forcibly detained in relocation centers, and many lost their land claims and returned to their former homes as tenant farmers and migrants laborers.[14] According to the *History of the Washington Township,* written by the local country club, which was clearly anxious about their presence, Japanese Americans in the township were never "numerous enough to warrant trouble."[15] A small number of families of Chinese, Filipino, Indian, and Hawaiian ancestry, most of whom came among different waves of agricultural workers, could also be found scattered throughout the township (Figure 3). As the central focus of White nativist fervor in prewar California, Asian Americans were, however, excluded from almost every facet of mainstream social and political life.[16]

The post–World War II period radically reshaped the character of Silicon Valley. As the primary gateway to the Pacific Rim, the nine counties that comprise the Bay Area boomed, swelling in population by about 500,000 people during the conflict.[17] Like many western Sunbelt regions, Santa Clara Valley was a popular site for postwar growth.[18] Core Bay Area cities such as San Francisco, Oakland, Alameda, and Berkeley, which before the war contained up to four-fifths of the region's population, lost their favored status to expanding suburbs.[19] Leaving behind increasingly overcrowded, dilapidated inner-city housing, many young middle-class families moved into suburban homes and neighborhoods being built on the South Bay's former agricultural

FIGURE 3. This class picture from the Irvington Grammar School's eighth-grade class of 1939 shows Asian Americans' long roots in Fremont. Six students and one adult pictured here have Japanese last names, and the student in the upper right corner is listed as "unknown." Image published in Hammond (2003).

empire. In San Jose, the population increased more than sixfold in only three decades—from fewer than 70,000 in 1940 to nearly 450,000 in 1970—as the city annexed surrounding farms to make room for new neighborhoods of single-family homes. While the Bay Area doubled in size between 1930 and 1960 to over 2.6 million residents, the percentage of residents living in core Bay Area cities shrunk to less than half.[20]

Postwar suburbanization, however, did little to relieve Silicon Valley's entrenched patterns of racial segregation. If anything, it deepened them. While Federal Housing Administration and Veterans Administration loans drove an unprecedented suburban building boom that accommodated returning White veterans and provided new homeownership options for many White working- and middle-class families, such loans were systematically denied to neighborhoods of color, particularly those in the inner city with older housing stock such as San Francisco's Chinatown. For many White Americans, suburbanization represented a class shift up that, according to anthropologist Rachel Heiman, "sealed their whiteness" and their identity with the middle-class American Dream. In the postwar period, this dream came to include good schools, nice homes, quiet neighborhoods, and the absence of lower-class and non-White residents.[21]

New transportation technologies and federally underwritten infrastructure investments encouraged South Bay suburbanization, while federal policy favoring slum clearance and the dispersion of "blighted" poor and minority communities razed inner-city housing in neighborhoods whose residents had few options in suburbia. In the 1940s San Francisco's Japantown was part of the urban renewal plans for the Western Addition, which became one of the largest slum-clearance projects in the nation. By the end of the 1960s, over 8,000 residents and 6,000 housing units in Japantown had been displaced. Replaced by large-scale commercial buildings and upscale residential condominiums, few residents or affordable housing units returned to the neighborhood.[22]

Discriminatory lending and real estate practices such as racial steering, blockbusting, and redlining as well as individual and collective acts of discrimination and violence often denied Asian Americans and other racial minorities access to suburban housing and a growing number of suburban jobs. Racially restrictive covenants, which were applied with increasing frequency in the immediate postwar period, were ruled unconstitutional in 1948 in *Shelley v. Kraemer,* yet many remained on home deeds. Moreover, homeowners who were intent on avoiding integration continued practices promoting de facto segregation well into the 1970s.[23] While exclusionary measures were in place before the war, postwar suburbanization crystalized America's racial order across metropolitan spaces as never before.[24]

Fremont followed a pattern of postwar racial and class segregation similar to that of many other South Bay suburbs. These battles often began at the time of municipal incorporation. As Robert Self has shown, incorporation proved to be among the most effective means of exclusion that many South Bay municipalities had at their disposal. As both industry and their working-class employees expanded out of cities such as Oakland and San Francisco, suburban municipalities incorporated to control growth and adopt standards for development that secured their borders against poor and minority encroachment.[25]

Leaders of the incorporation movement in Washington Township clearly understood issues of race and class integration to be at stake. By the mid-1950s several cities north and south of the township had incorporated, and residents were feeling the pressures of growth, including potential annexation from fast-growing neighboring municipalities. Supporters of incorporation trumpeted the value of local control over the character of growth, taxes, and their "way of life."[26] A 1952 editorial titled "Halt Toadstool Growth" exemplified the tone of the debates: "This Township wants its master plan [from the County Planning Commission] and wants it in a hurry—before shacks over-run our industrial land, before factories are jammed against our homes."[27] The Citizens' Committee, which favored incorporation, suggested that it would allow the township to solve "the troublesome 'fringe' problem which vexes so many communities."[28] The "urban-rural fringe problem," as California agricultural economist Stephen Smith explained during the period, was clearly about the desire of suburbanites to protect their property values against decline, including that brought about by race and class integration. Yet the problem was often posed as issues related to public health, welfare, amenity values, and, in Washington Township, maintaining their "way of life."[29] While praising growth liberalism that would allow the township to capitalize off of impending development, many officials and residents emphasized strong local control over the character of that growth, in part to restrict the influx of lower-class minority residents and other "undesirables."

In 1956, five of the eight unincorporated towns coalesced to form the City of Fremont—the third-largest city by land area in California at the time. While the new city was geographically large, its population was small and largely White. It had only about 22,000 residents and, according to the 1960 census, less than a 2% non-White population. With incorporation, the city took control of its land use and the power to shape new development. Officials inscribed their vision of the city as a middle-class suburb by zoning many of its neighborhoods for large lots of about two to four and a half families per acre. Seeking to boost its tax base, the city also zoned about 5,400 acres of land in its southern border for light industry. For its active planning efforts, Fremont received national recognition with an award from the American Institute of Planners in 1962.

Jack Stevenson, the first mayor, argued that Fremont was to be an antidote to the problems of city life. "Fremont stirs the imagination of those who fled the city to seek a better life beyond. It must excite those who look upon the tangled problems of the nation's older cities and wish they could start again," he proclaimed.[30] With the Second Great Migration of African Americans from the rural South to western cities such as San Francisco well under way, the "tangled problems" that many White suburbanites fled included the increasing interracial mix of urban neighborhoods.

Though a few Asian Americans were able to bypass Fremont's exclusive planning regime and various other discriminatory housing practices during the city's early years, their experiences were far different than the experiences of their White neighbors. Paula Jones and Sam Phillips, both middle-class Whites raised in Fremont in the 1960s, described the city as an idyllic place to grow up. Paula likened her experience to "growing up in a Garden of Eden." She recalled that most of her childhood in Mission San Jose was spent playing outside and climbing fruit trees. "It was a bucolic environment for a child," she explained. Likewise Sam, who grew up just down the road in Irvington, recalled that it had the feeling of a small agricultural community where a curious kid on a bike could roam free, as he did. But Asian Americans lived in the shadows of Silicon Valley. Their experiences were marked by daily social and psychological indignities and a clear sense that they were "alien neighbors" in their own communities.[31] Despite their hardships, pioneers such as the Nikitas, Hondas, and Fudennas paved important pathways for the next waves of Asian American suburbanites who would forever change the face of the valley.

CIVIL RIGHTS SUBURBANIZATION (1965–1980)

As in much of the rest of the country, Silicon Valley suburbia was the site of sometimes violent resistance to integration during the civil rights era.[32] To a far lesser degree than African Americans, but no less important, Asian Americans faced fierce opposition when purchasing homes and otherwise settling in suburbia. But the same period marked Asian Americans' first widespread success in pushing out of the urban center. As they broke through many historic dividing lines, communities such as Fremont became the front lines of debate over Asian Americans' new claims to their rights as suburbanites.

Like other minorities, Asian Americans' suburban struggle was born out of harsh inner-city conditions. In the 1960s when many South Bay suburbs were busy planning for new growth, San Francisco and Oakland were in the midst of an urban crisis. Dollars directed to housing and industrial development on the urban fringe took jobs, residents, and taxes away from central cities. Between the 1950s and 1970s, federal and local policies gutted many inner-city neighborhoods to make way for shopping malls, office towers, highways, and other downtown urban renewal schemes.[33] In Los Angeles and San Francisco, processes of Latino and "Asian removal" were as much at issue as "Negro removal" in many redevelopment projects.[34] Much of the housing replacement promised under the 1954 Housing Act never materialized, while racially segregated high-rise public housing projects became more prominent

FIGURE 4. The General Motors Company relocated from Oakland to Fremont, bringing with it many working- and middle-class families. This picture shows the plant after its opening in 1963 surrounded by miles of agricultural land. Image courtesy of Arnold del Carlo, photographer, Sourisseau Academy for State and Local History, San Jose State University.

fixtures within increasingly poor, racially segregated neighborhoods. New transportation technologies and federal support for highway construction that eased the downtown commute for suburbanites displaced residents and disrupted life in many urban communities. The Nimitz Freeway that brought rapid development to Fremont cut directly through West Oakland, leaving the once thriving African American mecca in ruins while also displacing many residents of nearby Chinatown.[35]

Economic restructuring and deindustrialization further hastened the outward migration of middle-class residents and jobs and exacerbated the conditions of the growing "urban underclass."[36] Industries once located in Oakland and San Francisco moved to the suburbs or headed overseas. General Motors (GM), for instance, moved its main West Coast production facility from Oakland to Fremont in the early 1960s (Figure 4).

By 1964, the plant employed more than 4,100 people and was the city's largest employer, laying the foundation for Fremont's early reputation as a blue-collar industrial suburb.[37] The racially integrated United Automobile Workers (UAW) union promised new employment opportunities for minorities in the city, but GM's initial policy of prioritizing local residents for new positions limited the effectiveness of the UAW's policies.[38]

The decline of central-city neighborhoods, their stark contrast to the suburbs, and various race riots in Oakland, Los Angeles, and elsewhere were important impetuses for civil rights reforms, including the Civil Rights Housing Act of 1964 and the Fair Housing Act of 1968, which prohibited discrimination by race in the administration of both public and private housing.[39] Anticipating these changes, California passed its own fair housing act in 1963 with similar provisions.[40] Further, in an important precedent-setting decision, in 1975 the New Jersey Supreme Court ruled in *Southern Burlington County NAACP v. Mount Laurel Township* (commonly known as *Mount Laurel I*) that exclusionary zoning was unconstitutional.

Judiciary rulings and legislation, however, were slow to impact conditions on the ground. In the absence of racially restrictive covenants, common interest developments put in place homeowners' associations and covenants, codes, and restrictions, requiring the maintenance of certain standards of home and neighborhood development and design. In high-end developments such as the many being built in Fremont during the period, such practices translated race-based forms of exclusion into more sophisticated class-based mechanisms.[41] In some of Fremont's earliest subdivisions such as Mission Ranch and Glenmoor Gardens, these tools helped maintain their exclusivity as largely upper-middle-class White neighborhoods well into the 1990s.

Suburban communities also banded together to enforce de facto segregation, forming neighborhood block groups and associations that provided vehicles for organized resistance. Real estate agents steered minorities away from certain neighborhoods, homeowners refused to sell their properties to non-Whites, and violence continued as an active threat to minorities seeking to move into many suburbs. In 1968 Tom Parks, who is African American, was looking to move out of his apartment in Oakland. He and his wife began by looking at over 100 apartments in Hayward and were consistently told that they were unavailable or required extraordinary security deposits. They were also steered away from purchasing a house in Fremont, where only 398 African Americans lived in 1970. When they bought in Newark instead, Tom recalled paying about $4,000 more than his neighbors and being harassed by five local police officers who launched a community-wide petition to prevent their purchase.[42] "There is nothing much that has been done in the way of the force of law that has terribly altered the practices that are in place. They have just shifted in how they implement those practices," Tom explained to me more than four decades later. As Arnold Hirsh argued, violence and intimidation, especially toward African Americans, might have actually increased as the legal restrictions waned.[43] Certainly, the language of exclusion shifted during the period from a focus on race to property values. As historian David Freund has pointed out, doing so provided cover to White suburbanites to deny personal malice toward racial minorities and support exclusive practices in the name of "rational" market logic.[44]

Just as the rationales of suburban racial exclusion were changing, so too were perceptions about Asian Americans as suburban neighbors. In the 1930s and 1940s, the strategic alliance of the United States with China led many White Americans to consider the acceptance of Chinese Americans into their neighborhoods as part of their patriotic duty. In the face of rising demands for civil rights, stereotypes about Asian Americans as compliant and industrial laborers who were unlikely to challenge the social order added to their exceptionalism from the otherwise clear rules of postwar segregation, which affected African Americans most particularly.[45] Tom recalled, for instance, that in 1949 when his family moved to San Mateo, a suburban community less than 20 miles south of San Francisco, his parents purchased their home through a "straw buyer," a Chinese American friend who bought the home on the family's behalf because the owners refused to sell to African Americans.

By the 1970s, changing attitudes regarding Asian American exceptionalism vis-à-vis other racial minorities had begun to ease their passage into new suburbs. This was most robust in inner suburbs such as Daly City, which abuts San Francisco's southern border. There, the Asian American population went from only around 4,000 in 1970 to more than 22,000 by 1980—from less than 7% to nearly 29% of the city's population. But even with such dramatic changes taking shape in some suburban communities, historian Charlotte Brooks notes that Asian Americans' acceptance was conditional—oftentimes prefaced on the expectation that Asian Americans would quietly stay in their place and adopt the norms of their White middle-class neighbors.[46]

Further, many Asian Americans continued to meet resistance as they settled into new suburban communities. Indra Singh, an Indian American senior, recalled that when he and his wife moved to Fremont in 1972, children threw eggs at their home and toilet-papered their yard. A friend of his who was also Indian American had rocks thrown at their house and, as a result, moved out of Fremont.

By the late 1970s and early 1980s, however, many more Asian Americans were beginning to make their way from other inner-ring suburbs such as Daly City or neighborhoods in San Francisco such as the Richmond District, where they had gained a foothold in the postwar period. The main factors pulling Asian Americans to the South Bay were the increasing availability of jobs and access to quality, affordable homes. Joe and Judy Wu are both American-born Chinese mathematicians who in 1973 were living and working in Oakland. In 1974 Judy got a job in South San Jose, and the couple made their way down the Nimitz Freeway, completed less than two decades earlier to connect Oakland to San Jose. Midway along their route, they discovered Fremont. There they found that they were able to purchase a two-bedroom home and pay less on their mortgage than they were spending to rent in Oakland. Joe could keep his job, commuting by car or Bay Area Rapid Transit, which opened a new station in Fremont in 1972, connecting the city to San Francisco and Oakland.

Andrew Li, an immigrant from Taiwan, was selling real estate and developing new homes in the 1980s in the Northgate neighborhood, where Judy and Joe settled two years after moving to Fremont. Andrew reported that while the low cost of new homes and job accessibility were the main draws for Asian Americans moving to the city during the period, one could not discount the important role that pioneers such as the Wus also played:

> Chinese, Filipinos—they may have a townhome or house in Daly City. They got invited by their friends and they bought a home in Fremont. They would invite them over for Saturday afternoon barbecues. It would be 80 degrees. They enjoyed it tremendously. They would go back to Daly City where it would be 45 degrees on Saturday night.... Sunday morning, they would drive to Fremont again, looking for a house.... The house prices were comparable, and the weather was much better.

As Andrew noted, social networks drew many Asian Americans southward and to particular Silicon Valley communities. The easiest places to settle were often those with or in close proximity to extant minority populations. In Fremont, the long history of Chinese American, Japanese American, and Filipino American farmworkers increased its popularity among Asian American newcomers. Many came by word of mouth, following family members and friends to neighborhoods such as Northgate. David Li, whose

Chinese American roots in the Bay Area date back to the 1850s, recalled that one of the things that convinced his parents to move from Berkeley to Fremont in the mid-1960s was that his mother's cousin had recently relocated there.

Social relations were not the only factor that drove David's parents to Fremont. Like many other Asian Americans, they were attracted to the range of possibilities that suburbia seemed to promise its residents. They wanted better schools and larger homes in safe, less crowded neighborhoods and also wanted to escape the same "urban ills" as their White neighbors. This no doubt included the growing concentration of poor communities of color. David stressed his parents' desire for a quiet, semirural lifestyle. Shortly after he was born, his working-class parents purchased a four-bedroom home in Irvington that supported their growing family and a different sort of lifestyle than they had enjoyed in Berkeley. David explained:

> I think it was just different. Fremont was just starting out. It was already a city, but it was a spread out community. "Spread out" meaning in between the neighborhoods that had sprung up at the time, we had farms and cow pastures. It was a different kind of living. It was country living. We just wanted to get away from the inner city, so to speak, and get back to the country. . . . I think [my parents] wanted a fresh start. . . . They decided there may be a better future for us there. It was a growing community with a lot of possibility.

In Fremont, David moved into a new home on a new street, with a new high school nearby. In all its novelty, suburbia invoked an endless sense of possibility, especially for those who had long been denied its benefits.

Though many Asian Americans held high hopes for their new suburban lives, they all too often found themselves surrounded by a sea of circumspect White faces. In 1970 Fremont's population was 97% White, including about 10% of the population that categorized themselves as being of "Spanish origin." In Fremont, this likely included a large percentage of Portuguese farmers, who had worked the land for generations. Asian Americans were less than 2% of the population. By 1980 Asian Americans had made significant inroads, growing to about 9,600 people, or roughly 7% of the population. Still, Asian Americans were a distinct minority, and they felt it. Having entered elementary school in Fremont in the early 1970s, David recalled being 1 of only 2 Chinese American boys at his school. Though his family was "acculturated"—eating meat loaf and pizza for dinner most nights, "not rice bowls"—he grew up with the nagging feeling that he was different. While he did not recall any direct acts of racial discrimination, he felt his difference in simple, everyday activities such as looking at his class pictures year after year in which everyone but him was blond or brunette.

Whether driven by feelings of isolation or hostility, many early Asian American suburban pioneers looked for communities to which they could belong outside of their local neighborhoods. To establish a stronger sense of community and retain their cultural ties, several early ethnic and cultural associations developed in Fremont. The South Bay Chinese Club (SBCC) was founded in Fremont in 1965 to preserve Chinese culture and customs while also fostering and encouraging better understanding among Chinese Americans of their civic responsibilities and the "American way of life."[47] The SBCC was and continues to be largely a social club for American-born Chinese. The Organization of Chinese Americans (OCA) started its first California chapter in Fremont in 1974, drawing its members from across the South Bay and the East Bay. Inspired by groups such as the National Association for the Advancement of Colored People and the Japanese American Civics League, the OCA had a far more political agenda than the SBCC. The OCA was concerned with both the civil rights and political representation of Chinese Americans. Judy Wu was among the California chapter's founding members. Having grown up on the East Coast, where her parents were active in the organization, Judy was concerned with the lack of Asian American political representation in Fremont, a cause that she and her husband fought hard for. With their support, Yoshio Fujiwara became the first Asian American elected to the city council in 1978.

Religious institutions also became an important part of the emerging cultural and community fabric. In 1978, Gurdwara Sahib was founded in Fremont to serve the religious needs of the region's growing Sikh American population. By the mid-1980s, Fremont's diverse faith institutions had come to include Wat Buddhanusorm, a Thai Buddhist temple; Vedic Dharma Samaj, a Hindu temple; and a host of small mosques and Asian ethnic Christian churches scattered throughout the city.

Despite Asian Americans' efforts to develop a sense of community rooted in their common suburban experiences, many continued to rely on established urban centers for their daily necessities and social support. Fremont's Chinese American residents still regularly traveled 30 miles or more to Oakland's and San Francisco's Chinatowns on the weekends to do their grocery shopping, eat out, or get a haircut. Indian Americans would head to University Avenue in Berkeley, where clusters of retailers and restaurants could be found near the University of California campus. These neighbor-hoods were not just service centers; they also served as important social and cultural hubs that provided moments of relief and a meeting point for those who had left their communities behind when they moved to the South Bay suburbs. This generation of Asian American pioneers consisted of largely young families headed by U.S.-born householders who had struggled to afford entry into the suburbs and build the community and cultural infra-structure they needed to thrive. They were quickly joined by a generation of recently arrived Asian immigrants who were doing the same.

NEW IMMIGRANT GATEWAY (1970–1990)

By the 1970s the technology industry in Silicon Valley was blossoming, and so too was Asian immigration. New laws made way for fresh waves of émi-grés, while a growing number of high-tech companies ensured plentiful opportunities for their employment. As the valley's population grew, so too did its reputation as a place that was "good for immigrants." As they had done for generations, Asian immigrants imagined the Bay Area as a land of bountiful wealth and opportunity. But now their visions centered on the possibilities arising in South Bay, not in San Francisco. The New Gold Mountain was, in fact, not gold at all—it was silicon.

By the 1970s, Santa Clara Valley was fully engaged in its transformation from an economy based on agriculture to defense and aerospace contracting. Facilitated by alliances that began during the early Cold War period, Stanford University engineering professor and future provost Frederick E. Terman, the so-called "father of Silicon Valley," pioneered efforts to pair talented university researchers and engineers with the needs of emerging industries to create a "community of technical scholars."[48] Thriving off its unique culture of competition and collaboration, the region became a hub of innovation that gave birth to some of the most important technological milestones of the late 20th century. From microelectronics and the semicon-ductor to the personal computer, the region broke ground in technology that became the hallmark of a new information age.[49]

Early Silicon Valley companies clustered in exclusive suburbs and employed an almost all-White labor force, especially among white-collar engineers and managers.[50] The valley was a dream landscape for many early high-tech employees who were enticed not only by its well-paying jobs but also by the promise of orderly and manicured suburban neighborhoods and high-end office parks designed around the same principals.[51] In 1970, for instance, the elite suburb of Palo Alto just beyond the Stanford University campus was 93% White. The community also housed the Stanford Research Park, a 700-acre site that was home to many of Silicon Valley's most prominent companies, including Bell Labs, Varian Associates, Hewlett-Packard, General Electric, and Lockheed.

Silicon Valley's rise to global prominence also came at a time of massive immigration from many parts of the world, particularly Asia. Immigrants were pushed by ongoing political and social turmoil and harsh economic conditions abroad and were pulled by the valley's mild climate, extant Asian American populations, and wealth of new job opportunities. Following the passage of the historic 1965 Immigration and Naturalization Act, émigrés began arriving in record numbers. Commonly known as Hart-Celler, the act opened the floodgates of Asian immigration by lifting restrictive quotas from non-European countries and instituting new policies aimed at family reunification and attracting skilled labor.[52] The population of Latino and Asian immigrants in the United States expanded rapidly—far faster, in fact, than Congress had anticipated. "The bill will not flood our cities with immigrants," Senator Edward Kennedy assured his colleagues. "It will not upset the ethnic mix of our society."[53] Facing pressure from civil rights advocates but expecting little change, Congress passed a bill that has had one of the most significant effects on the numbers and diversity of immigrants ever since.

More educated and skilled than previous generations, post–Hart-Celler immigrants were far more likely to bypass central-city destinations to settle directly into suburbs, such as those in Santa Clara County.[54] Between 1970 and 1980 the population of Asian Americans in the county grew threefold, from around 30,000 to more than 100,000, making up just under 8% of the population. In the subsequent decade the population more than doubled to over 260,000, comprising nearly 18% of the county's population. Fremont saw similarly dramatic trends, with Asian Americans growing from fewer than 2,000 residents in 1970 to more than 33,000 in 1990, comprising about one-fifth of the city's population. During the same period, the city's immigrant population went from less than 5% to about 20% of the population (Table 1).

Santa Clara County's first major wave of Asian immigrants were a diverse lot but highly stratified by occupation, education, and skill level. The valley's

		1960	1970	1980	1990	2000	2010
Fremont	White*	98%	97%	85%	70%	48%	33%
	Asian	2%	2%	7%	19%	37%	51%
	Hispanic	12%	10%	14%	13%	14%	15%
	Black	0%	0%	3%	4%	3%	3%
	Other	0%	1%	5%	6%	12%	13%
	Foreign-born	5%	5%	10%	20%	37%	43%
	Median household income	—	—	$25,342	$51,231	$76,579	$87,385
Metro	White	90%	86%	76%	69%	58%	52%
	Asian	3%	5%	9%	15%	20%	24%
	Hispanic	—	8%	12%	15%	19%	24%
	Black	7%	8%	9%	9%	8%	3%
	Other	0%	1%	6%	7%	15%	17%
	Foreign-born	10%	10%	15%	20%	27%	32%
	Median household income	—	—	$20,607	$41,595	$62,024	$73,027

*ALL racial categories include Hispanic populations to facilitate comparison of data across time. The U.S. census did not account for non-Hispanic groups by race until 1990. Source: All data for 1960–2000 is based on U.S. decennial census and, for 2010, the American Community Survey five-year data.

TABLE I. Over the last half century, Fremont grew from a predominantly White middle-class suburb to a hub for highly educated high-income immigrants from around the world. The table compares Fremont's racial composition, foreign-born population, and median household income to the San Francisco-Oakland-San Jose Metropolitan Statistical Area between 1960 and 2010.

"barbell economy" tended to concentrate jobs at the top and at the bottom—clearly dividing the workforce between manual and mental laborers.[55] Chinese from Hong Kong and Taiwan as well as Indians, to a lesser extent, were those most likely to be employed in the higher-end positions, entering into the ranks as scientists and engineers. Many arrived under professional visas known as the third and sixth preference, which prioritized admissions for those with "exceptional abilities" and in occupations with short labor supply in the United States. They came seeking better jobs and educational opportunities than they had in their home countries and oftentimes greater political stability and freedoms. Filipinos fled far more dire circumstances, including the deteriorating economic and political conditions in the Philippines under the dictatorship of Ferdinand Marcos (1965–1986). Still, those who emigrated tended to be among the professional class and entered semiskilled professions that supported the valley's economy, such as nursing and medical technology.[56] They were later joined by a rush of political refugees from Indochina, particularly Vietnam, who arrived in several successive waves after the fall of Saigon in 1975 and throughout the 1990s.[57] Often lacking formal education, many Indochinese refugees took jobs in manufacturing or other service-sector occupations such as construction, landscaping, and dishwashing. While plentiful and requiring little English-language skills, these jobs were often temporary, offered few legal protections, and had hazardous working conditions and little opportunity for upward mobility.[58]

While many recent arrivals initially settled into various communities in and around San Jose, their geographies quickly became as divided as their occupations. Southeast Asian immigrants, including Vietnamese and Filipinos, tended to cluster in "South County," an area of Santa Clara County that stretched all the way south to Gilroy and whose core was in San Jose. Despite San Jose's attempt to attract high-tech companies, its inexpensive housing, land, infrastructure, labor, and taxes compared to other Silicon Valley cities was attractive to many computer component manufacturing firms and their blue-collar workers.[59] These included not only many Southeast Asian Americans but also Latinos and, to a lesser extent, African Americans.[60] By 1990, Vietnamese Americans and Filipino Americans made up nearly half of the 152,000 Asian Americans in the city of San Jose.[61]

With growing presences in high-tech professions, Chinese and Indian Americans, however, bucked these trends. Instead, their primary geographies tended toward the more exclusive "North County" suburbs. Like Fremont, these communities had built their prestige on restrictive zoning that historically prevented race and class intermixing. By the mid-1970s when Asian immigration had reached new heights, however, many of the North County suburbs closest to Stanford University had already closed their borders to residential growth. By adopting strict no- and slow-growth policies, these close-in communities effectively raised the cost of land and pushed new development farther out. By 1975, 84,000 people commuted daily to the core Silicon Valley suburbs of Sunnyvale, Palo Alto, Mountain View, and Santa Clara.[62] While shunning residential expansion and density, many of these same communities welcomed new high-tech firms. Municipal bonds supported infrastructural investments needed for white-collar office parks, while tough environmental regulations ensured that manufacturing firms would not set up shop.[63]

Fremont was one of the few North County suburbs to welcome new residential development. In fact, the city courted it. Progrowth elected officials wanted Fremont to join the ranks of its prosperous neighbors and encouraged property owners to make residential and industrial land available to help it do so. "The welcome mat is out," announced Mayor Gus Morrison in 1989. "If someone wants to build a quality project here, I mean a quality project, they'll never have a reason to be disappointed with Fremont."[64] Stressing the need for "quality" development that matched their middle-class aspirations, the city fast-tracked business permits, rezoned much of its industrial land to industrial research, made significant infrastructure investments, and provided generous tax incentives to high-tech companies.[65] In an effort to attract new Silicon Valley wealth, Fremont radically shifted its development policies—going from one of the state's most highly recognized planned-growth communities to one of its most progrowth communities in only three decades.

The city's efforts paid off. New Silicon Valley residents and companies saw clear advantages to locating in Fremont. It was strategically located directly across San Francisco Bay from Palo Alto and just north of San Jose. Further, its large quantity of undeveloped land allowed new homes and industrial land to be sold at about half the price as in core Silicon Valley towns.[66] High-tech businesses boomed in Fremont from the 1980s to the late 1990s. In the early 1980s the city became home to Apple®, which produced its first Macintosh computer there.[67] It also attracted other large high-tech firms such as NEXT and Everex computer manufacturing. By 1989 Fremont was the fastest-growing city in the region for new high-tech firms, with roughly 6,200 acres of its industrial land occupied, primarily by manufacturers of computer-related electronics.[68] Officials projected Fremont as "Silicon Valley North"—a moniker that reflected both its changing character and their hopes for the city's economic future.

Fremont's residential population was also booming. Between 1970 and 1990 while the populations of many core Silicon Valley communities hardly budged, Fremont's nearly doubled from just over 100,000 people to nearly 175,000. During one of Santa Clara County's most significant periods of growth, Fremont outpaced the county's population growth rate 3.6% to 2.0%. "We're a sleeping giant," declared Gus Morrison. "Fremont isn't that blue-collar town of old. That label just doesn't fit anymore."[69]

With its ample stock of new and affordable homes, good schools, and an increasingly sophisticated array of community and cultural amenities,

Fremont was especially popular among newly arrived Asian immigrants. As evidence of the city's popularity among Indian Americans, Indra Agarwal, an Indian immigrant who moved to Fremont in 1972, recalled becoming the 16th subscriber to *India West,* an Indo-American newspaper that started in Fremont in the early 1970s and now circulates throughout California. By the 1980s, the city had developed a reputation in many Asian immigrant circles as a good place to live. Like prior generations, these groups arrived by word of mouth to stay with friends, family members, or university classmates from overseas and eventually settled in the city.[70]

These newcomers started businesses together, networked among each other, moved into common neighborhoods, and began to build their own versions of the American Dream. When I asked Ishan Shah, a second-generation Indian American, why his family had relocated from Chicago to Fremont in the early 1990s, he spoke of both the importance of immigrant networks and what Fremont meant to families such as his. "We had heard that's where all the immigrants went," he explained. "It was a community of people driven by the same principles. [My parents] really connected with that. They felt that this was going to be a good place with people like us." While Ishan's father was trained as a computer engineer, he moved to Fremont to pursue his lifelong dream of starting his own business. In 2009, Ishan announced his bid for Fremont City Council. At the age of 17, he became the youngest declared candidate to ever run for public office in the United States. According to Ishan, it could only have happened in Fremont. For both he and his father, the city represented a land of opportunity and was key to their American Dream.[71]

S. Mitra Kalita argues that for many post-1965 Indian immigrants, the American Dream and the suburban dream have been deeply intertwined. "For many, homeownership in a place with a good school district and soccer leagues, strip malls and picket fences, signified the completion of the American Dream," she wrote.[72] According to Kalita, what most post-1965 Indian immigrants wanted from suburbia was similar to that of most other Americans.[73] But there were also important differences. The first waves of post-1965 Asian immigrants were looking for suburbs with, as Ishan said, "people like us." It was a generation who in large part had come to the United States for higher education. They were high-achieving, upwardly mobile, and more culturally "assimilated" than previous generations. They had saved up and sacrificed to purchase new homes in quiet suburban neighborhoods with good schools that were easily accessible to their jobs. But they also sought out places in proximity to their cultural touchstones: Asian grocery stores, restaurants, community institutions, places of worship, and other professional Asian Americans.

These amenities and their shared value among others of similar racial, ethnic, and class backgrounds gave Asian American suburbanites a sense of home, place, and security. These amenities were not just part of Asian American suburbanites' dreams; they served as critical supports in their pursuit of them. Asian Americans have long used their ethnic communities and resources not just as a refuge but also as a platform for social mobility.[74] The community and cultural infrastructure being built in places such as Fremont was, as much as the suburbs themselves, their launching pads.

Taking stock of just how much Fremont changed over two decades of rapid immigration was not so easy for those who lived through it. But for those just coming to the area, the contrast between it and other American suburbs was clear. When Irene Yang arrived in Fremont in the mid-1980s from New Jersey after emigrating from Taiwan, she could not believe what she found:

> I almost felt like I'd moved to another country. This [was] not the America that I was used to. When I [went] to the playgrounds, the people [spoke] in their different languages. The Indian moms would be together speaking in Punjabi or whatever, and the Chinese moms—the Taiwanese moms—would be speaking Taiwanese dialect to each other (the ones from back then, very few from mainland China). And then, very few already, very few Caucasian moms.

For many Asian immigrants, even those such as Irene who had lived in the United States for many years, moving to Fremont changed the way they perceived of the suburbs and their relationship to it. Entering a city that was fully entrenched in its transformation from a White working- and middle-class community to a global hub for skilled migrants from all over the world, Irene was faced with a kind of diversity that she had never seen before. Amid such diversity, she saw both new opportunities for connecting with those similar to herself but also new challenges of negotiating the separate spheres that were beginning to take shape among Asian Americans and between Asian Americans and Whites. Such experiences marked the new social realities faced by Asian American suburbanites of this generation as distinct from all those who had come before them.

By 1990, Silicon Valley was entering its boom years. A decade later the ride was over, and the region was dealing with the aftermath of the dot-com bust and ongoing effects of the Great Recession. But throughout this period of rapid economic expansion and contraction, the region was constantly being reshaped by its role as a popular immigrant gateway, especially for highly educated, geographically mobile immigrants from mainland China and India. Compared to previous generations who often left their homelands behind, these migrants remained closely tied to their friends, families, and even workplaces abroad. In only two decades, they turned many valley suburbs into cosmopolitan places that were more dynamic, globally connected, and ethnically diverse than ever before.

The year 1990 marked a critical turning point in the history of immigration policy for highly skilled immigrants. That year, Congress signed a new immigration and naturalization act focused on attracting skilled laborers. The act tripled annual immigrant quotas for professional employment-based visas from 54,000 to 140,000 and initiated the H-1B, a visa that permitted foreign nationals with "special skills" that were in demand among American companies to work in the United States for six years with the option of pursuing a green card.[75] The initial cap on new visas was set at 65,000 but continued to rise throughout the decade, reaching 195,000 by 2001.[76] Policy changes coincided with improved foreign relations with both India and China and booming economies in both countries that produced large numbers of highly trained engineers, researchers, and other information technology professionals.

While national and international forces propelled Asian immigration, high-tech companies played a significant role in facilitating their migration to Silicon Valley. During the dot-com boom (1995–2000), over 168,000 new jobs were created in Santa Clara County—more than had been produced in the previous 15 years of a thriving electronics industry.[77] Arguing that there were insufficient American-born employees to fill these positions, Silicon Valley companies pressed Congress to raise the cap on H-1B visas and allocate a larger portion of those visas to high-tech employers. Their lobbying efforts proved effective.[78] In the first few decades of the program, Silicon Valley companies ranked among the nation's top employers of visa holders, and computer-related occupations received the bulk of all H-1B visas.[79] In 1999, for example, 57% of all H-1B visas went to workers employed in information technology.[80]

As more visas were granted, Silicon Valley began to use them to aggressively recruit skilled foreign-born workers. Some placed ads in overseas trade journals and newspapers announcing the availability of jobs and employer-sponsored visas.[81] Indian and Chinese workers were the primary beneficiaries of these efforts. Between 1990 and 2010 Indian nationals, whose educational system shifted in the 1990s to train more highly educated engineers, dominated the ranks of recipients, receiving 46% of all visas.[82] During the same period, émigrés from China came in a far second, receiving only about 6% of H-1B visas.[83]

Asian immigrants profoundly transformed the face of high-tech work. Between 1990 and 2000, the percentage of foreign-born engineers in Santa Clara County rose from 33% to 53%. Among them, nearly 40% were of Asian descent.[84] Asian immigrants were not only hired by companies; they also launched new firms. Between 1995 and 2005, over half of all Silicon Valley companies had one or more immigrants as a key founder. Indian and Chinese immigrants founded nearly one-third of new high-tech firms during the period.[85] Thus, while many recognized that the integrated circuit (IC) fueled the valley's success, when locals referred to the region as "being built on ICs," they were oftentimes referencing the region's large number of Indian and Chinese immigrants, who were commonly described as the engines that drove the industry.[86]

Immigration slowed during the dot-com bust in 2000 and the subsequent Great Recession. During these challenging times, many migrants were forced to return to their home countries, including many H-1B workers who were unable to remain in the United States without an employer sponsor. Immigration was further restricted by Congress's 2003 downgrade on new H-1B visas from a cap of 195,000 to the original 65,000.[87] With thriving technology sectors abroad—in places such as Bangalore, India; Chengdu and Dalian, China; and Hsinchu, Taiwan—many immigrants were also lured back to their home countries for better employment opportunities.[88] But even as Asian immigration rates slowed, the Asian American population in the valley rose. Between 2000 and 2010, the Asian American population in Santa Clara County increased by 32% to around 565,000.

Though they predominantly came from mainland China and India, the diversity among Asian immigrants in the region was striking, including many South Koreans, Filipinos, Pakistanis, Vietnamese, and Malaysians as well as Chinese and Indians from many different parts of the world. As Lisa Lowe argued, the abolishing of national origin quotas and exclusions that began with the Immigration and Nationality Act of 1965 brought in many groups that widened the definition of "Asian American."[89] By 2009, Fremont's residents came from as many as 147 different countries and spoke over 150 different languages.[90] Irene Yang's neighborhood is exemplary of such diversity, as it took shape in some of Fremont's more well-to-do neighborhoods. Sitting in her custom-built house in the Mission San Jose hills, which she described as Frank Lloyd Wright–inspired with feng shui touches, Irene pointed out the diverse families who surrounded her. She counted one White family; two Indian families, one from India and the other from Pakistan; and six Chinese families, including those from Vietnam, Singapore, Hong Kong, Taiwan, and mainland China. Irene's family also reflected this diversity. She was born in Taiwan but grew up in Japan and married a second-generation Chinese American. Held together by their class status, this potpourri became the norm in Silicon Valley neighborhoods by the first decade of the 21st century.

Diverse as they were, these newcomers shared one important similarity. They were far more likely than previous generations to regularly travel across the Pacific Rim for work and family. A 2002 study found that approximately half of all Silicon Valley foreign-born professionals traveled to their native countries for business yearly, and 5% made the trip five times or more per year.[91] Among these, Taiwanese were the most likely nationality to return home on a regular or even permanent basis, followed by Indians and Chinese mainlanders.[92] For many of these families, life was lived on both sides of the Pacific. Aiwah Ong describes late 20th-century globalization as producing generations of elite "hypermobile cosmopolitans" whose sense of citizenship has been grounded in their economic ties as much as, or even more so, than ethnic or national allegiances.[93] Among this generation of Silicon Valley newcomers, many found themselves at home both in the American suburbs and abroad. Their bicultural identities and transnational landscapes reflected their transpacific lifestyles.[94] As Wei Li put it, these global sojourners were as comfortable crossing oceans and countries as Main Street, USA.[95]

The mobility of many Silicon Valley newcomers changed their pattern of sociability and community. It was increasingly common, Andrew Li noted, to find Taiwanese Americans who ran companies in which the manufacturing was done in China, their business headquarters were in Taiwan, and the family home was in Silicon Valley. Asian Americans' frequent border crossings fostered important social networks, business ties, and familial connections that expanded their sense of place and home.[96] At the same time, they also disrupted old social patterns. Comparing his friends' lives to previous generations of Taiwanese immigrants, Andrew explained that overseas travel had become such a regular part of their lifestyles that it was difficult to get people together, even for a weekend barbeque.

Among this class of global cosmopolitans, the North County suburbs served as important gateway communities, especially those that were already popular among the Asian American middle class such as Milpitas, Cupertino, and Fremont. Word of mouth and established connections reinforced these suburbs as popular immigrant destinations. This extended to Taiwan, India, and mainland China, where the zip codes of these suburbs were well known.[97] Ellie Cho, a second-generation Chinese American who was a young student at Mission San Jose High School in Fremont when we met, understood the importance of immigrant succession in affecting the decision of families such as hers to settle in Fremont. "Immigrants who are moving in America, they are thinking like, oh, where am I going to fit in?," she explained. "Where am I going to make a transition the easiest?" For her parents, she understood the answer to be clear: "In Fremont, [the] Bay Area, because there's so many Asians here already."

Not everyone came to Fremont with the intention of settling in an Asian American community, but many found the city's ethnic diversity and its now-established ethnic businesses and social institutions comfortable and convenient. This included Timothy Hu, an immigrant from Taiwan who had spent most of his life working in the American Midwest. He explained that during his three decades there, he always "felt like a minority." Upon retirement, he and his wife Doreen decided to move closer to their daughter and other family members who lived in the Bay Area. Having found a residential subdivision that was close to his daughter that Doreen liked and that had new homes (which both Timothy and Doreen wanted) and good feng shui, they settled in the Fremont hills. Quickly, their lifestyles began to change. As they were now located close to three major airports with direct flights to Asia, the Hus began making more frequent trips to mainland China, Hong Kong, and Taiwan, where they held important social and business connections. Within a 15-minute drive they could be at any one of four Asian shopping centers, where they frequently ate out at restaurants that Timothy claimed were far better than those in San Francisco's and Oakland's Chinatowns. Just down the road in Milpitas, his wife began frequenting a Chinese Buddhist temple that was located along the city's historic main street. Once a week, Timothy made a longer drive across the bay to Millbrae, a suburb south of San Francisco, where he joined a Chinese opera club. While they had not planned on it, the Hus stayed in Fremont because they discovered that it was "good for Asians." They had all the community and cultural amenities they desired. Just as important, living in a city where "everyone is a minority," Timothy noted, he no longer felt like one himself.

With plenty of room for new residential, commercial, and office development, Asian American newcomers shaped the character of Fremont far more than in most Silicon Valley suburbs. For its growth between 1990 and 2000, Robert Lang and Jennifer LeFurgy ranked Fremont fourth among the nation's "boomburbs," cities with populations over 100,000 that were growing rapidly.[98] In the same study, Fremont ranked as the nation's number one "cosmoburb" growing suburbs with particularly high numbers of foreign-born, highly educated residents, especially non-Hispanic Whites and Asian Americans.[99]

By 2010, Fremont was the largest Asian American–majority city in Silicon Valley and, in fact, the largest majority Asian American municipality in the continental United States.[100] Known to many as "Little Taipei" and "Little India," Fremont had become a popular meeting ground for successful young Asian Americans. Along with many other Silicon Valley suburbs, Fremont ranked among the wealthiest municipalities in the country, and among the city's residents, Asian Americans were some of the most prosperous. In 2014, the American Community Survey estimated the median income of Asian Americans in Fremont to be nearly $125,000, compared to around $100,000 for the city as a whole.[101] Asian American newcomers congregated in some of Fremont's most prestigious neighborhoods, including Avalon, the 275-home gated community in which Timothy and Doreen lived and where homes regularly sold for upwards of $2 million (Figure 5).[102]

Fremont had become popular not only among Asian Americans working in high tech but also for high-tech businesses, especially those run by Asian Americans. Between 1990 and 2000, around 1,200 high-tech firms set up shop in Fremont.[103] According to former mayor Bob Wasserman, before the tech crash in 2000, the city had more high-tech headquarters than San Francisco.[104] That same year, it was also reportedly the most popular city in the United States for Taiwanese high-tech companies, with over 100 firms with connections to Taiwan.[105] Like many before them, companies that were relocating or expanding their operations from overseas found advantage in Fremont's inexpensive industrial and warehouse space and strategic location within Silicon Valley. Increasingly, they were also attracted to the city's easy

FIGURE 5. Inside the Avalon, one of Fremont's gated communities, signs of Asian Americans' presence are readily apparent in many homes. Photo by author.

access to emerging Pacific Rim high-tech hubs and its growing population of highly skilled immigrants. To locate where the technology startups are the thickest, wrote Mark Hendricks, a writer for a blog run by American Express®, "Go west, young entrepreneur. When you reach Fremont, California, you're there." In 2012, the credit card giant reported that Fremont had more than 21 technology startups for every 100,000 people—a ratio that was nearly as much as the next three cities combined.[106]

By 2010, the transformation of Silicon Valley from a landscape of cauliflower fields and White working- and middle-class suburban communities to the hub of Asian American life in northern California was complete. Nearly a half century of immigration had transformed once-fledgling Asian American destinations into mature immigrant gateways (Maps 2 and 3).

Between 2000 and 2010, while Santa Clara County's Asian American population grew by 140,000 to over 565,000, San Francisco County added only 28,000 new Asian American residents, with a population totaling less than half that of Santa Clara. By 2010, Santa Clara County had also eclipsed San Francisco in its percentage of foreign-born residents, 37% to 36%. As historian Margaret O'Mara observed, the rise of Silicon Valley resulted in a

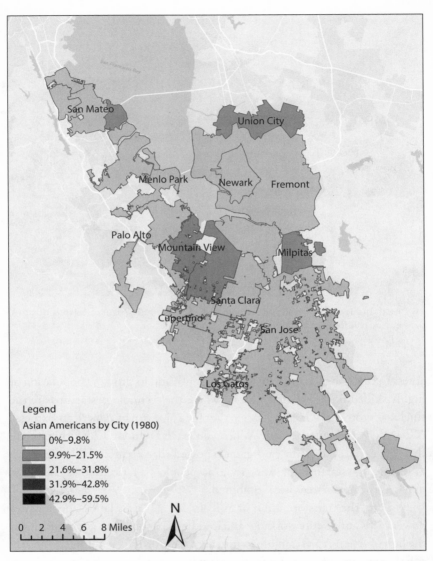

Legend

Asian Americans by City (1980)

- 0%–9.8%
- 9.9%–21.5%
- 21.6%–31.8%
- 31.9%–42.8%
- 42.9%–59.5%

0   2   4   6   8 Miles

N

MAP 2. In 1980, Asian Americans could be found in limited numbers throughout many Silicon Valley communities. Image by the author.

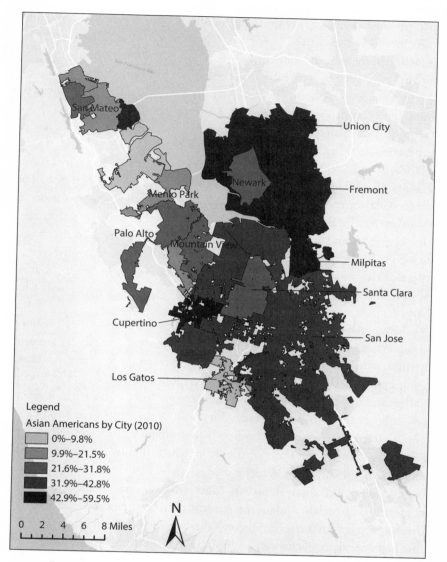

Legend

Asian Americans by City (2010)

- 0%–9.8%
- 9.9%–21.5%
- 21.6%–31.8%
- 31.9%–42.8%
- 42.9%–59.5%

0 2 4 6 8 Miles

N

MAP 3. By 2010, the Asian American population in Silicon Valley exploded. Chinese Americans and Indian Americans, who tend to be employed as scientists and engineers in the valley, made up the bulk of new migrants, particularly in the region's middle-class suburbs such as Fremont. Image by author.

pattern of residents moving from the "suburbs in which they live to the suburbs in which they work."[107] For a new generation of middle-class Asian Americans, the suburbs were the only America they knew or needed.

This new geography widened generational and ethnic divides among Asian Americans. Among Chinese Americans, while earlier generations of immigrants tended to concentrate in relatively poor urban enclaves, speak Cantonese, and hail from Hong Kong or China's Guangdong Province, latter generations tended to live in middle-class Silicon Valley suburbs, speak Mandarin and fluent English, and come from major urban centers in Taiwan and mainland China. These two groups coexist but with very little social or professional interaction.[108] Whereas Asian Americans' social isolation in suburbia once led them to find common cause with their urban counterparts, the geographic and social distance between generations increased the chasm to a gulf. While San Francisco and Oakland Chinatowns struggled to survive amid a long process of bleeding businesses and residents to the suburbs, Silicon Valley suburbs thrived as destinations for young professionals who had a far different sense of what it was to be Asian American.

The emergence of middle-class Silicon Valley suburbs such as Fremont also increasingly separated Asian Americans from African Americans and Latinos, who had not suburbanized at the same rates. When they did, these groups tended to live in more working-class suburbs farther from the Silicon Valley core. By 2010, African Americans comprised 3% and Latinos about 15% of Fremont's population. Asian Americans were learning to build community in more diverse neighborhoods than many had left behind in Bay Area urban centers and the countries from which they hailed, and certainly more so than the waves of White Americans who had moved to the suburbs before them. But their suburban communities were also more diverse ethnically than racially and more so racially than economically. The diversity that had come to characterize Silicon Valley softened the racial and class lines that had once defined cities and suburbs but, at the same time, also signaled the creation of more complex spatial and social geographies *within* suburbia.

. . .

The path to the New Gold Mountain, like the old, has been littered with stumbling blocks and stop signs. Prior to 1965, Asian Americans' struggles in Silicon Valley were defined primarily by their efforts to find permanence and avoid the threat of displacement. They toiled on the land, seeking through their labor to legitimate their claims to it. But they were constantly threatened by their tenuous legal status as citizens and property owners. For civil rights–era Asian Americans, hard-won battles settled many legal questions, but their status as suburbanites was still widely questioned. They lived in constant tension with neighbors who openly fought for communities that did not include them. Excluded from one suburban dream, Asian Americans began to carve out another.

It was not until the birth of high-tech industry in Santa Clara Valley that Asian Americans' claims to the region finally seemed settled. Among this generation, their challenge was to build homes and communities in suburbs that had not yet established a comfortable place for people like them. They did so at a time of great dynamism, when waves of immigrants with little resemblance to those who had come in previous decades were flooding into the region. More likely upwardly mobile, educated, and professional, these migrants brought their own American Dream with them. Together they started restaurants, travel companies, banks, real estate firms, language schools, ethnic newspapers, and cultural and religious institutions. This generation was no longer fighting *for* suburbia; they were building it anew.

Today, Asian Americans are moving into Silicon Valley suburbs in which they are in the majority and where the landscape is beginning to affirm their desired lifestyles. Chinese and Indian Americans now dominate the engineering and research sector of high-tech firms, and many have broken through the infamous "bamboo ceiling" to enter positions in management and launch their own firms.[109] Shopping malls, restaurants, and stores catering to the needs and desires of Asian Americans abound. Asian American students are in the majority at many of the region's top-performing schools. They now live in some of the valley's most exclusive neighborhoods and, in general, feel far less pressure than previous generations to shed their ethnic identities and customs during their move to the suburbs.[110]

Asian Americans' inclusion in suburban life, however, has never been on equal terms to that of White Americans, nor has it been complete.[111] As the remaining chapters make clear, despite their many advantages, Asian Americans are still fighting to make the valley their home and for broader recognition of their rights as suburbanites. Just as Japanese American tenant farmers once hoped to put down roots and leave their mark on the land upon which they worked and raised their families, so too are today's Silicon Valley migrants. Their challenge is to build communities that reflect their identities, broad geographic ties, mobile lifestyles, extended social and familial networks, and everyday social and cultural practices. They struggle with how to express their dreams in a suburban landscape precast for a different set of dreamers. Their battles are not fought on the streets or with neighbors openly hostile to their presence and instead are waged more quietly in city council meetings, with planning commissions, in development reviews hearings, in school board meetings, at parent-teacher conferences, and over the white picket fences of their well-manicured lawns.

Undoubtedly one of the arenas in which Asian Americans' pursuit of their suburban dreams have been the most rigorously pursued and hotly contested has been local schools. In the next chapter, I explore how the premium that Chinese Americans and Indian Americans have often placed on enrolling their children in high-performing schools has reshaped Silicon Valley neighborhoods, Fremont city politics, and the lives of Asian American youths. The chapter shows how the changing racial and ethnic composition of some of the region's most competitive schools has raised tough questions about what constitutes a quality education and equitable schools in Silicon Valley's diverse suburbs.

TWO

A Quality Education for Whom?

Education has always been at the center of suburban politics.

MICHAEL JONES-CORREA

NESTLED AMONG FREMONT'S southern foothills is Mission San Jose, a neighborhood that has long been known for the 18th-century Spanish mission, which marks the main intersection of its historic downtown.[1] More recently, the neighborhood has become internationally recognized for another landmark—Mission San Jose High School. Until the mid-1990s Mission High was a prototypical suburban American school, made up of a largely White middle-class student body. Today it is a premier destination for highly educated families from all over the world, especially Asia, and one of the highest-ranked schools in California (Figure 6).

Over the last few decades Asian Americans have transformed the face of many American public schools, especially those at the top. In 2010, California's five highest-ranking public schools all had majority Asian American student bodies.[2] The academic performance of Asian American students in schools across the United States has raised a host of scholarly debates about the factors that constrain and promote their educational achievement—the role of the model minority myth, culture, parenting, income, selective immigration, and other individual and structural factors.[3] But there are other important questions to ask about the forces behind these trends and their impacts.

In this chapter, I examine how schools figured into the aspirations that many Asian American families brought with them to Silicon Valley and the ways in which their desires and decisions about education reshaped the region's schools, neighborhoods, and development politics. By taking a close look at changes that have engulfed Mission San Jose High and its wider neighborhood over the past few decades, I argue that schools have been a major catalyst for the remapping of regional racial geographies and a critical battleground for Asian American suburban politics.

FIGURE 6. Mission San Jose High School has become an internationally renowned public high school, especially popular among Asian American families. Photo by author.

For many Asian American families, high-performing schools such as those in Mission San Jose were the dominant factor drawing them to relocate to Fremont from around Silicon Valley, the United States, and even abroad. Schools were key to many Asian Americans' visions of success in the United States and their newly adopted suburban communities. Many viewed education as their primary means of cementing their social and economic status and made highly strategic, calculated decisions to place their children in Mission San Jose schools, often at great personal and economic expense. Once there, Asian American parents worked hard to ensure that the schools met their expectations in terms of their academic culture, curriculum, and high academic standards. Like generations of White Americans before them, "good schools" were a key part of their suburban dream.

But many Asian American families in Fremont also held different ideas about what constituted good schools than those of their White neighbors. As well-educated, technically skilled professionals, many Asian Americans parents placed priority on a rigorous education, especially in math and the sciences, that would prepare their children to enter professions like their own. Whereas many established White families claimed to want less competitive schools that offered a more "well-rounded" and "balanced" education, Asian American families were widely associated with an increasing sense of academic competition, stress, and a culture that placed a premium on high grades and academic rigor. Tensions over these differences catalyzed racial and ethnic tensions within the Mission San Jose schools and led a number of White families to leave the neighborhood and the district. This was also true for a number of native-born Asian Americans, who perceived the area as becoming too heavily driven by Asian immigrant values.

The social reshuffling sparked by Asian Americans migration to Mission San Jose schools runs counter to the typical narrative of suburban segregation. Most scholarship has focused on Whites' efforts to seal themselves off from racial integration in schools, especially with African Americans, because of racism, fears of property value decline, and reduced educational quality.[4] The traditional narrative of White flight focuses on the movement of Whites away from inner-city schools and the battles fought to give students of color greater access to White suburban schools through policies such as busing and regional redistricting. The dynamics of White flight explored in this chapter are different. In Mission San Jose, academic competition and the perception of disparate educational values between White and Asian American families have produced and reinforced racial divisions. This fragmentation occurred within suburbs as well as among two relatively economically privileged groups often thought to exist on the same side of the educational divide. Such divisions contributed to the racialization of Mission San Jose schools as spaces that seemingly marked Asian Americans' inability or unwillingness to assimilate the dominant culture of American education and instead introduce "foreign" practices that many established families claimed were "inappropriate" and "unhealthy" in American suburban schools.

The racial undertones of educational debates in Fremont were also evident in the public deliberation over school boundaries. As Whites left Mission San Jose and the schools became increasingly dominated by Asian American students, Asian American families found themselves, somewhat inadvertently, competing for spots within increasingly racially "segregated" schools. When the Fremont School District tried to redraw the Mission San Jose attendance boundaries to address population and achievement imbalances across the district, the uproar that ensued showed that Asian American educational practices and ideas continued to be marginalized as out of place and foreign. But the case also showed that education has been an important arena in which Asian Americans have defended their right to helping to craft the culture and character of suburban space.

FROM WHITE TO ASIAN AMERICAN SCHOOLS AND NEIGHBORHOODS

Asian Americans' decisions about education have transformed the social geography of Silicon Valley and the neighborhoods in which they have settled. While immigration reform, globalization, and economic restructuring in the latter half of the 20th century forever changed the face of the valley, not all neighborhoods were equally affected. Mission San Jose quickly rose to the top as Fremont's hub of Asian American families. According to the 2014 American Community Survey, Mission San Jose had the highest concentration of Asian American residents of any neighborhood in Fremont, with Asian Americans comprising 71% of the population.

Asian Americans of various ethnic backgrounds consistently reported that schools were their top reason for locating to Mission San Jose and, for many, to Fremont. In the 1980s, Asian Americans employed in high tech tended to move to Cupertino, Sunnyvale, and Menlo Park—more established communities closer to the valley core that had higher-ranking public schools. But Fremont, and more particularly Mission San Jose, offered families an enticing alternative—increasingly good schools and new upper-end housing at a more affordable price. Looking for a nice neighborhood with good schools for their young son, Dan and Elaine Chan had been convinced that Mission San Jose schools were worth a try when they purchased their home in the neighborhood in the early 1980s. They quickly realized what a wise decision they had made. Over the next few decades, many other Asian American families followed suit.

The path that Irene Yang took to Mission San Jose was typical of many Asian Americans who arrived in Fremont in the 1980s and 1990s. As we chatted over tea in her kitchen, she recalled her early days in Fremont. Irene had recently finished her graduate degree, gotten married to Henry, and had her first son. The Yangs then decided to move from New York to Fremont. Irene's brother and mother were already living in the city, and Irene and Henry felt that as Asian Americans, they would have better job prospects on the West Coast than in the East. In the mid-1990s the Yangs rented a home in Ardenwood, a neighborhood in northern Fremont with smaller and more affordable homes than those in Mission San Jose. The neighborhood, however, had highly ranked elementary schools, which was the major draw for Irene, just as it had been for her brother who lived nearby. Irene enrolled her son in the Mandarin bilingual program at Forest Park Elementary, which in 1993 was one of the first of its kind in the state. Many credited the program with helping to make the neighborhood attractive to Chinese American families such as the Yangs. After several years Irene's husband's real estate business was booming, and they had saved enough to purchase a house in Mission San Jose—a neighborhood where, Irene explained, most Asian Americans in Fremont aspired to live. The Yangs made the move right after their son graduated from elementary school so as to avoid sending him to a lesser-ranked middle school in Ardenwood and place him on track to attend Mission High.

Asian Americans' migration into Mission San Jose schools compounded year after year. As more families moved into the neighborhood for the schools, test scores rose—and as test scores rose, more Asian American families located within the neighborhood (Map 4).

In a few short decades, Mission High became one of the highest ranking schools in California, with an internationally recognized reputation. In 2008, 2009, and 2010, Mission High was ranked the number one comprehensive high school in the state, based on its standardized test scores. In 2009, *US News and World Report* rated Mission High as the 36th best academic school (among both public and private schools) and 4th best public open-enrollment high school in the nation. William Hopkins Junior High, its feeder school, had the highest standardized test scores among public junior high schools in California in 2005 and 2007. Mission San Jose's four elementary schools have also been consistently ranked among the highest in the state.

Mission High's academic ascent happened as quickly as its demographic transformation. When the California Board of Education first began recording racial demographics in 1981, Mission High was 84% White. Mexican Americans and Japanese Americans who had lived on and worked the land for generations made up the majority of its non-White students. Having grown up in the area, Paula Jones, who now teaches at Mission High, recalled that well into the 1980s, the school was referred to as "Little Scandinavia" for its predominance of blond-haired, blue-eyed students. But as Maria Lewis, a longtime Mission San Jose resident and now a teacher at Mission High,

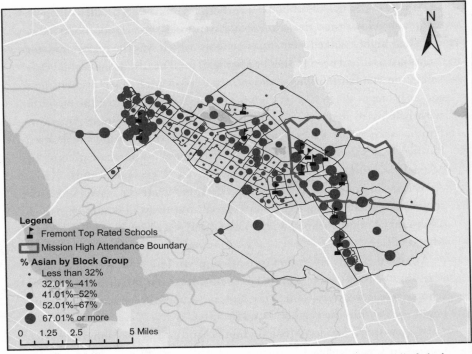

MAP 4. Asian Americans have clustered near Fremont's top performing schools, all of which rank 10 out of 10 on California's Academic Performance Index, the state's standard measure of academic achievement. The Mission High attendance area also has the city's largest concentration of Asian American residents. Image by author.

observed, "The 1990s marked the end of the dominance of the White, blond-haired group at Mission High."

Between 1981 and 2009, Mission High's White population declined from 84% to 14%, while its Asian American population soared from 7% to 83%. Growth among students of Chinese and Indian descent far outpaced those of other Asian American groups. In 2009, Chinese Americans made up 49% of Mission High's Asian American student body, and Indian Americans made up another 17%. Roughly a quarter identified as "other," a category that likely includes a large number of students of mixed Asian and Caucasian ancestry, which Mission High students commonly refer to as "Wasians" and "Hybrids." Although neither the school nor the district record parental country of origin, most Chinese American families are reportedly from Taiwan, a trend consistent with the larger neighborhood.[5] Most students are native-born, second-generation Asian Americans, and a number are among the so-called

		1981**	1985	1990	1995	2000	2005	2010
Race	White*	84%	81%	71%	53%	39%	19%	12%
	Asian	7%	10%	25%	41%	57%	58%	84%
	Hispanic	7%	6%	3%	4%	3%	2%	2%
	Black	1%	1%	1%	2%	1%	1%	1%
	Other	1%	1%	1%	0%	0%	20%	1%
API Scores*		—	—	—	—	882	935	951

*ALL non-Hispanic categories exclude Hispanic populations.

**1981 is the first year that the State of California recorded school racial demographics.

***CALIFORNIA'S current Academic Performance Index standardized testing system began in 1999.

TABLE 2. Mission San Jose High's student population went from predominantly White to Asian American in only a few decades. During the same period, the standardized tests scores for the school rose sharply.

1.5-generation, who were born overseas but raised in the United States. In 2010, 76% of Mission High's Asian American students were born in the United States, but over two-thirds spoke a non-English language at home, an indication of their parents' immigrant status. Latinos and African Americans made up only 2% and 0.5% of the student body, respectively (Table 2).

As evidence of Mission High's changing student body, at graduation time administrators often ask students to line up by C's and W's because of the large number of graduating students with common Chinese last names such as Chen and Wong.

With many parents employed as Silicon Valley engineers and researchers, Asian Americans have also raised the class status of the school and the neighborhood. In 2014, 70% of Mission San Jose residents age 25 and over held a bachelor's degree or higher, and among these nearly 40% held a graduate degree or higher. Among employed adults, 73% worked in management, business, science, and arts-related occupations, with over half of these related to computer technology, engineering, or science.[6] In 2005, the neighborhood appeared on *Forbes* magazine's list of the 500 most affluent communities in the United States with a median income of over $114,000. By 2014, this had risen to $144,000.[7] That same year, less than 4% of Mission High students qualified for free and reduced lunch, compared to 17% across the district and 58% in the state.

David Li reminded me of just how much had changed in Mission San Jose since he had grown up there in the late 1960s and 1970s. We gathered at Mission Coffee, a trendy and upbeat café just steps from the original mission—an ideal place to think about old and new. Here, Mission High teens crowded around overstuffed couches and rustic tables piled high with laptops, textbooks, and lattes, while old-timers discussed the local landscape paintings that lined the walls, read, and visited with neighbors and members of the various local civic and social clubs that regularly met there. Over the hum of these many voices, David recounted tales of his early school life and reflected on how much had changed. He recalled that when he graduated from Mission High in the early 1980s, "everyone just drove a car to get around." But during his most recent visit to the school, students were sporting fancier cars than his. Many arrived in Lexuses, Audis, and BMWs, the latter of which is commonly known to students as "Basic Mission Wheels."

The popularity of Mission San Jose schools has also driven up the neighborhood's home prices. In June 2016, the neighborhood's median home sales value was over $1.4 million, compared to around $905,000 for the city as a whole. Houses in Mission San Jose regularly sell for upwards of $400,000 above those of other Fremont neighborhoods. While the neighborhood has long maintained a reputation for large expensive homes, the gap in home values has become more extreme over time. In September 1996, for example, Mission San Jose homes sold, on average, for just over $100,000 more than other homes in Fremont—$326,800 compared to $212,000.[8] Because of its highly ranked schools, real estate agents now commonly describe Mission San Jose as a "diamond area," a neighborhood where prices simply will not drop.[9] While median home prices actually did decline during the Great Recession, they lost less value than homes in the rest of the city, only 11% compared to 16%, respectively.[10] Schools have come to define so much of the culture and identity of the area that residents will often simply refer to their neighborhood by their local elementary school—Gomes, Mission Valley, Chadbourne, or Weibel. In Mission San Jose, even the subtle differences among these schools carry real social cachet.

GLOBAL AND LOCAL EDUCATION STRATEGIES

The concentration of Asian American families within Mission San Jose is no accident. Various scholars have shown that the education of young children is a major driver of Asian emigration, especially to the United States or Canada.[11] Taiwanese families often plot out decisions regarding their

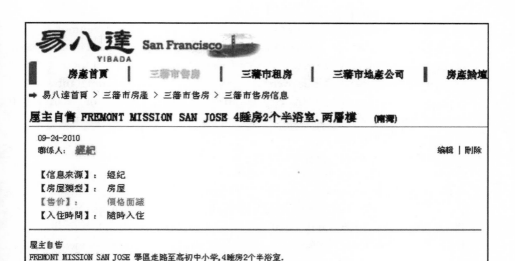

易八達 San Francisco
YIBADA

| 房產首頁 | 三藩市售房 | 三藩市租房 | 三藩市地產公司 | 房產論壇 |

➡ 易八達首頁 ＞ 三藩市房產 ＞ 三藩市售房 ＞ 三藩市售房信息

屋主自售 FREMONT MISSION SAN JOSE 4睡房2个半浴室. 两層樓 (南灣)

09-24-2010
聯係人： 經紀   编辑 | 删除

【信息來源】： 經紀
【房屋類型】： 房屋
【售价】： 價格面議
【入住時間】： 隨時入住

屋主自售
FREMONT MISSION SAN JOSE 學區走路至高初中小学, 4睡房2个半浴室.
两層樓 雙車庫另有BONUS ROOM 300SF. 售999,500元
請洽510-493-8180 馬先生

FIGURE 7. Mission San Jose homes often appear on television and in print ads in Taiwan, India, and China. This listing for a single-family home on a Taiwanese real estate website emphasizes its location within the Mission San Jose school district (Yibada, 2010).

children's education from a very young age based on their desires for dual citizenship, bilingual education, Chinese cultural education, and American university degrees.[12]

Formal channels for information sharing and social networks play a critical role in informing these decisions. Ads for Mission San Jose homes and schools regularly appear in Hong Kong, Taiwan, and India (Figure 7).

Many residents reported that news about Mission San Jose schools' Academic Performance Index (API) scores, California standardized measure of academic performance, was widely circulated abroad and among Asian immigrants in the United States. For instance, John and Tina Cho, who both emigrated from Taiwan, had heard about the "good schools" in Fremont from friends while they were living in Texas. In the late 1980s when John's company, a geotechnical engineering firm, transferred his position to San Jose, they immediately began house hunting in Fremont. The *Chinese New Home Buyers Guide,* a free bimonthly newsletter that is circulated widely throughout Silicon Valley, undoubtedly influences the decision of home buyers with ads for homes in the neighborhood commonly displaying the tagline "Mission San Jose schools."

Within Fremont, news about test scores and school quality are common-place. Diana Li, who emigrated from Taiwan, suggested that for Asian immi-grants in Fremont, "If you ask them 'What's the score of this and that for this school?,' they all know." While overstating the case for all Asian immigrants, Diana also emphasized that the city has attracted a large number of Asian American families who place a premium on high-performing schools, often as measured by test scores.[13]

Parents sometimes go to great lengths to enroll their children in Fremont schools. A number of Mission High parents regularly shuttle back and forth between multiple countries, while their children remain in the neighborhood to attend school. Though the number is difficult to estimate, Principal Sandy Prairie explained that it was not at all uncommon for her to receive phone calls from Taiwan or China in response to parents' concerns about poor grades or test scores.[14] School administrators also expressed concerns about Mission High's increasing number of "parachute kids," youths left in the United States with relatives, friends, or caretakers to pursue their education while their par-ents remained abroad. In other popular Asian immigrant destinations such as Vancouver and Los Angeles, this has been found to be a common educational strategy but one that has serious potential consequences.[15] Children are some-times targets of crime and become unruly, and marital affairs and divorce are more frequent than in other Asian immigrant families.[16]

To enroll their children in Mission San Jose schools, families have been known to rent or buy much smaller homes than they can afford or shuttle several related or unrelated families through a single house in order to stay within the attendance boundaries. For families from India, doubling or tripling up families into homes or converting rooms into garages in order to afford homes in prized neighborhoods with good schools has been found to be common in Silicon Valley and elsewhere.[17] Likewise, several interviewees reported that it was com-mon for immigrant families to pool their resources to buy homes in Mission San Jose in order to enroll their children in the local schools.

The schools in Mission San Jose are in such high demand that they have also become the focus of citywide debates about unscrupulous attendance practices. In 2004, an exposé in Mission High's student newspaper, the *Smoke Signal,* found that 34% of Mission High students surveyed knew someone who attended Mission High illegally.[18] Some described such prac-tices as commonplace. Among them was Sally Park, a second-generation Korean American who admitted that she attended Mission San Jose schools for years by using her aunt's address. Her mother was a single parent with two children who could not afford to purchase a home in the neighborhood when they first relocated from Los Angeles to Fremont. Even after she saved up and was able to purchase a home in Mission San Jose, Sally's mother continued to work two to three jobs to pay the mortgage. Some I spoke to charged that Asian Americans were more likely than other groups to engage in these practices, though this could not be substantiated.

Because so many families have come to the Mission San Jose neighborhood for its schools, some say that the schools have contributed to unusually high neighborhood turnover. Mary Walker, an Indian American with two sons enrolled at Mission High, could not attest to whether this was true for the neighborhood as a whole but suggested that her own experiences seemed to fit the stereotype. Her youngest son was a freshman at Mission High when we met, and thus Mary explained that she and her husband "only need Mission for another four years." After that they will likely move to a neighborhood with less expensive homes, she projected. "I think that the majority of the families will just move out when their kids are done with their school unless they want to keep the homes for their kids, to send their grandkids [to Mission High]," she explained.

Stories often circulate throughout the neighborhood about immigrants arriving in Mission San Jose with suitcases of cash to purchase homes for exorbitant prices in order to enroll their kids in its schools. Most families I met, however, worked hard to make ends meet. Mary was one of the few stay-at-home moms with whom I spoke. Her husband, who sat poring over a mound of paperwork at the dining room table on the weekend we met, was able to support her decision to remain at home thanks to the six-figure income he earned working for the high-tech giant Google. Mary pointed out, however, that in most Asian American families she knew in the neighborhood, both parents worked long hours in stressful jobs and relied on their salaries as their "sole means of survival." Some even hired drivers to shuttle their children around to various after-school programs. Their detailed planning underscored the importance many Asian American parents in Mission San Jose placed on their children's education and how hard they worked to support it.

While many Mission San Jose families agreed on the trends that were reshaping the neighborhood, they held different interpretations of the forces that drove them and their impacts. Many White families with whom I spoke set their stories of neighborhood change against a backdrop of the tight-knit and stable middle-class community they remembered. They often saw skyrocketing housing prices amid what they perceive as a decreasing quality of life in the neighborhood. They read the overcrowded houses that now pack the hillsides, unscrupulous school attendance practices, and a lack of neighborhood cohesion brought on by rapid neighborhood turnover as a cost being borne on the backs of themselves and their children for the benefit of moneyed immigrants with a laser-like focus on the schools. Many questioned whether the neighborhood still held the values and character that drew them to it in the first place. In contrast, Asian American parents tended to emphasize the many sacrifices they had made for their children's education and the value for their children of receiving a quality American education.

THE VALUE OF AN AMERICAN EDUCATION

Why do so many Asian Americans in Fremont seem to place such weight on high-performing schools? Both cultural and structural forces play formative roles. That is, the beliefs, customs, habits, and practices of Asian Americans matter, as do the social, economic, and political forces that have helped to shape these ideas over time. Yet, the former have often been the focus of efforts to explain Asian Americans' high levels of education and economic success in the United States relative to other groups, propelling Asian Americans' status as a model minority.[19]

Since the term "model minority" was first coined in the 1960s, it has been applied to various ethnic and religious groups to highlight their "success," as typically measured by income, education, occupation, and other socioeconomic indicators, relative to other racial minority groups. Asian Americans, especially East Asians, have been its prime targets. While superficially casting Asian Americans in a positive light, scholars have long recognized the fallacies behind the myth and the harm it causes for both those to whom it is applied and those to whom it is not. For nonmodel groups, the model minority myth tends to collectively fault them for failing to achieve in the same ways and to the same degree as the model group, erasing the unequal barriers to and indicators of achievement. For model groups, the myth tends to hold all to the high standards achieved by a few, downplaying wide intragroup variation as well as individual and institutional hurdles, including those based on race and class.[20] The high academic performance of Asian American students is a commonly cited feature of the myth. Looking at the emphasis that many Asian American families place on education through a more multifaceted lens creates a more complex picture and underscores the vulnerability they face within the American social and economic order.

In Mission San Jose, many residents related Asian Americans parents' focus on high-performing schools to educational practices in Asia. In much of Asia, one's level of education often serves as the primary indicator of one's social status, and one's test scores often serve as the primary signifier of academic achievement.[21] Excelling academically is the major vehicle for gaining social status and socioeconomic privilege. Randy Zeng, an immigrant from Taiwan, explained that many Asian countries have extremely competitive testing cultures in which "you take the one test and that decides your life." He described the rigorous exam system that he went through in Taiwan that allowed him to attend graduate school in the United States:

> You have only one chance to take the high school exam nationwide and rank it. Number one high school, number two high school, all based on your score. It [has] nothing to do with your activity, nothing else, talent, nothing. Strictly that. When you apply to college, it's the same. One exam decide[s] everything.

In both Taiwan and China, exams at the elementary level often determine what high school students will attend and if they will be able to go to college. Exam time is treated as seriously as many national holidays.[22] In India, only students scoring the highest on college entrance exams are able to study medicine and engineering. The next best can study business, and those at the bottom have far fewer options. Further, such degrees often carry real social weight. "For Indians, it's more like, if you're not a doctor or an engineer then you're nothing," one Mission High student told National Public Radio reporter Claudio Sanchez.[23] In Vietnamese, one of the biggest insults you can give someone is "Do mat day," which means that one has lost his or her education.[24]

Education is also often a critical part of the success stories of Asian American parents in Mission San Jose and one of the only ways that they know of to help their children succeed. Irene Yang brought this point home. While contemplating why parents at Mission High seemed to hold such high expectations for their children, she reflected on how powerfully her experiences as an Asian immigrant had shaped her views:

> I'm first generation. The way I see it is I did well. I did fine so far in life, you know? I progressed, did well, because I have a pretty good education from school. So I don't really know any other way of achieving.

Both Irene and her husband were graduates of Columbia University in New York. To her, their large home, stable jobs, and comfortable middle-class lifestyle seemed a testament of the value of a "good" American education in achieving wealth and success in the United States.

Other Asian American parents said that education was an important legacy they wanted to pass on to their children. "[For the] majority of immigrants, there is no family wealth, there is no inheritance," Mary Walker explained. "The only thing that you can give [your kids] is the skill to make it on their own." Even though many Asian Americans in Silicon Valley are highly educated professionals, they are often also the first in their families to "succeed," and their class status is still precarious. Anthropologist Sarah Heiman documented a high degree of anxiety among newly minted middle-class suburbanites who often fear "falling back" into the lower classes from which they came. This group, she argued, feels a constant need to fight to maintain their privilege.[25] Having children who thrive educationally is one way of securing that status. Indeed, it is common for all U.S. immigrant groups, not only Asians, to emphasize education among the second generation.[26]

American degrees can also translate to high social status and economic mobility. Degrees from American colleges are important forms of social capital that demand monetary returns and job security in Asian countries.[27] Aiwah Ong argues that among Asian immigrants, good schools "ethnicize and index their cosmopolitan citizenship."[28] A family's ability to place its children in good American schools shows that they have "made it" within the global economic system.

Education also serves as a means by which some Asian American parents seek to protect their children from the effects of racial discrimination.[29] If their children can excel in education, many believe that they will stand a much better chance of being accepted into American society and withstanding the inevitable blows of racism.

Education can even help Asian immigrants gain American citizenship or temporary residency in the United States, as most now enter on educational or professional work visas. Natalie Tindo's experience is indicative of the chain migrations that often accompany educational visas. Like many Indonesians of Chinese descent, Natalie was sent to the United States for college in the 1970s, both to get an American education and to avoid social unrest in her home country. After she became a citizen, she was able to use the family reunification provision of the immigration law to get visas for the rest of her family to come to the United States. Hong Kong immigrants often strategically use their children as a kind of "health insurance" by selecting different sites for their education that will help them obtain Green Cards and expand their real estate holdings.[30] For the parents of children who are not able to gain entry into competitive secondary schools in Asia, placing their kids in U.S. schools can help to ensure that their kids can still attend college.[31] For students from Taiwan, an American education can even serve as a means of avoiding compulsory military service.[32]

Thus, for many Asian American families in Mission San Jose, education is not considered among the many credentials upon which they can rely; it is the primary vehicle to raise their social and class status and ensure their families' economic and political security. For many families, education is key to the ways in which they conceive of their own success and that of their children.[33] It is not something to be taken lightly or for granted. The value that many Asian American families place on education has reshaped the culture at Mission San Jose schools and raised tough questions about what a quality education means at Mission High.

A CHANGED SCHOOL CULTURE

In its early years, Mission High was widely viewed as an average neighborhood high school, roughly equal to two of the other five high schools in the Fremont Unified School District.[34] In 1974 it was well regarded locally, but students' level of academic achievement was still poor by today's standards, with grade point averages (GPAs) ranging between 2.0 and 3.0.[35] Shane Taylor, a 35-year Fremont resident, recalled that when his kids were going to school at Mission High in the early 1980s, a time that he describes as before its "transition," there were many students who performed quite poorly, especially compared to today. In 1987, 65% of students went to college, 40% went to four-year institutions, and 25% went to community colleges.[36] But since 2000, Mission High has maintained a near 100% graduation rate and in 2010 had 31 valedictorians (out of 512 total graduates), all with GPAs above a 4.0; 81% of students were on the honor roll, and 94% of the graduating class enrolled in college. Sixty-four students went on to study at the University of California, Berkeley, and several others went to prestigious institutions such as Stanford, Princeton, Harvard, Cornell, and the Massachusetts Institute of Technology (MIT). "All the Ivy Leagues know about Mission," explained Annie Tan, a Chinese American parent of two Mission High students.

Mission High's curriculum is one indication of change. Once-popular classes in woodworking, auto, electrical, and metalworking skills are no longer taught at Mission High. Instead, Mission High now offers a vast array of honors and advanced placement (AP) courses, particularly in math and sciences. In the 2009–2010 academic year, 77% of juniors and seniors completed one of Mission High's 52 AP sections, 85% of which were math- and science-related. In 2011, Mission High was rated as number one among *US News and World Report's* "Best High Schools for Math and Science." The school administers around 1,800 AP exams per year (for a student body of 2,150 students).[37] And in 2005, Mission High had the highest AP statistics exam pass rate of any school of its size in the world.[38] Principal Sandy Prairie attributed their success in part to the school's policy of insisting that students take basic prerequisites before enrolling in APs but admitted that the policy has faced heavy parental criticism. "It's been a huge fight and struggle with our parents group because they don't understand why their kid can't take [AP biology or chemistry] in the 10th grade," she explained.[39]

As students have advanced academically, so too have the credentials of Mission High faculty. Jan Frydendahl, who grew up in the area and graduated from Mission High in the 1980s, is among 4 math teachers at Mission with a doctorate. Sitting in his classroom with various mathematical equations pinned to the wall that I could not even begin to decipher, Frydendahl explained that he pursued his PhD while teaching at Mission High because he realized that he needed to "evolve" to better meet the needs of his students.[40] Now he teaches only AP math classes. And in 2010, 8 out of the 31 students in his AP finite mathematics class went on to study at MIT.

In response to heightened demand, the neighborhood has developed a robust network of supplementary education. Ohlone Community College is popularly known as "Mission on the Hill" because of the large number of Mission High students who attend classes there on weekends and over the summer. Scholastic Achievement Test (SAT) prep classes, professional tutors, and other academic services are scattered among the neighborhoods' many strip malls. Students often attend after-school and weekend Chinese classes and academic summer camps and are even known to study their textbooks and be tutored on coursework the summer before classes begin.[41] A popular Mission High cheer reaffirms the school's reputation: "Cosine, sine—cosine, sine—3.14159—2400s on SATs—and yes, we all take five APs."

The social life at Mission High has also been transformed. In the 1970s, Mission High held a reputation as a somewhat wild school with regular reports about girls' locker room break-ins and wild homecoming parties. One *Smoke Signal* reporter described it as a place where "profanity bounces off the walls in the hallways and during lunchtime [and] students are ambushed with food in daily lunchroom free-for-alls."[42] Administrators also regularly complained about the lack of student involvement in clubs. One student joked that the most popular clubs were those with "no constitution, no officers, no dues, and no meetings."[43] Today, administrators debate whether students start too many clubs to pad their college resumes. Mission High's long list of clubs includes a range of social, cultural, and philanthropic activities that include bangra dance, Bollywood cinema, Chinese yo-yo, Japanese animae, Asian pop music, and raising money for Chinese orphans.

Sports serve as another indicator of change. Up until the 1980s, Mission High was largely known as a football school and was ranked among California's top teams for several years running. But for the past couple of years the school has struggled to even field a varsity team, and in 2002 coaches canceled the season for lack of interest among upper classmen. According to Coach Kevin Lydon, trying to muster enthusiasm for football on the Mission High campus was "like trying to sell electricity to the Amish."[44] Students commonly joke with one another that the only reason to go to a football game is to get physics extra credit (as the physics teacher is also the football coach). Meanwhile, the badminton team is larger than the football team and, like Mission High's chess and debate teams, is highly competitive regionally and nationally.

In only a few short decades, Mission High transformed from a typical White suburban American high school into an internationally renowned academic institution made up of predominantly Asian American students from middle- and upper-middle-class immigrant families, many of whom placed great weight on their academic success in a competitive and rigorous environment.

The Pressure to Succeed

Swelling Asian American student populations at Mission High corresponded with rising academic expectations and an increasing pressure to succeed. While stress in top-performing high schools is not unusual, the particularly high levels of stress and stressors facing many Asian American students are one of the downsides of "success stories" such as Mission High.

Mission High has been recognized as one of the first schools in the nation to participate in Stressed Out Students (SOS), a program started by a former Mission High teacher that instructs students and parents on managing stress. Noting troubling trends in the numbers of students seeking permission to study at home because of stress and severe mental health problems, SOS was brought to Mission High in 2007 by then vice principal Sandy Prairie.[45] By 2010, it was one of the school's most active student clubs. According to an SOS survey of 1,175 Mission High students, more than half showed signs of depression or burnout.[46] Another Mission High study found that students average about five hours of sleep per night.[47] And some say that stress has led to rampant problems with cheating. In one extreme case in 2003, six Mission High students broke into the district's server and altered their grades and official transcripts to improve their chances of getting into the colleges of their choice.[48] The *Smoke Signal* now regularly dishes out advice on managing academic stress and getting enough sleep while also keeping up grades and selecting the right college.

High levels of stress are common to many Mission High students, but many with whom I spoke reported that Asian Americans face more stress, or at least a different set of stressors, than many of their White peers. I met up with Paula Jones, a seasoned Mission High teacher, in a break between her classes. Paula, who is White, was surprisingly candid when it came to matters of race on campus. She argued that SOS was particularly helpful for Asian American students and parents "because it addresses stress and Asian ethnicity and the pressure that these Asian students are under." Further, she noted that levels of attempted suicides and other self-destructive behaviors in her classroom were more prevalent among her Asian American students, particularly Taiwanese Americans. She recalled one Taiwanese American student who passed out in her class over a B grade and another who tried to hang herself in the bathroom over stress and grades. Such extreme cases underscored for Paula and other administrators the need for outreach to Asian American students and parents, an area where Paula believes that SOS has been particularly effective.

One source of stress for many Asian American students is their parents. Asian American parents are often stereotyped as overbearing and strict—the prototypical tiger moms. Made popular by the controversial book by Amy Chua, *The Battle Hymn of the Tiger Mom,* the term "tiger moms" refers to the stereotypically rigid style of Asian parenting as opposed to the more relaxed styles of Western parents.[49] Having been raised by strict Chinese immigrant parents who coupled high expectations with unconditional love, Chua describes how her experiences influenced the high bar she set for her own children. Her kids were expected to earn straight A's, speak fluent Chinese, and compete internationally in violin and piano and were not allowed to have sleepovers or play dates, participate in school plays, watch television, or play computer games, like many of their White friends. Similarly, students at Mission High often share stories of Asian American parents who go to extremes to ensure their children's academic success. They talk about those who coach their kids to be valedictorians, scrutinize every grade, quiz and test, call or e-mail their teachers on a weekly basis, and request extra-credit homework and will even do homework assignments for them. They joke about gray-haired, stressed-out students who will throw away an A-minus for fear of getting punished by parents willing to withhold meals from children with bad grades. And they poke fun at the "Asian grade scale," wherein A = Average, B = Bad, C = Catastrophe, D = Disowned, and F = Forever Forgotten.[50]

However, this strict definition of success is only one of the many frames that middle-class Asian Americans adopt in order to promote success among the next generation.[51] In fact, few of the Asian American parents with whom I spoke fit the tiger mom trope, and most believed that the stereotype was overblown. Several spent countless hours volunteering in the children's classrooms and did not consider themselves particularly overbearing when it came to their children's education. Still, many also felt that they held higher, or at least different, expectations for their children than did White parents. John Cho, who said that his friends often questioned his nontraditional Asian parenting style, explained: "We give our kids freedom, but not as [much] freedom as White people give their children."

For many Asian American parents, trying to figure out how to strike the right balance between the educational values by which they were raised and prospects facing their children in the United States can be quite difficult.[52] While contemplating the struggles that she had with her own son over grades and homework, Irene reflected that "Maybe if I was a third or fourth generation here, maybe I would be more relaxed about it, because I know not everybody has to go to a good college to be successful." With her son now enrolled in a California state university and majoring in advertising, Irene had finally come to some resolve. She was able to see the value in the path that her son had chosen given the opportunities he had available to him, which were distinctly different from her own. Yet, she also felt proud that she had helped him get to this point by sometimes pushing him when he did not want to be pushed—a trait she attributed to the way she had been raised.

The pressure that many Asian American students feel is not only parental but also cultural. A *Smoke Signal* survey found that most Mission High students cited pressure from family related to culture as the number one cause of their stress, anxiety, and depression.[53] In a *CNN* report provocatively titled "Are Asian Students Smarter?" that featured Mission San Jose High, Stanford University cultural psychologist Hazel Marcus argued that many Asian American families consider academic success a child's duty to the family. "It's the most important role. It's your job. It's what you are supposed to do, is to bring honor to the family by becoming educated," she said.[54] Min Zhou and Xi-Yuan Li argue that Chinese immigrant parents often measure their own success by their children's educational achievements. "If a child goes to an Ivy League college, his or her parents will feel rewarded and are admired and respected as successful parents. If their children are less successful, they lose face," they note.[55]

Stress is also self-imposed, especially among students who are aware of the many sacrifices their parents have made for their education. For instance, in response to a 2006 *Wall Street Journal* article on hyperinvolved "helicopter parents," Melony Fong, a second-generation Chinese American student at Mission High, wrote:

> When I think about everything my parents have been through in order to provide me with the opportunities that I have, I'm extremely grateful and, in turn, put pressure on myself to excel. This is the main force that propels me into taking challenging courses and achieving good grades.[56]

Melony pushed herself not because it was what her parents expected but also because it was what she felt she owed them. Upset by a 2004 National Public Radio report about Mission High that she felt implied that Asian American parents were to blame for the high levels of stress at Mission High, *Smoke Signal* columnist Rebecca Gao explained that "We aim towards our definition of success not because our parents expect us to, but rather because we know what we are capable of."[57] Joining me at Mission Coffee, Rebecca later explained that while Asian American parents may foster in their children a desire to succeed and a respect for hard work, by the time they get to high school, most Asian American students push themselves. "By that point it becomes so ingrained in our personalities, in our characters. How do we know that this desire to succeed isn't us?," she asked.[58]

FIGURE 8. Mission High students often experience high levels of stress over their grades. This cartoon published in the student newspaper, the *Smoke Signal,* illustrates the high standards to which many students hold themselves. Image by Cassie Zhang, artist, *Smoke Signal,* Mission San Jose High School, Fremont, California.

Asian American students' stress is also compounded by the model minority myth. Many Mission High students clearly understood both the upsides and downsides of the stereotype. "Since we're Asian, we like all the benefits that [go] with being a model minority. Except we also have all the pressures as well," Cindy Wei, a Chinese American senior at Mission High explained. "We always have to be perfect. We've got to get those A's" (Figure 8).

Cindy not only earned good grades but was editor in chief of the student newspaper, producer of the Mission High television station, and a regionally competitive volleyball player. Her efforts were propelled by both her family's dreams and those of a society that constantly told her that she could and should do better. Various scholars have documented how Asian Americans benefit, in terms of their confidence levels, teacher perceptions, and student tracking, from the stereotypes around their academic exceptionalism.[59] While stereotype threat tends to weaken the academic performance of some groups, particularly African Americans, stereotype performance tends to enhance the academic achievements of Asian Americans. But it also adds to stress and anxiety for Asian Americans who do not meet the high standards as well as those who do.[60]

The Ethno-Academic Divide

Academic stress, competition, and changes in social and academic culture impact everyday social relations at Mission High. Over the years, tensions have flared among parents and students over issues such as the school's curriculum, homework, extracurricular activities, and parental involvement. These issues, especially those centered on academics, often divide White and Asian American families and fuel racial and ethnic tensions in the school and the neighborhood.

Racial and ethnic identity play an important role in students experience at Mission High. A 2010 *Smoke Signal* survey found that 72% of Mission High students thought that ethnicity played at least a "somewhat important" role in social relations on campus.[61] Social groups tend to segregate themselves along racial and ethnic lines, with the primary divisions being among White, Chinese American, and Indian American students. Indian Americans are sometimes accused of thinking of themselves as White and more assimilated than Chinese Americans and, according to many, mix better with White students. Immigrants are often labeled as "FOBs" (fresh off the boat) or "fobby," suggesting that they are nonassimilated and thus uncool. Among immigrant students, social lines are often further delineated based on familial histories in different regions, social castes, and language groups. While students from mainland China sometimes refuse to work with students from Taiwan, students from Hong Kong sometimes reject Chinese mainlanders. Cindy quipped that at Mission High, "instead of the Bloods versus Crips, we have Chinese versus Taiwanese." Differences in language, skin color, caste, and religion among Indian Americans can determine who students will work with in class and are critical identity markers.[62] For instance, Mary Walker reported that Indian American students often accuse her son of not being a "real Indian" because he is Christian.

Racial and ethnic divisions are common in many schools, often stemming from several factors, including peer pressure and socioeconomic and cultural differences. For African American and Latino students, tracking into lower-division and special education classes, parental education, income levels, and teacher biases are commonly noted issues that often physically and psychologically divide them from their White and Asian American peers. At Mission High, however, competition over grades and stereotypes about academic intelligence drive wedges between and among White and Asian American students. "Mission High is made up of two student bodies," explained *Smoke Signal* reporter Jennifer Kao, "those in Honors and those in non-Honors classes."[63] At Mission High, these are racial and ethnic dividing lines as well.

Mission High's academic disparities are most evident between White and Asian American students, whom the California Department of Education considers to be its only "statistically significant" racial groups. In 2009 Mission High's Asian American students had a base score of 966 compared to 890 for non-Hispanic White students on California's standard API. Whites make up the majority of students in the lower-division and special education courses, while Asian American students are overrepresented in the honors and advanced placement courses, particularly those related to math and science. This academic divide means that White and Asian American students are less likely to be in the same classes, form friendships, and build social capital.

The academic divide has also generated crude stereotypes about students' intelligence and work ethic that reinforce their social divisions. White students are often labeled the "dumb White kids," "blonds," "jocks," "rah-rahs," and "theater kids," while Asian American students are referred to as "curve busters," "nerds," and "grade robots." The labels extend to all kinds of social actions. Those perceived as being studious and academically oriented are frequently deemed "Asian," those considered nonacademic are called "White," and those Asian American students who do not fit their assigned academic label are allegedly "Whitewashed."

These derisive racial labels reinforce social divisions and the model minority myth about Asian American academic success and, in contrast, a prevalent assumption that White kids, especially White girls, do not earn good grades or study hard. "My best friend and I are blonde, light-eyed and in honors' classes. When we walk into the room, you can tell from the body language [that Asian students are] thinking 'Why are you in this class'?," explained one Mission San Jose student.[64] In a controversial *Smoke Signal* article, staff writer Anamarie Farr argued that "I am part of a minority that is the object of discrimination at [Mission High]. No, I'm not a Gupta, Chan, Chen, Wu, or Wong. I am Farr and non-Asian. . . . Just because I don't weigh myself down with 4 or 5 or even 6 AP classes does not mean that I lack intelligence."[65] Anamarie's charge of "reverse racism" exhibited one of the many ways that White students and parents have pushed back against what they see as the dominant Asian culture in Mission San Jose schools. Many Whites have adopted the language of racial oppression to describe their sense of powerlessness in the face of rising academic expectations. Such claims, however, too often dismiss the ways in which White students still hold a privileged status at Mission High as the "normal" students, to which many Asian American students are often compared and judged.

These debates also played themselves out in the classroom. Alice Mitchell described her anger at discovering that when her daughter was in elementary school, students organized a class vote to decide who was the smartest and most "superior race"—Chinese, Taiwanese, Indians, or Caucasians. Her daughter, one of only a few White students in the class, chose not to participate. But as Alice recalled, the Chinese American and Taiwanese American students clearly outvoted the Indian American students. "I don't remember who won between China and Taiwan," she added. At Mission High, the racial divide has become so enmeshed within the academic divide that it lends itself to such biological fallacies.

Academic performance also plays a significant role in shaping students' ethnic identities and peer groups. Among Asian Americans, those students who perform well are commonly valorized by their peers, whereas those who perform poorly are more likely to be marginalized. Maxine Frank, who is of mixed Chinese and Caucasian ancestry, relayed that because she is in honors classes, active in school clubs, and hangs out with mostly other Asian American students, she feels more Asian than White at Mission High. Alice Mitchell suggested that because her daughter had high test scores and grades, she is sometimes deemed an "honorary Chinese" or "blond Chinese" and is more accepted by her Asian American peers than many other White students. In contrast, Sally Park, who is Korean American and described herself as nearly failing out of Mission High, said that her poor academic performance made her feel like an outsider and led her to hang out primarily among the few African American and Latino kids at school. As is typical for many Asian Americans who do not fit the model minority stereotype, Sally distanced herself from her coethnic and racial peers.[66]

Sally's struggle also demonstrates the intersection between race, class, and academic performance that further cements social divisions. At Mission High, it was not only her grades but also her family's income that led Sally to feel like an outsider. Her mother was a single parent and was not able to provide Sally with the same advantages as those of many other Mission High students. Now a successful undergraduate student at the University of California, Berkeley, Sally struggled to make sense of how her family's income had affected her experience at Mission:

> I felt like my experience was so much more different than the average student there. They were involved in so many things. I mean, these kids are just so busy with things. They would be playing some instruments. They would have some sort of lesson like flute, or cello, or whatever have you. And then they would have some sort of sporting thing or ballet or whatever. And they all took prep courses for SATs. My mom couldn't afford any of that. I felt like I don't really belong here and I felt like that what they were doing was how it's supposed to be. This is what successful students do.

As Sally demonstrates, differences in income are an important indicator of academic achievement not only because of the actual resources that families are able to bring to the table but also because of the ways that "frames of success" are internalized. In Mission San Jose such class divides are subtle, marked sometimes by simply whether one is picked up from campus or not. "The Hill kids," as they are often called, must be driven to campus, whereas students who live in "the flats" or "the Apartments," the neighborhood's one and only subsidized public housing project, more often walk or take the bus to school. "Students are very conscious of their geographies," Paula Jones explained.

While many students do not conform to the given racial stereotypes at Mission High, their social lives are still shaped by them. Several students noted how hanging out with White students, or hanging out in general, can be interpreted as a sign of one's academic failure. Alternatively, hanging out with the Asian American students tends to suggest that one has no social life at all. Alice explained that even though her son is in honors classes with mostly Asian American students, he does not have many Asian American friends because they usually talk about homework, and "he's not willing to become one of those robots." Sam Phillips, who grew up in Fremont just minutes away from his current home in the Mission San Jose hills, attributed "Asian" educational values to his son's struggle to live a "normal" teenage life at Mission High:

> The Asian culture does not operate like ours in a social sense. They don't come over to visit [my son] after school. . . . I wouldn't say that they're not

allowed, but they're not *encouraged* to go and hang out with—I don't think that they're encouraged to hang out, even with other Asian families. There's a lot of studying that takes place. Most of the extracurricular activity is pretty limited to either music or traditional stuff like tae kwon do or martial arts or things like that.

Sam's understanding of Asian culture framed Asian American students as strict, homogeneous, and foreign while also helping to reinforce his claim that his son's activities were normal. While many of the Asian American parents and students with whom I spoke rebutted Sam's stereotypes, his comments point to the prevalent perceptions about Asian Americans that drive the social positioning of Asian American and White students at Mission High as well as the relationships among them.

Academic competition also often affects social relations among different racial and ethnic groups. Though both Indian American and Chinese American students tend to do well academically, their performance is still subject to intraracial stereotypes. Mary explained that several Indian American parents have made comments to her about Chinese American students being more competitive and have felt threatened by their academic success. Ellie Cho, John and Tina's daughter, commented that while racial and ethnic stereotypes surround the academic performance of different groups, most people compete with their friends and those in their classes who more than likely are of the same ethnicity. Between White and Chinese Americans, she explained, "We don't really compete with them because we're not like friends with them."[67]

Competition, the pressure to succeed, and different ideas about and expectations of academic success contribute to striking social divisions between and among Asian American and White students and parents both inside and outside of Mission High.[68] Stereotypes about intelligence and real disparities in academic performance affect students' identities, social lives, and, as I will show in the next section, their lived geographies.

NEW NEIGHBORHOOD GEOGRAPHIES OF RACE

The changing culture of Mission San Jose schools and increasing racial and ethnic tensions have created divides not only inside schools but also within the larger neighborhood and region. While many Asian American families have moved to the area in search of competitive, academically rigorous schools, many established White families have left in search of less competitive schools that they perceived as offering a more well-rounded and balanced education in a less stressful academic environment. In a clear departure from the traditional pattern of White flight, in Mission San Jose the rapid decline in the White population has proceeded amid rising home values and the entry of more well-to-do residents.[69]

These patterns have been driven in part by educational competition and differences between Asian American and White parents' ideas about what constitutes a quality education and how their children can succeed. A far less recognizable trend is that even some native-born Asian American families are leaving the area for the very same reasons. The departure of both White and non-White families from the area underscores the importance of schools in shaping patterns of suburban racial and ethnic geographies that reinforce the racialization of Asian American space. As more and more White families have left, Mission High has even more clearly evidenced the ways that Asian Americans, and particularly Asian immigrants, are critiqued for their failure to integrate with and adopt the social and spatial norms of their middle-class White peers.

The New White Flight

In a 2005 *Wall Street Journal* article titled "The New White Flight," Suien Hwang argued that non-Hispanic Whites were leaving Silicon Valley schools that they perceived to be too competitive and narrowly focused on academics, especially math and sciences, at the expense of liberal arts and extracurricular activities.[70] The article focused on Monta Vista High and Lynbrook High in Cupertino. Few scholars analyzed the issue, but residents and the news media picked up on the debate—some claiming that White flight was a reality and others claiming that it was not.[71] The controversy became so heated in Cupertino that comments made by district superintendent Steve Rowley during the debate, which were critiqued as blaming Asian Americans students for the increasing pressure felt by White students, were cited by some as a reason for his firing two years later.[72] In an interview with the newspaper *India-West,* former Mission High principal Stewart Kew weighed in on the issue. According to Principal Kew, because Asian American students were leaving the district at the same rate as White students and because the drop in White enrollment had been, in his words, "gradual," there was no support for the White flight thesis.[73] However, nearly every parent, student, neighbor, and school administrator with whom I spoke believed that White flight was real at Mission High.

A common maxim among the Mission San Jose residents was "every time a White family moves out of the neighborhood, a Chinese or Indian American family moves in." While not statistically accurate, their point underscores the common perception about who the in-movers and out-movers are in the neighborhood. Some described this change as natural neighborhood turnover. Older residents who have lived in the neighborhood for years and no longer have children living at home sell their homes to younger families. Especially since housing prices have shot up in recent years, in part because of the schools, residents who have owned their homes for a long time can cash out and purchase homes in other areas that better meet their current priorities.

However, these explanations do not fully explain the trends in the declining percentage of young White families and students in Mission San Jose schools. Between 1981 and 2010 non-Hispanic Whites declined from 84% to 12% of the Mission High population, representing a drop from 1,405 to 273 White students. During the same period, overall enrollment grew by 471 students.

These trends were not just about White families failing to move into the neighborhood but also about some who already lived there deciding to move out. While these moves could have been motivated by job relocations, housing prices, or other factors, many of the Asian American and White families with whom I spoke believed that a significant part of this trend included families leaving the area for communities that are within only a few miles of Mission San Jose, such as Pleasanton, Livermore, Foothill, and Sunol. These are areas that have high-ranking schools (but not as high as Mission High) and high-end homes but more White students and what Leslie Clark, a White Mission High student, described as more of a "feeling for the White community."[74] What explains the departure of families to these nearby neighborhoods? Some credit Mission High's increasing class sizes.[75] Two parents with whom I spoke said that Mission High's overcrowding and poor facilities have reduced the quality of its learning environment. Newer schools in the surrounding areas offer smaller class sizes, better facilities, and additional funding for extracurricular activities, academic enrichment, and other amenities.[76]

A more commonly cited reason, however, was that many White families simply felt uncomfortable living in a predominantly Asian American and especially immigrant community. Several White parents in Mission San Jose shared stories about friends who left the neighborhood because their son or daughter did not get invited to birthday parties or otherwise felt that they did not fit in with the neighborhood's dominant Asian American culture. Nina Young, a White Mission High senior, explained the sense of discomfort that both she and her mother sometimes felt living in an Asian American–majority neighborhood:

> When I was going to school in elementary school, like walking to school, like all the parents and all the kids would be speaking Chinese or another language so like I couldn't even understand them. And like my mom, I know that she would get kind of like kind of upset because she felt kind of like excluded in a way. 'Cause like there would be like a few White moms, but that is it. And most of them, like Asian[s], talked their language and you don't know what they're saying. So that bothered me, too, because people did it in school sometimes.

Unused to feeling like outsiders in their own neighborhoods, some White parents and students took aim at the use of Asian languages in schools and elsewhere. Alice Mitchell recalled that when her children were in elementary school, she would sometimes hear other White parents make comments such as "What are they saying behind our backs?" when parents spoke together in Chinese. These comments reflect the sense of social displacement, isolation, and xenophobia that may have contributed to some White families' decisions to leave the area.

While multiple factors play into White students' declining populations at Mission High, overwhelmingly the most commonly cited reasons among parents, students, and administrators with whom I spoke were academic competition, stress, and the culture of Mission San Jose schools. Many White parents expressed grave concerns about the amount of homework assigned to students, the selection of courses available to nonhonors students, students' opportunities to participate in nonacademic activities, the level of academic stress, and a desire for their children to have a "normal" high school experience and receive a "well-rounded" education. By "well-rounded," parents generally referenced their desire for a greater focus on sports, extracurricular activities, and the liberal arts, especially music and theater. "Normal" typically referred to more active social lives and extracurricular activities such as football games and homecoming dances. White parents' narratives about what it is to be a normal, well-rounded American teen privileged the actions and practices of their own children as both commonplace and desirable while implicitly critiquing Asian American students and parents for failing to conform.

White Americans' power to label and be labeled as normal and well-rounded was buttressed by a host of social stereotypes of suburban American teens and by dominant educational norms in the United States.[77] George Lipitz argued that Whiteness secures its power by virtue of its invisibility. "As the unmarked category against which difference is constructed," he wrote, "whiteness never has to speak its name, never has to acknowledge its role as an organizing principle in social and cultural relations."[78] At Mission High, the invisible power that White students and parents held included their quiet acceptance of their own normativity. Meanwhile, despite being in the numerical majority, Asian American students at Mission High were constantly reminded by their classmates, administrators, and neighbors that they operated on the margins of normal suburban American life.

Many school administrators and parents who had watched family after family leave the school also believed that academic competition was a central concern, particularly White students' declining academic performance relative to that of Asian American students. Principal Sandy Prairie said that she had spoken to many White parents over the years who had decided to transfer their children from Mission High to nearby Irvington High, a school with a much higher percentage of White students, more lower-division classes, and a reputation for less stringent courses and homework through its magnet arts program. In explaining their reasoning, she said that many felt that "there wasn't any way their kids could compete [at Mission], so why bother?" The bar at Mission High was simply too high. In order to get their children into a top-tier college, most parents wanted them to graduate in the top 15% of their class and knew that they stood a better chance of doing so at Irvington.[79]

Others spoke about families they knew who had moved out of Fremont altogether because they felt that their children could not or did not want to compete. Natalie Tindo explained that a common attitude among the White families she knew who had left Mission San Jose schools was that their children would be "a bigger fish" somewhere else. Alice Mitchell, who had lived in Mission San Jose since 1989, described the strategies she had seen families use to keep their children competitive. One White couple had two children—one who was performing well in Mission San Jose schools and the other who was not. While maintaining their house in Mission San Jose for their higher-achieving child to attend Mission High, they purchased a condo in Pleasanton for the other child to enroll in a less rigorous school. "They felt pretty strongly that [their younger kid] would do just fine in a normal school," she explained. Invoking the term "normal," Alice reiterated the perspective I heard over and over again among White parents at Mission High. The competitive culture fostered by Asian American parents and students at Mission High was abnormal, if not unhealthy, for their children and was not one that set their children up for success.

Others spoke of White students and parents they knew who were concerned about Mission High's academic focus, including its heavy math- and science-based curriculum, the small number of lower-division courses, and significant homework and academic stress. Mission High teacher Paula Jones recalled discussions she had with White parents who elected to send their children to Irvington High instead of Mission High. They explained to her that they were making the move because Mission High "catered to the Asian students." She described their sentiment as follows:

> You don't honor the needs of the White students. You've shut down all electives. The wood shop is shut down, which only the White kids sign up for. There are no electives available for the White students that the parents felt were appropriate. All you're doing is upping the advanced placement this, advanced placement that. This is no longer a traditional, regular high school that is amenable to a regular kid.

Claiming their values and practices as "regular" and "appropriate," many White parents had left Mission High with a clear sense that the unconventional and unwelcome educational practices of Asian American families drove their decision. Maxine Wan felt this deeply. As a Chinese American student at Mission High who had watched many of her White peers leave the neighborhood, she reasoned that it was because "They would rather go to a school that's not so amped up on Chinese culture." Clearly, she was part of the problem. Mary Walker added that not only were Asian Americans often seen as the problem, but they were also used as scapegoats for changes in the school that they had nothing to do with, such as wood shop. Wood shop was not shut down because of Asian American students, she argued, but because of statewide education budget cuts. "There are kids that are just regular kids among Asian kids. They are in nonhonors classes and would have preferred those classes," she said. "This has nothing to do with Asian and non-Asian." Mary's claim that there were "regular kids" among Asian American students at Mission High was a rebuke of the criticism and racial stereotypes often aimed at Asian Americans but one that simultaneously reinforced the dominant norms about what is it to be a "regular" American teen.

Social issues also topped the list of concerns among many White students and parents. Leslie Clark and Brandy Patterson, two White Mission High seniors I met with in a cramped but comfortable teachers' lounge, were clear about why they had considered transferring to Irvington High. Leslie said that her central concern was having a more diverse student body that included more White and non–Asian American students, which she felt would allow her to grow more socially. Brandy thought that at Irvington she would be less likely to be stereotyped. "You're not every day hearing that you're White, you're dumb. There, you might hear it once a week," she explained. Alice Mitchell expressed relief that her two children were at Irvington High and not in the Mission High "pressure cooker." Her daughter is a cheerleader, and her son plays baseball. Because of the lack of academic pressure at Irvington High, she felt that she has seen them grow a lot "in the social side of things."

Often enough, however, the distinctions between wanting a different type of education and less competitive and stressful schools and feeling uncomfortable about living in a predominantly Asian American neighborhood can be a bit blurry. Alice said that the families she knew who sent their children to the nearby schools in Sunol were either White or mixed White–Asian American couples who said that they were looking for "less homework," "more balance," and "more Caucasians." "And they're pretty direct about it," she noted. Lisa Bell added that while clearly White flight at Mission High had multiple causes, at its base it was driven by one simple fact: "Parents want their kids to be surrounded by students like them. It's as complicated and as simple as that."

White families leaving Mission San Jose schools appear to be making the same kind of strategic educational decisions as Asian American parents to try to give their children the most educational, social, and economic advantages they can. But differences in their perceptions about how to best prepare and position their children to compete invite consideration of how privilege and advantage may accrue to Asian Americans and Whites differently. I have shown that the experience of most Asian Americans suggests that education plays a key role in their economic and social mobility, but this may not be as critical for Whites. Scholars have long documented the advantages that historical and contemporary neighborhood segregation provide to White Americans, including not only access to higher-performing schools but also neighborhoods with lower crime, higher housing values, more public resources, stronger social networks, and greater social and cultural capital.[80] As George Lipsitz points out, the "possessive investment in whiteness" is something that White Americans carry with them wherever they go, producing unfair gains and unearned rewards in whatever spaces they occupy.[81] Meanwhile, other groups do not receive the same gains by virtue of their skin color and in fact often experience social and economic devaluation of their spaces. While Asian Americans may have benefited in many respects from their access to Mission San Jose's high-performing schools, their presence seemed to increasingly devalue the neighborhood for many White Americans. As their White neighbors left, many Asian Americans also began to wonder if they might too might be losing out on some of the privileges that living in well-to-do suburban neighborhoods was supposed to afford them.

Asian Overflow

The neighborhoods in Pleasanton and Livermore to which many White families have relocated are beginning to attract more Asian American families as well—a trends that some families call the "Asian overflow" out of Fremont. For instance, between 1990 and 2010 while the overall population in Pleasanton grew by about 40%, the percentage of Whites decreased from 91% to 67% and the Asian American population grew from 6% to 23%. In addition to changes in overall immigration in the region, Asian American population growth, particularly among new families settling into the area, can be explained by some of the very same factors that led to the rapid rise of the Asian American population in Mission San Jose—the availability of high-performing schools and new homes. But among those Asian American families who have left the Mission San Jose attendance area for these neighborhoods, the trend also underscores intraracial divides between native-born Asian Americans and Asian immigrants regarding Fremont's schools.

A point made by several interviewees is that some Asian American families, particularly those born in the United States, leave Mission San Jose schools for the very same reasons as White families. They tend to see the intense pressure to succeed educationally as an Asian immigrant value and, like White families, feel out of place in a predominately immigrant community. Born in Indonesia but raised in the United States, Natalie said that she considered leaving Mission San Jose because even though she is of

Chinese descent, she neither speaks Chinese nor feels that it is "healthy" to have her children in such a competitive academic environment. She also felt isolated from her many American-born Chinese friends who moved out to Pleasanton and Livermore and often encouraged her to do the same:

> They all left. I could name like five families that I used to know, lived here, our girls grew up together, and one day they just kind of go "Uh, no we're not coming here anymore" because it's foreign to them. They don't feel comfortable. Being an American, they don't speak Chinese anymore.

Several 1.5- and second-generation Asian Americans adopted the language, practices, and preferences of their White American peers, further distancing themselves socially and spatially from their coethnic neighbors.

Like White flight, this created divisions between Fremont and other suburban communities and also within Fremont. Maureen Xu, who came to the United States from Taiwan at the age of five, lives in the Mission High attendance area but chose to send her eldest son to Irvington High. She cited a number of reasons for her decision, including her son's learning disability, a desire for less homework and competition, and more family time, social diversity, and space to have a social life and pursue his personal passion—marching band. "I thought, 'You know, it would really suck to play in the marching band for a constantly losing team,'" she explained. Interestingly, however, Maureen noted that her youngest son is getting ready to graduate from middle school and wants to continue on to Mission High with his friends. Maureen said that she was considering allowing him to do so, mostly because he looks "more Asian," has more Asian American friends, and performs better in school than his brother. But she added that she and her husband (who is White) decided that if he does make the move, he will not be allowed to take honors classes. "We don't need him to be so stressed out that all the academic curiosity is squeezed out of him," she explained. "I don't believe that's healthy."

The geography of race in Mission San Jose and its surrounding areas has been impacted by academic competition and residents' differing definitions about a quality education. Academic competition and differing social and cultural ideas about what constitutes a good education have become filters through which the varied racial and class interests of Asian American and White families are understood and enacted. As both groups attempt to maximize their perceived interests, they have created and exacerbated patterns of racial segregation between Whites and Asians Americans and even among Asian Americans.

THE POLITICS OF SCHOOL BOUNDARIES

In 2000, a new school boundary plan announced by the Fremont School Board catalyzed race and class tensions that had engulfed Mission San Jose schools for decades. Like patterns of White flight out of the district, the boundary controversy showed how the changing culture of Mission San Jose schools had raised tense race relations and helped to restructure social geographies that reinforced extant racialized stereotypes about Asian Americans in schools. But it also showed how Asian Americans fought back against the mounting criticism to proclaim the value of their spaces and their right to the type and quality of education they had come to expect at Mission High. Ironically, however, as Whites continued to leave Mission San Jose schools, Asian Americans found themselves fighting hard to maintain what some perceived as racially segregated schools that were, nonetheless, high-performing. This ironic twist in the long and sordid tale of American racial segregation in suburban schools exposed how new dynamics of race and class have challenged the ways public policy makers often understand issues of educational equity.

For nearly a decade, between 1991 and 2000, boundary disputes embittered and embattled the Fremont Unified School District. The central focus of the debate was the Mission San Jose schools. In 1991, Mission San Jose schools had the highest test scores, the largest percentage of Asian American students, and the highest rates of overenrollment and overcrowding among all five Fremont attendance areas.[82] With the goals of equalizing enrollment, facilities, and curriculum across the district, the Fremont School Board began discussions about redrawing school attendance boundaries. Early talks signaled that some Mission San Jose students would no longer be tracked into the esteemed Mission High. After several years of debating which Mission San Jose elementary school was to leave the attendance area and flip-flopping on whether boundary changes would occur at all, in 2000 the school board finally settled on Fred E. Weibel Elementary. Weibel was then the highest-ranked Fremont elementary school and the third highest-ranking elementary school in the state and had the largest percentage of Asian American students of any school in the district, with a 75% Asian American student body. Drafted in 1999, the plan would direct students from Weibel to Irvington High, where API scores were more than 200 points lower than Mission High and non-Hispanic White students were in the majority.

The reaction of Mission San Jose parents was immediate and intense. When the school board was deciding which Mission elementary school was to be redirected to Irvington High, Ellie Cho, who was enrolled in a Mission San Jose elementary school, recalled heated parent meetings that sometimes spilled over into arguments between parents at her brother's Boy Scout meetings. School board meetings often brought out hundreds of angry parents opposing any changes to the Mission San Jose attendance boundaries. Various protests were organized, including one in which around 175 cars drove around Irvington High to highlight the long commutes and traffic that would be caused by the change. Susan Barnett, a Mission High teacher, recalled several cars displaying placards reading "Our kids will never go here!" "It got very nasty," she explained.

At least four different groups opposing the proposed boundaries were formed, mostly among parents at Weibel. Stacy Zhong, an immigrant from Hong Kong who had moved into the Weibel attendance area primarily for the schools, was heavily involved in one of these groups. She described how she and other parents sent fliers to every home in the neighborhood, collected donations, built a website, organized parents to attend Fremont Unified School District meetings, and began a campaign to recall several school board members. Among many other things, parents accused Superintendent Sharon Jones, who proposed and defended the plan, of "social engineering," or purposive manipulation of the school system by moving students for the sole purpose of raising test scores across the district rather than investing in improving schools.[83]

In the lead-up to the decision, parents booed, hissed, and shouted profanities at board members during public meetings while bearing signs that read "No, no, no boundary change or see you in court."[84] Witnesses recalled meetings in which students, parents, and school board members were crying. Police officers were present at several meetings that lasted well into the evening during which hundreds of parents signed up to address the board. Tanya Saito, a Japanese American student at Mission High who served as a representative to the board, said that she was sometimes scared to leave the meetings alone and had to be escorted out. "We were definitely hated at the time," she recalled. Even 15 years later, she was still visibly upset by the memory of how those times divided her community.

The views of Weibel parents were not, however, uniform. Though some residents argued that both Asian American and White parents were equally upset by the proposed boundary changes, most agreed that Asian American parents were the most upset and active in opposing them. Part of the reason was simply because Weibel was a 75% Asian American school. But there were other reasons as well. Sitting in the home that she had custom built only blocks from Mission High in order to ensure that her children would receive a coveted spot in the school, Stacy Zhong explained that Asian Americans were the most involved because "the whole reason that they had moved to the area is because of the schools." In contrast, working on the campaign against the boundary changes, Stacy was shocked to find that there were White parents who thought that sending their children to Irvington High was a good idea because it was less competitive and their children would have a better chance to "shine." None of the Asian American families she knew felt the same. "Asian parents want to give their child [the] most, how do you say, competition. They think that you challenge the children in order for them to succeed. You don't put them in an easy environment so they could feel good," she explained. Stacy clearly overestimated the extent to which all Asian American parents agreed with her position, yet she also pointed out the differences that seemed to animate both sides of the debate.

Alice Mitchell, who is White, had two children enrolled at Weibel and did not oppose the boundary changes because she felt that her kids would do better at a more "well-rounded" school. She explained that her struggle had not been over whether to send her children to Irvington but rather her initial decision to enroll them at Weibel:

> We were actually concerned about going to Weibel because of the whole pressure cooker elementary school mentality. Not really so sure that I want to do that to my children. Not really so sure that I want to send my children to a school where [when my daughter] was in her kindergarten, there were 120 students in her class. They still had a lottery to get into the school. People camping out at the school to get their ticket to get their child in. And if you didn't get in, then you [were] overloaded somewhere else. For the 120 kids in her class, I think she was 1 of 5 Caucasians. There was a little bit of concern of being that much of [a] minority. I was like, "Is this really a good thing, not a good thing?" We almost thought that in spite of great tests scores, [it] might not really be what we wanted.

Alice said that she was more concerned with her daughter's shyness at that point than her academics and was looking for a place that would allow her to "fill out on the social side of things." "We weren't concerned about her ability to keep up academically," she explained. "We just wanted to make sure she was going to be able to make friends and explore things socially." Ultimately, that priority led them to sit out the attendance boundary debate. But as Alice's comments point out, her social priorities were conflated with the racial dynamics of Mission San Jose schools in which White students were increasingly in the minority.

Like their opinions about White flight, the opinions of neither Asian Americans nor White parents about the boundary issues were as simple as these examples suggest. Indeed, parents support for or opposition to the boundary changes were motivated by a complex intersection of various interests and values. The boundary dispute, however, helped to show that many White and Asian American parents saw themselves as benefiting from Mission San Jose schools differently. Further, the dispute evidenced the ways in which their views about the kind of education that such schools provided were becoming more and more racially polarized both within Mission San Jose and across the city.

Many Asian American parents were not only upset by the prospect of moving to Irvington High but also took offense at the ways in which school board members approached the issue of the move with parents. Letha Saldanha, an Indian American who served on the Fremont Unified School District's Equity Commission during the boundary dispute explained to National Public Radio reporter Claudio Sanchez how Asian American parents thought differently about the issue than members of the school board who were, at the time, mostly White:

> [Asian American parents] just don't take a chance with our children's education and most of us make a lot of sacrifices. This is one of the cultural differences. . . . You don't go into a meeting with Asian parents and tell them that test scores are not important and that it really doesn't matter—your child will do well wherever they go—which is what the traditional administration tries to tell us.[85]

The failure of administrators to understand the weight of the boundary decision for many Asian American parents further fueled racial tensions about the issue.

Asian American parents were also deeply offended by comments made during various public hearings. They complained of residents who mimicked and mocked their accents, accused them of abusing their children by forcing them to study, and charged them with making Fremont into another Chinatown. Weibel parents were referred to as excessively wealthy, elitist immigrants who were not assimilating into American culture. "The fact that [Mission San Jose parents] feel Irvington area schools are somehow inferior to theirs is insulting," Lunette Rawlin, an Irvington High parent, told a *San Jose Mercury News* reporter during the debates. "They feel that we somehow don't value our children's education as much as they do, and I find this attitude elitist."[86] In a similar way, Katherine Newman documented how White baby boomers in a New Jersey suburb who were not able to afford the middle-class lifestyles that they enjoyed as kids tended to direct their anger toward wealthy Asian American families whom they described as "illegitimate elites."[87] The description displayed their sense of Asian Americans as foreigners who were taking advantage of an unearned but privileged position in the United States.

Like the battles fought inside Mission High, the district-wide debate played on many residents' sense that Asian Americans' income, education, and academic achievement were leading to an uneven playing field for Whites. And yet, it also showed how the actions of Asian American families were cast as falling outside the norms of "acceptable" behavior. Comments made about Asian Americans in Mission San Jose schools repeated long-held narratives about Asian Americans as foreigners who were exercising undue control over the fate of the city and introducing ideas and practices that were simply un-American.

The boundary changes were finalized by a vote of four to one by the school board in early 2000. Anna Muh, the first and only Chinese American member of the school board and the first successful Chinese immigrant to run for office in Fremont, cast the lone vote against the plan. The boundary issue, many said, figured prominently into her election to the school board, as it helped to galvanize Asian Americans around an issue.[88] The other four members of the board were White, and three were known longtime advocates for Irvington High.[89] When the boundary changes were announced, angry Weibel parents stormed out of the meetings, shouting statements such as "lynch the board" as they left—a biting phrase given the torrid racial history of school desegregation in the United States.[90]

In response, Weibel parents initiated a series of legal battles. Among them was a racial discrimination suit filed by 20 Asian American parents against the Fremont Unified School District, the school board, and the superintendent. The suit alleged that the district's plan was racially motivated and designed to divert high-performing Asian American students to other schools to boost academic scores around the district. The lawsuit read as follows:

> The basis of the new boundaries was not equal convenience or equal facilities, but in fact to remove Asian students from the higher performing schools to schools that needed performance scores boosted. The board and Superintendent Jones implemented the boundary changes for the purpose of singling out Asian students.[91]

The suit claimed that the district's effort to seek a racial balance was a violation of the equal protection clause of the 14th Amendment and sought compensatory damages related to any loss in home property values.[92]

Meanwhile, some Weibel parents shifted their focus away from legal action to the creation of a separate Mission San Jose school district. Weibel parents collected over 7,000 signatures in support of the district (as many signatures as the proposed student population), raised over $100,000 in donations, and filed their petition in Alameda County.[93] This was the first time that California had ever seen a new school district petition sponsored by a majority Asian American coalition of parents. The proposed district would be over 60% Asian American.

In an ironic twist, race and class equity were the central grounds for the county's and state's concerns over, and ultimately their denial of, the proposed district. In an editorial to the *San Jose Mercury News,* Fremont superintendent Sharon Jones argued that the creation of a new Mission San Jose district would "promote racial segregation, cause substantive economic hardship to both resulting districts, and significantly erode educational opportunities for all students."[94] The Alameda County School Board unanimously rejected the proposal, stating in its report that such a district would carve out an "enclave of privilege" and violate state rules prohibiting racial imbalances.[95] On appeal, the California State Board of Education reversed Alameda County's finding regarding racial segregation, arguing that because the proposed district would match the racial composition of the neighborhood, this did not constitute segregation. The board, however, unanimously upheld the county's decision to deny the split. The denial was largely based on class rather than the racial composition of the new school district, as the board ruled that the proposed district would leave the Fremont Unified School District with more low-income students.

The various rulings and petitions brought into focus the awkward position of Asian Americans in educational politics in the city. As racial minorities, they were subject to forces such as White flight that threatened to isolate them spatially in ways that could disadvantage them. But as a high-income and highly educated group, such isolation might also serve to their advantage relative to less well-off groups, which included both lower-income Whites and other racial minorities. Asian Americans used the tools provided by both their class privilege and status as racial minorities to try to retain their place in Mission San Jose schools. The denial of their petition, however, evidenced the limits of their privilege vis-à-vis lower-income groups and other racial minorities in matters of school equity. But it left open questions about how equity is defined between high-income Asian Americans and similarly situated Whites as well as among groups that claim to hold such different definitions of a high-quality education.

In the end, the redistricting plan seemed to achieve the goal of promoting greater program equity across the district, at least in Irvington. By 2009, the percentage of Asian Americans at Irvington High had doubled to 50% of the student population. Meanwhile, Irvington's API scores rose from a base score of 715 in 2000 to 831 in 2010, earning it a ranking among *US News and World Report*'s top 1% of American public schools in 2009 and 2010. More AP classes were offered at Irvington, in part due to a compromise with Weibel parents to drop legal action in exchange for, among other things, increasing the number of honors and advanced placement courses at Irvington and allowing students to take classes at Mission High not offered at Irvington High. During the same period, Weibel Elementary dropped from the number three–rated elementary school in the state to the number three–rated elementary in the district.

However, the plan left many highly upset Asian American parents in its wake. Mission High principal Sandy Prairie contrasted the experiences of White parents whose children went to Irvington, who for the most part were "very, very happy," with the experience of Asian American parents, who "resolved their issues" and "made it work." Letha Saldanha expressed the disappointment felt by many Asian American parents over the school board's handling of the issue:

> There is a myth going on that everything is so peaceful in Fremont after the boundary change and everybody is happy. It's not that everybody is happy. It's that the people who were impacted have given up and aren't seething and have just said, "Hey, they're not going to listen to us so, we are going to work through it."[96]

Ironically, one of the ways in which many Asian families chose to "work through it" has reinforced the racial divisions between Mission San Jose and the rest of the district, which were at issue in the boundary dispute. According to several residents, after redistricting, Asian American families were more likely than White families to send their children to private schools or move into the new Mission High attendance area or out of the district altogether. Sitting in his modest ranch-style home only blocks from Mission High, Randy Zeng explained how he and four other Chinese American families he knew moved from Weibel into the new Mission High boundaries after the plan was passed. To do so, he sold his 3,500-square-foot custom-built house and moved into a 1,500-square-foot older home in Mission Ranch, a neighborhood that he felt would be safe from future boundary disputes. Stacy Zhong did the same. She allowed her daughter to finish at Weibel and then sent her to private school for two years while her son completed his last two years there, and she and her husband remodeled a home in view of Mission High School. Right after her son graduated, they moved into their home inside the new Mission District. According to Principal Sandy Prairie, the district's underestimation of the value that people placed on Mission San Jose schools is why the plan failed to reach its population targets for the Mission District:

> What I think the superintendent and school board never dreamed would happen is that people then would be willing to sell their houses once they got out of junior high and move into the attendance area when they hit high school. And that's what we started to see happen. And that's why our population never, ever really went down.[97]

In 2001, the year when the boundary change first went into effect, the population at Mission High went down by about 140 students and continued to fall for the next two years. But by year three the numbers started to climb up again, such that by 2009 the school enrollment was back to its 2000 levels. Meanwhile, the Asian American student population and its relative portion of the student body continued to rise year after year.

While failing to reach its population goals for Mission San Jose schools, the boundary changes and the reactions of students, parents, and administrators to them heightened social tensions over the racial, ethnic, and class composition of the schools. Within the debates, Asian Americans continued to be stereotyped as high achieving but abnormal and out of place. But Asian American families fought back against these stereotypes and for a place in Mission San Jose schools. To many Fremont residents and city officials, the debates exposed how deeply Asian American families, particularly Chinese and Indian immigrant families, felt about the schools and what was at stake in their children's academic success. It cast into stark relief the differences between many White and Asian Americans' definitions of a "high-quality education" and how these differences are resolved in education politics.

. . .

In searching for solutions to 21st-century challenges of racial inequality, the past seems to hold fewer and fewer clues to the future. As rapid immigration and internal migration have stirred the American melting pot, old lines have been broken and new ones are emerging. These divisions do not look like or act like the old ones, nor are they driven by the same forces. In Silicon Valley, Asian American and White parents' interracial academic competition and different definitions of "good schools" are among the major drivers of their social geographies. While Asian American families struggle to provide their children with the most rigorous education they can afford, some White families are leaving these same schools that they view as too intense, stressful, and competitive. Just as the failure of schools often shapes suburban communities, so too does their success.[98]

Regardless of the source, however, the emerging racial divide in Silicon Valley schools and neighborhoods is troubling. Many of the Asian American parents with whom I spoke did not want their children to attend predominantly Asian American schools. Indeed, like most minorities, they held greater preferences for living in racially integrated communities than did White Americans.[99] Many Asian Americans felt that the departure of White families left them in a more "ghettoized" community that was subject to easy stereotyping. While many did not want their children spending their time in theater classes or playing football, they also did not have a problem with other children doing so and welcomed the diversity that White students had once brought to Mission San Jose schools. But after the exodus of so many White families, many Asian American parents, especially immigrants, felt that they had little choice. If they wanted to keep their children enrolled in a high-performing, academically rigorous school, they had to keep them in Mission San Jose schools. It was, after all, the reason why most had moved to the neighborhood in the first place.

During our conversations, some began to question the wisdom of their decisions. They worried that the Mission High "bubble" created a false sense of the world in which their children were in the majority and among the most successful but was not preparing them for the "real world." In a society where power and opportunity are not equally distributed based on one's merit (or test scores), these parents struggled to prepare their children with a useful skillset to navigate the terrain outside their neighborhoods. As Wendy Cheng has noted of Asian Americans in San Gabriel Valley, many did not "feel" their race or the limits of their racialized privilege until they left the boundaries of their community.[100] By encountering fewer and fewer Whites in their schools and neighborhoods, many worried that their children would lack the social capital and networks needed to break through the glass ceiling. And indeed, in a market in which 80% to 90% of jobs go unadvertised and are obtained through personal networks, their concerns seem all too justified.[101]

Just down the road from Mission San Jose in Cupertino, Tomás Jiménez and Adam Horowitz observed that Asian Americans' performance in schools challenged the characterization of Whites as the taken-for-granted benchmark population that sets achievement norms to which all other populations adjust.[102] While I agree that Asian Americans have challenged these norms, they have not completely upset them. Nor have they taken away the power of dominant educational norms to bestow benefits upon White Americans within contexts in which they are not in the minority. In leaving Mission San Jose for other neighborhoods, White Americans seems to be reasserting their benchmark status.

In tackling this divide, old policy paradigms of educational equity based on Black-White and urban-suburban divides fail to address new realities. The debates over school boundaries showed how awkward it was to fit Asian Americans into boxes of privilege that had largely been drawn for Whites. In applying established criteria to prevent segregation in schools, Asian American families received mixed messages about their place in the educational system. On the one hand, they were told that their status as racial minorities made them more vulnerable to the forces of segregation and therefore that they could not, even by their own will, voluntarily separate themselves from others. On the other hand, they were told that their desires to create their own school district was "elitist." Their economic status made for easy parallels to the NIMBY reactions of White communities past and present.[103]

Undoubtedly, class interests affected the desires of Asian Americans to remain in the Mission San Jose district, and their class status enabled their resistance to the boundary changes. But their racial privilege did not work in the same way that it did for Whites. While Asian Americans might have wanted to carve out an "enclave of privilege," their enclave was one in which racialized perceptions about them as foreigners, abnormal, and unwilling to adjust to the norms of middle-class suburban American life left them as the target of various forms of otherizing. As much as they prized Mission San Jose schools, Asian Americans also wanted to be able to live in diverse communities. Many remained in the face of White flight simply because they felt as though there were very few places in which their educational practices were understood and valued, such as at Mission High. But their decision came at the cost of living in more racially integrated neighborhoods—a cost that nagged at many residents as they considered the value of their newfound community.

The debate seemed to be a missed opportunity to have a meaningful conversation about the diversity of educational goals and interests that Asian Americans brought to Silicon Valley and how schools and neighborhoods could adapt. In this case it might not have meant that Asian American families would not have had to leave the Mission San Jose schools, but perhaps they felt better about doing so. It might have meant that they did not leave school board meetings bitter that their voices were not heard, that they believed that public officials were seeking out creative solutions to meet their needs, and that their core values were not sidelined or discounted. By helping residents work through their fears, policy makers can help communities not only find solutions to tough problems but also build respect and tolerance for difference in the process.[104]

While schools have been at the forefront of Silicon Valley's politics of development and demographic change, Asian Americans have also quietly made home in the region in other ways. Just down the road from Mission High are several ethnic shopping centers that are popular among Asian American students, who regularly gather there after school and on the weekends for a needed pause from their otherwise pressure-filled lives. These shopping centers are beloved and active in the lives of their parents and grandparents as well. These multigenerational gathering spaces, however, have not simply faded into the background of suburban shopping centers lining Fremont's freeway exits and major arteries. Like schools, these spaces have become flash points for larger politics over racial and ethnic change in the region. They have become places in which questions about what it means for communities to roll out the welcome mat and make a place for difference are being hashed out among friends, neighbors, and various political and economic interests.

THREE

Mainstreaming the Asian Mall

ON A TYPICAL FRIDAY AFTERNOON in Fremont's Mission Square Shopping Center, known to regulars as "Little Taipei," Chinese American grandmothers stake their turf on parking lot benches while chatting with friends and comparing their grandchildren's latest feats. Outside the 99 Ranch Market, elderly men smoke, play cards, scratch their lotto tickets, and read newspapers from hometowns such as Beijing, Saigon, and Manila. A few middle-aged women convene at outdoor tables wearing face masks, arm covers, and big-brimmed hats to shade them from the afternoon sun. By 3:00 many parents and elders have left, while students from nearby Mission San Jose High gather at *boba* milk tea and frozen yogurt shops. They listen to the blended beats of American, Taiwanese, and Hong Kong pop blaring over the shops' speakers and browse magazine racks for gossip on their teen idols from around the world. As the evening approaches, families arrive with three generations in tow—grandparents holding fast to their grandchildren while waiting in line outside popular restaurants such as the Aberdeen Café. A familiar parking lot dance begins as a swirl of Toyotas, Hondas, and Lexuses with lace-covered seats, Hello Kitty trinkets, Buddha figurines, and Ivy League decals fight for the few remaining spaces. Older youths replace the teens and fill the cafés until they close at 2:00 or even 3:00 in the morning.

Little Taipei is one of five shopping centers in Fremont that cater primarily to the city's growing Asian American population (Figure 9). Variously referred to as "Asian" or "Asian-themed" malls or by the predominance of certain ethnic groups, such as "Chinese malls" and "Vietnamese malls," these shopping centers have become common markers of popular Asian immigrant suburbs throughout the United States, Canada, Australia, and many other countries. At least 140 such centers have been documented

FIGURE 9. Fremont's "Little Taipei" is one of many Asian malls in Silicon Valley. Asian malls blend various traditions to create a uniquely Asian American suburban space. Photo by author.

throughout the United States.[1] In Silicon Valley these shopping centers have sprung up all over the region in the past several decades, neatly following Asian Americans' changing social geographies.[2]

This chapter explores how these shopping centers act as community gathering places that have helped to shape and are shaped by Asian Americans' emergent suburban identities and their sense of home and community in the region. Following my interviewees, I refer to these shopping centers as "Asian malls," though in neither form nor function are these malls particularly "Asian." They are vibrant hubs of Asian American social and community life for suburbanites from multiple ethnic, national, and c lass backgrounds. For many, these shopping centers offer a home away from home that fulfills their everyday needs while also meeting their desires for comfort, familiarity, and cultural affirmation. They are places where patrons strengthen the bonds of family, exchange stories of hardships and triumphs, make new friends, reunite with old classmates, and celebrate life's special moments. They enmesh and entangle the familiar and the strange, places near and far, and patrons across race, ethnic, class, cultural, and generational divides. They help to inform new sensibilities, social networks, cultural practices, and communities linked by common geographies and attachments that are sometimes located within but often go beyond the bounds of city and neighborhood. In a region as diverse as Silicon Valley, Asian malls have become central meeting grounds in which people of many different backgrounds have come together to define what it is to be Asian American.

While such collisions and negotiations may be taking place among Asian American groups within the mall, they are commonly occurring between Asian Americans and other groups about the mall. This chapter also examines the politics that have surrounded the development of Asian malls within the city of Fremont and demonstrates that they have been portrayed by many non–Asian American residents and city officials as nonnormative, undesirable, and even foreign spaces that do not fit into the existing character of retail in the city. These shopping centers have been treated as problem spaces that are out of character with the social and spatial norms of middle-class suburbia. Accordingly, new city planning policies and processes have reshaped Asian malls to fit more easily with traditional suburban shopping centers and accommodate non–Asian American customers. The public scrutiny and regulation of Asian malls exhibits how fears of cultural contamination and difference remain a powerful ideology shaping the spaces of Asian American public life in suburbia, just as they have for decades in the inner city.

City officials have also used Asian malls to evidence the multicultural character of Fremont for both economic and political gain. Public discourses over the building and design of Asian shopping centers show that places that seemingly mark ethnic and cultural difference often help to bolster narratives of multiracial and multiethnic inclusion. But city policy and processes aimed at inclusion have also worked to exclude certain expressions of Asian American public life and culture that are not in line with their projected image. In these beloved spaces of Asian American suburban life, new social practices and identities have taken root, and new debates over immigration and community change have emerged.

NOT YOUR TYPICAL SUBURBAN SHOPPING CENTER

Walking into an Asian mall in Fremont is not like walking through shopping centers in Asia, along the streets of urban ethnic enclaves such as Chinatown, or in any other mainstream shopping mall in Silicon Valley. The form, location, and management of Asian malls are a unique synthesis of these different traditions, designed around the needs, desires, and identities of Asian American suburbanites.

Like many urban Chinatowns, Asian malls typically host a wide range of independent retail businesses that sell music, jewelry, clothing, books, and herbal medicines from many different regions in Asia. They also offer a range of personal and professional services such as massage, acupuncture, hair, dentistry, travel, and banking.[3] In Asian malls, as in many Asian cultures, food is a central focus. Large banquet restaurants and Asian American supermarkets, like the popular 99 Ranch Market, anchor many Silicon Valley malls alongside a host of satellite restaurants, cafés, and bakeries.[4] "Asian malls are essentially food courts," explained Charles Wang, a Chinese American developer who has been involved in several Asian shopping center projects during his two-decade-long career in commercial real estate in Silicon Valley. In the popular Milpitas Square shopping center, for instance, approximately half of its 62 shops offer food-related services.

While these malls mimic many of the qualities of urban Chinatowns, they have adapted them to their suburban context. Tony Lo, who has developed two Asian shopping centers in Silicon Valley, explained that in urban Chinatowns, prices tend to be very low, the customers generally speak little English, parking is scarce, and the streets and stores are often undermaintained. "This is a couple of steps up from Chinatown," he said of the Asian mall in which we met, with a "totally different clientele." Lo referred to the popular perception of Asian malls as more modern shopping centers for middle-class Asian American consumers. Philip Su, the developer of both the largest Asian shopping center in southern California, San Gabriel Square, and the largest in northern California, Milpitas Square, explained that these malls meet a market niche outside of the central city for Asian-oriented products that are affordable and familiar to their patrons but in a more convenient location and with more upscale amenities.[5] In Silicon Valley, the footprint of many malls is similar to that of other suburban shopping centers—single-story neighborhood-style strip centers surrounded by a sea of parking spaces. At Milpitas Square, for instance, its 62 stores are supported by over 1,100 parking spaces.

While Asian malls may take on familiar suburban shopping center forms, they often operate quite differently financially. In many North American cities, malls have introduced a business model in which shopkeepers own rather than rent the spaces where they do business. In high-density Asian cities such as Hong Kong and Taiwan retail condominiums are typical, but these are new to Silicon Valley. Explanations for the popularity of this form of ownership vary. Charles Wang suggested that for Chinese Americans, it was a natural extension of their entrepreneurial ambitions. "The Chinese culture is made up of entrepreneurs," he argued, as we sat together in his office abuzz with contractors running in and out that gave rhythm to our conversation; "everyone is a hustler and wants to open a shop." Perhaps sensing my unease about the certainty with which he pronounced the cultural roots of the practice, Charles went on to explain that condo ownership also held practical benefits for their owners. It can help small business owners save money and avoid unexpected rent increases and possible evictions, he noted. Others pointed out that real estate can serve as an investment to help immigrants gain financial equity, stability, and even citizenship.[6] One store owner in Fremont Times Square who sold Chinese-language Christian texts and other religious products explained that purchasing her unit provided the stability that a niche business such as hers needed to get off the ground. For Asian shopping center developers, who tend to work on relatively small-scale projects, condos can lower their liability by reducing their long-term carrying costs.

Whether condo-owned or not, however, another distinguishing feature of these malls is the subdivision of space for multiple tenants. Pacific Mall located in the Toronto suburbs, the largest Asian mall in North America, includes over 500 condo-owned small businesses within its 270,000-square-foot center. For the many family-owned businesses that start up in these malls, the small spaces provide a launching point into more mainstream retail. They also allow business owners the opportunity to make additional revenue and sell a broader range of goods to attract clients. In Toronto and elsewhere, both the small size of retail spaces and condo ownership have been shown to support ethnic entrepreneurship and the development of suburban ethnic economies.[7]

Another quality of these malls that also supports many Asian-owned businesses is their flexible hours and management. Milpitas Square and its adjoining Ulfrets Center remain open until 2:00 a.m. on Friday and Saturday nights. At the Pacific East Mall in Richmond, a security guard reported that he often has to kick patrons out at 4:00 in the morning on weekends, when the mall finally shuts its doors. Die-hard singers from around the Bay Area patronize KTV Music Karaoke and mix with those attending the all-you-can-smoke hookah nights at Stogies' Smoke Shop. When I caught up with a Stogies' employee at one of these late-night parties, which was packed wall-to-wall with a diverse mix of both Asian American and non–Asian American youths, he explained how the flexible mall management had helped his business to thrive. He credited the ability of the store to supplement their tobacco-related products with lottery services and hookah parties to it being named "Retailer of the Year" for the highest-grossing sales of any small business in California during their first year. "You have to be very flexible," explained Pacific East's manager. "We are not a corporate mall. [It] gives you a survival edge."

While conventional location factors such as placement near a freeway with good visibility and access are important, the overriding factor dictating the location of Asian shopping centers is their proximity to large Asian American populations. "It's not rocket science," explained Charles Wang, "all you need to know is who's living there." John Luk agreed. John is an immigrant from Hong Kong and the president of GD Commercial, a brokerage firm in Silicon Valley that specializes in Asian shopping centers. He has worked on some of the largest Asian mall projects in the region. "Whenever the Asian population hits 30 to 40 percent, it's time to open an Asian mall," he explained.[8] In community after community, growing Asian American populations have been met by an increasing number and diversity of Asian shopping centers.[9] These shopping centers have reshaped not only the form of the Silicon Valley landscape but also the social and community life of the many suburbs within it.

CENTERS OF SUBURBAN SOCIAL AND CULTURAL LIFE

Asian malls serve as vibrant centers of public life for a diverse cross section of Asian Americans in Silicon Valley. These shopping centers are critical places of identity and community for many Asian American suburbanites that connect them both to their local communities and to the Asian diaspora. Asian malls have carved out a space within suburbia that has shaped the ways many Asian Americans conceive of and engage in suburban public life.

Places both Special and Mundane

Asian shopping centers are service centers that connect their patrons to resources that facilitate their everyday life functions. At the newspaper stands located outside many Asian supermarkets, patrons can pick up the

Chinese New Home Buyers' Guide or get information on food services, senior living care facilities, recreation, transportation, shopping, entertainment, and professional services. Billboards outside 99 Ranch Market and many other supermarkets are littered with handmade signs about houses for rent, babysitting services, tutoring, and items for sale.

These shopping centers fill a niche for affordable Asian-oriented products and services that are either unavailable or available only in a limited variety and at higher prices elsewhere. As Charles Wang put it, while many American Americans in the valley may go to Macy's or Kohl's to buy clothes, they will head to the Asian mall to purchase live fish, inexpensive vegetables, and an assortment of Asian products that they cannot find elsewhere.[10]

Asian shopping centers also typically offer a range of personal and professional services, such as medical, dental, and eye care, with attention to common cultural practices. At Fremont Times Square, the Asian Medical Clinic provides health care that combines an understanding of Eastern and Western medicines and tends to the common health concerns of Asian Americans. Their multilingual doctors speak Mandarin, Cantonese, Punjabi, and English. Also popular are the many legal, real estate, food-related, and educational services that tend to congregate at these malls. Youths are often shuttled to their local shopping centers to participate in Chinese-language, music, and other after-school activities, while adults make their ritual trips in and out of grocery stores and restaurants. Milpitas Square sponsors job fairs and career days, among many other events aimed at building social and economic capital among Asian Americans.

In 2010 the federal government stationed census takers in 99 Ranch Markets across the country, showing that malls are also important sites of Asian American political participation. Scholars have shown how Vietnamese American shopping centers have acted as spaces for protest and political action around issues such as the commemoration of the Vietnam War and geopolitical relations between the United States and the Socialist Republic of Vietnam.[11]

Malls also serve as sites for special occasions. In Silicon Valley, many go to the mall to get married or celebrate holidays, birthdays, graduations, and other life events. Weddings are such a popular part of the business of many banquet restaurants such as ABC in Milpitas's Ulfrets Center that they try to encourage customers to get married during off-peak times of the year. In addition to the restaurant's standard wedding package of a cake, a photographer, flowers, a karaoke machine, and entertainment by Leung's White

Crane Lion Dancers, one promotion offered a complimentary one-night hotel suite and a bottle of wine to any couple who got married between January and April.

Spaces of Comfort and Acceptance

For many immigrants who gather in these malls to purchase familiar goods and products from their home countries, Asian malls feel like home. Sally Park, the Korean American student who described her struggles to adjust to life at Mission High, noted that her mother faced similar struggles adjusting to life in the United States. When accompanying her mother to various Asian malls, however, Sally detected a palpable sense of relief, in contrast to her mother's experience at more mainstream shopping centers:

> When she looks at something, she knows exactly what it is. If she needs help, she knows how to ask for help and feels comfortable with that. With English, even though she's pretty good with English, pretty proficient, there's still just that moment of hesitation. If she needs to ask for help, she will probably just ask me to ask. . . . I think it just gives immigrants, specifically, comfort. Like you've come all this way but this doesn't have to be as foreign as you think it is. You can come into this little enclave that we've made and feel at least at home.

For Sally, Asian malls, like Chinatowns, are spaces that help immigrants adapt to life in a new place. In Asian malls, immigrants can speak their native language in a culturally familiar setting that provides a necessary reprieve from the daily negotiations they make as they attempt to blend multiple cultural worlds.

For second-generation youths, Asian malls connect them to their families, their ethnic heritage, and each other—it is a place, many said, where they go to "feel Asian." Several interviewees confirmed what one blogger described as feeling like he had been "practically raised" in 99 Ranch.[12] It is a place of first jobs, dates, and many childhood memories—an intimately known and familiar space. Many youths grew up being shuttled to and from these shopping centers for art and piano lessons, shopping, and eating out with their families. At Pacific Mall, I met four teens who all said that they had grown up coming to the mall with their families since they were in elementary or middle school. Though they noted that they sometimes hang out at other malls, they still came to Pacific Ranch up to three times per week. Taking a phone call during our interview, one teen referred to his location as simply "Ranch"—a destination that was apparently well known among his peers.

As adults, many return to these malls with their families during holidays and for other special occasions. Ethan Ding, a Chinese American college student whom I met at Pacific East Mall in Richmond, said that he spends most of the time during his trips home to Los Angeles being taken out by his parents to their local 99 Ranch mall, just as his family did for out-of-town guests for as long as he could remember. "They remember the Asian mall," said John Luk in reference to second-generation Asian American youths.[13]

These shopping centers reinforce Asian Americans' everyday cultural practices. At 99 Ranch, those wanting to celebrate Thanksgiving can pick up an entire meal consisting of roasted turkey, crispy fried shrimp balls, grilled short ribs, sautéed lotus root with Chinese cured pork, braised rock cod, and chow mein noodles. This alternative to the traditional American holiday celebrates Asian Americans' practices as part of American culture. "In Ranch 99, I don't feel I am a minority at all," explained one customer.[14] The proliferation of products and practices that bridge their multiple cultural identities help many Asian Americans see themselves not as "hyphenated" Americans but instead as constitutive in the very definition of American.

These shopping centers also act as a cultural bridge for Asian Americans as they straddle their Asian and American identities. Shenglin Chang and I have shown that Asian malls act as important spaces of identity for transnational youths who spend their lives shuttling back and forth between Taiwan and the United States.[15] Among many second-generation youths, urban ethnic enclaves are considered too "old-fashioned" or "traditional," whereas Asian shopping centers offer more "hip" and "modern" products, including cell phone gadgets and car accessories that reflect their lifestyle preferences. Boba milk tea shops featuring funky, modern decors and Taiwanese and American pop music are vibrant youth hangouts. At Milpitas Square, Quickly, an international chain of boba milk tea shops, large digital displays report on news of importance to Asian American youths, from the death of Apple® founder and CEO Steve Jobs to the latest Chinese pop star drama. Its shelves are lined with Asian American magazines such as *East 38,* which is written in Chinese about Chinese celebrities but marketed only in northern and southern California.

Philip Su described the importance of the food selections available at Asian shopping centers in light of his own experience and identity. Born in

Taiwan, Philip came to the United States for education and was groomed in the real estate industry by his parents' early investments in California. With various real estate holdings in both the United States and Asia, he has become all too familiar with the transpacific commuter lifestyle and the need to rein-force diverse aspects of his identity. "When I go back to Asia, maybe from time to time I want to have doughnuts. I feel like you need to have [a] burger to feel like [an] American," Philip explained. "And from time to time [in the United States] you feel like you need to have some rice to feel like Chinese." For many immigrants, Asian malls are an important space that allows them to retain their sense of themselves as Asians and Americans. They offer a welcome relief from what W. E. B. DuBois classically referred to for African Americans as "double-consciousness"—lessening the internal burden that weighs on many Asian Americans as they vie for a place in the national imagination and within their own suburban neighborhoods.[16]

It is common to see mallgoers appropriating spaces for their own purposes in ways that promote a sense of ownership and public belonging. On bill-boards at the J&S Coffee and Tea House in Pacific East Mall, youths leave love notes with Japanese anime characters and express their poetry and art or simply their love of boba in many different languages. The group of youths I met at Pacific East Mall were break-dancing in the hallway when I inter-rupted them. They noted that they generally felt welcomed within the mall, especially by a nearby café owner who sometimes played their requested songs. Outside 99 Ranch at Milpitas Square, employees and customers regu-larly gather around tables to smoke, gamble, talk, and play cards. Through their use and engagement, customers have transformed Asian malls into active reflections of their own spatial identities and meanings.

Spaces of Hybridity and Experimentation

At Asian malls, patrons encounter not only the culturally familiar but also people and practices that promote experimentation and border crossing. Patrons are not exclusively Asian Americans, nor are they from one Asian ethnic group. The ethnic orientation of the anchor store is generally a good indication of the predominant group that frequents these malls. Malls anchored by 99 Ranch Markets, for instance, tend to serve more Chinese American clientele, while those anchored by Lion Market tend to be more popular among Vietnamese Americans. Yet most attract diverse Asian and non–Asian American customers. At Fremont's Northgate Shopping Center,

FIGURE 10. Outside a 99 Ranch store in Fremont's Northgate Shopping Center, stands carry newspapers from twelve different language groups. This is an important place of everyday interethnic interaction. Photo by author.

which is anchored by a 99 Ranch, only about 50% of its clientele are Chinese American, according to one employee. Latinos, African Americans, and Indian Americans make up the majority of the other patrons.

This diversity is reflected in the mall patrons who gather around newspaper stands, grocery aisles, and parking lots. These daily encounters within the banal mall spaces help to build respect and tolerance for difference—a "cosmopolitan canopy" in which civility among difference prevails.[17] A Filipina immigrant I met who was browsing the stands outside the 99 Ranch at the Northgate Shopping Center said that she came to the mall mostly to pick up newspapers about Filipinos in the United States and abroad. But since the stands carry such a diverse array of ethnic newspapers, she often also picks up non-Filipino newspapers to "learn about other cultures" (Figure 10).

For many patrons, food is a primary medium of experimentation. Asian shopping centers generally maintain a broad selection of Pan-Asian cuisine, and their supermarkets sell foods from Asia, Latin America, and the United States. Two of the more popular restaurants in Milpitas Square are Coriya Hot Pot City and Darda Seafood. Coriya describes itself as an all-you-can-eat restaurant "where Japanese shabu shabu meets Korean barbecue to create Taiwanese hot pot." Darda is a popular Chinese halal restaurant where Islamic prayers and pictures of a ritual hajj hang alongside Chinese New Year banners. Philip Su explained that most patrons seek out opportunities to try new cuisines. "Every time we have a new restaurant that join our shopping center, there's always a draw because everybody wants to try something new," he noted.[18]

For non–Asian American customers, Asian shopping centers also offer a space to try out different ways of being and seeing the world. At Pacific East Mall I encountered Chris Cooper, a White teen who was wandering the halls. When I asked him about his familiarity with the mall, he explained that this was his first time visiting and that he does not like malls, "But this is different!" Chris was excited by all the different aspects of Asian American culture that he was exposed to—an experience that he counted as both unique and valuable. Asian mall patrons often try out new things and try on different roles. At KTV Music, a karaoke café that has a selection of over 110,000 English, Mandarin, Cantonese, Japanese, and Korean music videos, an employee reported that non–Asian American patrons were particularly drawn to singing in Japanese. During karaoke participants are able to inhabit their "vocal alter egos," argues communications scholar Rob Drew. They position themselves physically, socially, and culturally through the choice of songs and renderings.[19] While some may view these malls as places to experience the exotic pleasure of Asian culture, as spaces of everyday life and community among diverse racial and ethnic groups these malls resist cultural essentialization and fetishization.

Cultural and Community Meeting Grounds

At several of the Asian malls I visited, customers came from near and far and regularly spent several hours on a given visit especially on Friday and Saturday nights, when parking was hard to find. "It appears as if Asians do not go to the mall to shop, but rather to take their weekend vacations," quipped marketing scholar Roger Blackwell.[20] At Pacific East several shoppers reported that they visited every weekend, such as one Laotian American teen I met who visited the mall every Sunday and several times during the week to eat and meet up with friends. Many of these shopping centers have the same draw as regional power centers anchored by big box retailers. Debbie Zeng and Denise Wei, two Chinese American college students I spoke to while they stood in line outside a Japanese noodle shop in Milpitas Square, reported that they regularly traveled around 30 miles to get to the mall, primarily to buy food and meet up with friends.

These malls are particularly popular during cultural holidays. In Silicon Valley, celebrations held at Asian malls around Lunar New Year and the Chinese Mid-Autumn Festival can draw crowds that are as large, if not larger, than those for similar events held in San Francisco and Oakland. In addition to special holidays, malls often host cultural events such as lantern- and kite-making workshops, calligraphy and fine art demonstrations, folk dances, puppet shows, and drama and music performances. The Asian Garden Mall in Los Angeles holds weekly night markets similar to those found in many Asian cities. "The objective of these planned events is to create a social atmosphere to expand the role of an Asian shopping center from purely commercial. By creating a gathering place, it is intended that the center form a social hub that attracts Asians from a wider trade area," concluded a report on Asian shopping centers commissioned by the City of Fremont.[21] On opening day for Milpitas Square, more than 10,000 residents from around Silicon Valley participated in the festivities, which included lion dancing, kung fu demonstrations, and a Chinese orchestra.[22]

Patrons come to the mall to socialize and build and renew friendships. They frequently come with friends and also run into others while there, even those from Taiwan and China.[23] The mall acts like a suburban Main Street—a place to see and be seen. On the weekends, the sidewalks and hallways are overrun with customers dressed in their Sunday best, with the symbols of their success apparent in the cars they drive, the clothes they wear, and the amount of dishes they order in local restaurants. "Food is the ostensible attraction [of Asian shopping centers] but the real draw is the chance to renew one's identity by casually rubbing elbows with other Asians," observed H. Y. Nahm in an online daily about Asian American parenting.[24] Shenglin Chang observed that 99 Ranch serves as such an important social hub that a trip to the market by a dating couple can serve as almost their official "coming out" to the larger community.[25] Like bowling alleys, movie theaters, cafés, and other "third spaces" that critics suggest have been lost amid contemporary suburban sprawl, Asian shopping centers are places where Asian Americans connect with others to build a sense of community in their local neighborhoods.

These connections are important for both young and old. Walter Cai, a Chinese American senior I met at Northgate Shopping Center in Fremont who spoke little English and had no family in the area, said that the mall was an important space for him to connect with longtime friends and make new ones. He had found his apartment on a posting outside the 99 Ranch and now walks to the mall every day from his home. Recognizing the importance of these shopping centers for the elderly, several Bay Area groups that serve Asian American seniors provide transportation to and from local Asian malls. Debbie and Denise explained that Asian shopping centers are important places for suburban youths like themselves who have few other safe places to hang out, especially those with good, inexpensive, and familiar food options and a vibrant nightlife.

Asian shopping centers are also places to strengthen familial bonds that help retain cultural practices across generations. Roger Blackwell referred to them as "family places, symbolic of a culture that is able to take commercial and cultural interests and blend them."[26] Mary Walker, who grew up in India, said that her husband will not let her cook on the weekend so that their family can spend time together eating out, often at an Asian mall. The malls close to her home in Mission San Jose contain only a few Indian American stores and restaurants, but Mary noted that regardless of their ethnic orientation, she found comfort in Asian malls' focus on family and food that resonated with her own upbringing. "It's a family event on the weekend," explained John Luk. He reported that Asian American families from diverse ethnic backgrounds will often reward the grandparents for working hard during the week and watching the children by taking them to the mall. It is not at all uncommon to see families with three generations streaming in and out of mall restaurants and shops. These shopping centers help to bridge the generation gap, observed H. Y. Nahm: "they're a way to show our kids and their non-Asian pals that Asian culture offers shiny modern attractions as well as old dusty ones."[27] As first-generation parents struggle to keep cultural practices alive among the second generation, these malls provide a place where both their old and new worlds collide.

Asian shopping centers attract a robust mix of Asian Americans from different ethnicities, nationalities, and classes who come together to produce new Asian American cultures. While the constitution of Asian malls largely reflects differing patterns of ethnic migrations across the region, most malls contain a variety of Asian restaurants, customers, and stores that sell products ranging in quality from high-end jewelry to knock-off name brand purses and knickknacks. At Milpitas Square, luxury clothing boutiques adjoin gift shops selling inexpensive imports along narrow and packed aisles.

At most of the restaurants, even the most popular and seemingly exclusive ones, lunch can be bought for less than $10 a plate. "There is a sense of the mall integrating different waves of ethnic Chinese immigrants from all over Asia. They may come from different classes, but the mall represents common ground," argued anthropologist Aiwah Ong; "it is a place where different streams of Asians become Asian-American."[28]

Asian malls provide a platform upon which important connections have been built among Asian American suburbanites. Within them many migrants' old attachments have been shed or transformed, while new ones have taken root. To become Asian American is to attach oneself to a set of experiences, practices, and values beyond one's ethnic and national group. For Asian Americans who arrive in Silicon Valley from disparate places, carrying with them different migration stories, languages, and traditions, Asian malls are one of the few places of common ground.

Translocal and Transnational Connections

Asian malls rely on and support social and economic networks that extend from the local to the transnational. In Silicon Valley, businesses and customers regularly come from ethnic enclaves in San Francisco, Oakland, and San Jose. Several popular mall restaurants got their start in San Francisco's Chinatown and still have branches there. Many businesses also come from outside the Bay Area, especially San Gabriel Valley. Philip Su explained that when building San Gabriel Square near Los Angeles in the 1980s, he recruited about 20 stores from northern California to open new branches there. Likewise, when building Milpitas Square he recruited many successful businesses from San Gabriel Square that were "anxious to get on the waiting list."[29] Businesses that had made a name for themselves in southern California ethnoburbs recognized the growing market for their products in northern California. Likewise, many Asian mall businesses looking to expand rely on a growing number of Asian shopping center developers and brokers to help them find suitable locations beyond Silicon Valley.

Asian malls not only connect Asian Americans to their local and regional ethnic communities but also provide a bridge to loved ones overseas and everyday life in their countries of origin. The malls are points of connection to places that are geographically distant but ever present in the minds of their patrons. Many popular retail chains originated in Asia, while others adopted the names of popular stores from overseas. Malls help their patrons stay abreast of trends in Asia. Popular youth magazines such as *éf* and *Body* arrive hot off the Taiwanese presses with the latest in overseas news and fashion, while recently released Japanese and Korean animated comics and films are widely available. Dan Chan reported that when he and Elaine first moved to Fremont in 1982, they used to bring back lots of things that they missed when visiting family in Taiwan. Now they can find everything they need at their local Asian mall. For many immigrants such as the Chans, such vibrant connections to their homelands help them feel more settled in their newly adopted homes.

Mall patrons can also virtually link to everyday life in Asia. Televisions in several restaurants broadcast overseas news and popular Korean, Chinese, and Taiwanese dramas and music videos, which can also be seen streaming from laptops and smartphones in mall cafés. At i.tv in Fremont Times Square, customers can sign up for 12 channels of Chinese television, while an employee reported that some of their competitors offer as many as 88 channels. Inexpensive phone cards can be bought for calls to Asia, travel arrangements can be made for return visits, and money can be easily sent to relatives at the many Asian bank branches typically found in Asian shopping centers. East West Bank, which specializes in international banking, bills itself as a "financial bridge." Its patrons can use ATMs anywhere in the world without fees and change money into almost any Asian currency. Asian mall developers also often rely on the support of overseas banks to make their projects work. According to Joe Fong, Asian banks "provide the missing link between the global hemispheric domains and the Asian diasporic regional field."[30] They connect the local to the global and the global to the local.

The lived experience of Asian malls also provides a touchstone to distant places. To some, watching the neon lights come on at night, getting stuck in an overcrowded vegetable isle, or passing a door plastered with fliers and advertisements recalls the feeling of everyday street life in Asian cities. "It's amazing how much like Singapore or Hong Kong these malls are," observed Aiwah Ong.[31] Similar to what one might see on the streets of Shanghai, during the Lunar New Year the mall is filled with red banners and signs wishing patrons good luck in the coming year. Fights break out in the grocery aisles and parking lots, and just like in China, everyone stops to stare. A violin and piano duet plays classical Chinese ballads outside a music store, while an ad hoc group of mall patrons begins ballroom dancing in the hallway (Figure 11).

FIGURE 11. Asian malls help their patrons stay connected to everyday life and culture in many Asian countries. Outside a music store in one Silicon Valley mall, patrons listen to a band playing traditional Chinese ballads. Photo by author.

ASIAN MALL BACKLASH AND REGULATION

While Asian malls are important sites of identity and meaning for a cross section of Silicon Valley's diverse Asian American communities, they have not always been warmly received.[32] In Fremont, non–Asian American residents as well as city officials have been highly critical of them—commonly depicting them as racially exclusionary spaces that are unwelcoming to non–Asian Americans and an eyesore within an otherwise orderly suburban landscape. They have also adopted regulations and review processes that reinforce these perceptions. Implicit within these debates are assumptions about Asian Americans as foreigners who refuse to assimilate to suburban American culture.

While city officials have used regulations to mark Asian malls as spaces of difference, they have also laid claim to these malls as markers of an inclusive multicultural city. In the United States multicultural ideologies gained political traction in the late 1980s and 1990s, a time of neoliberal retrenchment, the rollback of state welfare, and deep racial and economic turmoil in

American cities. Though hailed for its embrace tolerance and respect for difference, many scholars have noted that multicultural rhetoric has all too often been used to undermine calls for racial justice and equity and divert attention away from structural imbalances.[33] In practice, multicultural policies that have been adopted by cities and countries around the world have often helped to reinforce the illusion of cultural practices as authentic expressions of difference and promote them as objects of spectacle to be observed and consumed by others. In Fremont, Asian malls have served as an outlet for public officials' to celebrate the city's social diversity while simultaneously undermining calls for more authentic expressions of difference in its retail landscape.

Problem Spaces

A thread on the *Tri-City Beat,* a popular Fremont blog, sums up many non–Asian American residents' complaints about Asian malls. These include charges that they are racially or ethnically segregated spaces and are unwelcoming to non–Asian American customers and that there are simply too many of them in the city. Ironically, a posting discussing the failure of the city to successfully attract Whole Foods, a high-end organic grocer, led to heated criticisms of Asian malls.[34] One poster, Jen, asked, "Why does every center around have to become Asian themed? I think there are enough of those."[35] Marty commented that "I don't take issue with a demographic being represented. But I take issue when an entire retail project is dedicated to a specific ethnic group. It promotes segregation and a fractional community." Jen complained that "Asian shopping centers are not exactly welcoming to those [who] are not (primarily) Chinese" and that too many of the new centers in Fremont "catered to Asians." "Why is it so many of the Chinese retail establishments are so inclined to put the name of their store in Chinese characters on their store fronts?," asked Vor. "It certainly tells me who the owner is attempting to attract and who they are not."

As these posts suggest, Asian malls have been a socially and politically divisive issue in Fremont. Among non–Asian Americans, many have depicted the city as being "taken over" by an overwhelming number of new Asian malls and stores. I counted only four Asian shopping centers among the city's 5.9 million square feet of commercial retail space. Residents' overestimation of the number of Asian malls in the city recalls the prevalent fear of Asian cultural contamination that has followed Asian American space since the Yellow Peril of the late 19th and early 20th centuries.[36] The portrayal of Asian malls as racially exclusionary mirrored the claims of "reverse racism" and the unwelcoming environment that Asian American students and parents were creating within Mission San Jose schools, some of which were born of White Americans' sense of alienation and xenophobia. While these malls include diverse Asian American and non–Asian American businesses and customers, they have been often portrayed as actively constructing barriers to social mixing. The presence of various Asian languages on retail signs, even when accompanied by English as is often the case, has been read as a rebuke of non–Asian American patrons. Meanwhile, more mainstream shopping centers with English-only signage in a majority Asian American city have avoided such reproach.

Fremont city officials have their own concerns about these malls, particularly their design, management, configuration, and retail and customer mix. Most of their concerns relate to those contained in the 2005 *Assessment of Asian-Themed Retail: City of Fremont*. These included their "poor quality of maintenance," "excessive" signage that is of a "lower quality," a poor tenant mix, and a lack of non–Asian American customers.[37]

The *Assessment of Asian-Themed Retail* was commissioned by the Fremont Economic Development Department to assess "the potential for Asian-themed retail centers in Fremont, particularly vis-à-vis their suitability to the City's intended strategy [for retail development]."[38] After several developers approached the city with interests in developing Asian malls, the city contracted Thomas Consultants, a Canadian development strategy group known for its work with several shopping centers in Canada, Asia, and other countries around the world, to conduct the assessment. After analyzing the retail environments of Chinatowns in San Francisco and Oakland as well as Asian malls across the Bay Area, the group concluded that the city should use its design review processes to address the issues raised in the report and promote a high quality of maintenance and design. While the report praised the potential for Asian malls and noted that Asian retail "clearly plays an important function for Bay Area Asians," its recommendations focused on attracting centers that mirrored the orderly design of the existing landscape and would appeal to diverse middle-class consumers.

A key concern for city officials raised by the *Assessment of Asian-Themed Retail* was retail condominiums. According to the report, city officials should "ensure that the proposed developments will be leased rather than sold in order to ensure that standards are maintained."[39] The lack of centralized management was a key concern with condominium ownership that, the report concluded, lent itself to inadequate maintenance. This and other issues about Asian malls raised in the *Assessment of Asian-Themed Retail* were reinforced by another report commissioned by the economic development department, the *Fremont Market Analysis and Retail Strategy*. Published in 2008, the report provided an economic assessment of Fremont's retail landscape, including an assessment of issues related to retail condominiums. The report concluded that retail condos promote excessive use of signage that is "visually unappealing" as well as an "undesirable clustering of businesses" that can lead to "overpowering competition" among businesses and higher turnover rates.[40] The latter referred to the tendency of several similar businesses to cluster within Asian malls.

The city's concerns about retail condos were not only about their aesthetics, tenant mix, and turnover but also their potential for redevelopment. The *Fremont Market Analysis and Retail Strategy* pointed out the difficulty imposed by the retail condominiums for the city's control of its land uses:

> Historically, cities could use their power of eminent domain to assemble such centers for redevelopment. As the courts and public opinion have pushed for limiting the use of eminent domain, however, this tool for facilitating redevelopment is no longer viable. Therefore, retail condo projects have a built in functional obsolescence that will be almost impossible to address.[41]

The report warned against the "blight" that might be caused by the city's inability to easily work with multiple owners to address high vacancies or other nuisance issues in condoized shopping centers. More broadly, the report cautioned that the condominium ownership threatened to loosen the strict control that the city was able to impose over its commercial landscape, compromising its ability to promote its desired retail form and aesthetics. According to Fremont Economic Development coordinator Angela Tsui, from a planning perspective, retail condos are simply "too hard to control."[42] Though not prevalent in Fremont at the time, retail condos were becoming popular in other Silicon Valley cities—a scenario that, the report concluded, the City of Fremont should avoid.

The focus of both reports on promoting a "high-quality" and controlled retail environment shows the ways in which Asian malls challenged the city's vision of desirable retail form. Like many other suburban communities, Fremont had long used land-use controls to avoid the visual disorder more commonly associated with inner-city and low-income communities. Orderly, cohesive, and well-manicured landscapes have long served as markers of race and class privilege in the United States. Adopted from the estates of European elites, these principles have shaped suburban form as well as a sense of who belongs and who does not within suburbia.[43] The reports' recommendations reinforced these ideologies. The city, they suggested, should use its powers of design and development review to avoid the symbols of lower-class Asian malls and bolster its ability to continue to do so. Further, the Asian malls that were most appropriate for the city were those that could adapt themselves to the look and form of their more mainstream counterparts.

The reports resulted in a number of changes in the review process for Asian malls in Fremont. First, the recommendations from the *Assessment of Asian-Themed Retail* were shared with the planning and economic development department to assist in its review of potential Asian mall projects. The concerns raised about retail condominiums in the *Fremont Market Analysis and Retail Strategy* resulted in even stricter regulations. "Although this is relatively new territory as most cities have not adopted such policies," advised the report, "Fremont would be well served by taking a proactive approach to the future and actively addressing the retail condominium issue as quickly as possible, rather than waiting for more serious problems to arise."[44] Though Fremont had no Asian malls with retail condominiums at the time, there were a number that were approved, were in the final approval stages, or were under review. In 2009 by a unanimous city council vote, the city adopted two new regulations that would shape the location and character of future retail condominiums.

The first was a zoning text amendment that established new standards for the design and operation of all new retail condominiums or condo conversions in the city. Under the new law, retail condos are issued a conditional use permit, which subjects them to an additional level of planning review. To receive full approval, developers need to show their compliance with a set of standards that includes a review of the size of the units to ensure that they are "typical and customary to the zoning district." Developers must also establish a property owner's association "to warrant the continued viability of the project, avoid conditions of neglect and blight, retain aesthetic consistency and conformity, and ensure a mechanism for funding the maintenance and replacement." The association is required to have initial reserve funds equal to five years of annual maintenance costs and to hire a licensed, professional management firm. In addition, associations are required to adopt covenants, codes, and restrictions (CC&Rs) that cover, among other things,

FIGURE 12. Fremont Times Square is the city's first condo-owned Asian mall. Because the city passed a retail condo ordinance just before the mall was built, planners exercised stricter control over the development process that gave the property a more traditional suburban shopping center form and ensured that it could be made more readily available for redevelopment. Photo by author.

"promoting a high quality and professional physical appearance and cohesive operation . . . that avoids deteriorating and inconsistent conditions including but not limited to design, architectural treatments and features, and signage."[45] Just as the CC&Rs have been used to control housing standards, raising the cost of homeownership and discouraging lower-income residents, retail CC&Rs raise the cost of business ownership in ways that discouraged smaller independent retailers and developers. In addition, CC&Rs, whether in residential subdivision or commercial districts, aim to standardize the look of development, often adopting and reinforcing dominant social and cultural norms of design.

Finally, new retail condo regulations addressed the city's desire to make way for future redevelopment opportunities. This was most clear in the second component of the ordinance, which applied additional standards to commercial, industrial, and other nonresidential condominiums within a half mile of current or proposed rapid transit stations. The ordinance emphasized the need to limit fractionalized ownership within zones designated by city plans as areas for future high-density development. According to one seasoned city planner, this component came as a direct response to the proposal to build Fremont Times Square, Fremont's first condo-owned Asian shopping center (Figure 12).

The resolution adopted in 2007 stated that part of the reason for the regulations was that the city "anticipated one or more condominium development applications in the coming months" and specified that the regulations would apply to any approved project whether or not regulations had been fully adopted at the time of approval.[46] Fearing that the retail condominium projects such as Fremont Times Square might stand in the way of their ability to control important development areas such as those close to transit, the city council zoned them out of some of Fremont's most valuable land.

The timing of the draft retail condominium ordinance gave the planning department the ability to work with the developers of Fremont Times Square to ensure that the project complied with the city's terms. To receive planning approval, the mall was required to adopt CC&Rs, have a management team in place, and ensure that its units were "appropriately sized." According to former planning director Jeff Schwob, the latter specification helped city staff negotiate a reduction in the number of units to nearly half the number originally proposed.[47] Another planner informed me that the city was also able to work directly with the developers to structure the CC&Rs to ensure that provisions were made for the units to maintain a minimum level of visibility and that the majority vote within the property association was vested with its anchor tenant, Marina Foods. Thus, if the city wanted to redevelop the site it only had 1 owner to contend with, bypassing potential dealings with the other 63 owners. "[The city] structured the voting rights so that we could cause change to occur more easily," Schwob explained.[48] Through the adoption of new regulations, the city directed Asian malls away from some of the city's most valuable land and was able to better control the structure and form of new shopping centers.

All of the Asian mall developers I spoke to were critical of Fremont's attempt to regulate Asian malls. Some saw the commissioning of the *Assessment of Asian-Themed Retail* as revealing city officials' biased views toward these shopping centers. Developer Charles Wang wondered why there was not a greater backlash to the city's decision to focus a study on Asian shopping centers in the first place:

> Now, what would the outcry be if they said "You know what? We're going to do [a study] about African Americans." Or, "We're going to do one about Native Americans." Why are you commissioning the study, and why are you spending the money on a firm that's not even in this area, from Vancouver, to come in here and give you an analysis of all the shopping centers here. Are you trying to inhibit their growth? Are you trying to control them

in a certain way rather than let the market dictate what it is? That, to me, was quite disturbing.

The city, he argued, had gone to great lengths to produce a report that itself evidenced its unfair treatment of Asian Americans. Further, the report was designed not to help Asian malls flourish but instead to regulate them. Charles believed in the market's ability to decide how a city should grow and change. Such laissez-faire attitudes were common among Asian mall developers. Most did not believe that government should play such a strong role in deciding what should go into a shopping center. The market, they said, was on the side of developing more and larger Asian malls.

Developers' complaints were not only with the regulation of Asian malls. They also complained that the City of Fremont was an extreme case when it came the scrutiny given to Asian mall projects. City officials' attitudes, some charged, were based on their biased views about the desirability of Asian malls. Diana Li, an immigrant from Taiwan who had been developing residential and commercial real estate in Silicon Valley for nearly two decades when we first met, felt that the city was skeptical of allowing Asian malls before any studies were conducted. "They don't like Asian center[s] to start with," she explained, "and then after that, they did a study." For her, it was the skepticism that city officials already had that drove the reports rather than the reports that drove the city's concerns.

Developers charged that the city's distaste for Asian malls had resulted in several potential projects having been turned down or delayed. They cited a propensity for stalled applications, excessive study periods, and additional planning requirements. "We fight through this, that, and then the city would just hold our application—just leave it as no, no, no; no Asian, no Asian," complained one frustrated developer. Referencing a proposed Asian mall project that was under planning review for nearly four years, another charged that the planning department "threw everything in the way." He described what he saw as an excessive number of traffic and environmental studies. Though such accusations are difficult to verify, the view of many developers I spoke to was that Asian malls were perceived by both city officials and many non–Asian American residents as unwelcome or at the very least a problematic addition to Fremont's commercial landscape. Rather than recognizing the social value that these properties served in the lives of their patrons and the economic value they brought to Fremont, they charged, city officials were blindsided by residents' complaints about these malls and their own desires to see them regulated.

Such views were even held by some Asian mall developers such as Tommy Feng, a major Silicon Valley shopping center developer, who agreed with some of the city's assessments about the downsides of retail condominiums. Tommy acknowledged that retail condominium projects might have a harder time succeeding financially compared to those that were centrally managed, but he viewed the city's reaction to the Fremont Times Square project with trepidation. He concluded that "The city hated the project." While city regulations allowed Fremont Times Square to include retail condominiums, Tommy believed that the city had effectively banned them by imposing such strict regulations. Regardless, the vehement opposition among city officials during the debates indicated that any future retail condominium projects would have a very hard time getting approved. "They would not allow another condo project in this area," he projected. The city's handling of the Fremont Times Square project, he thought, was a missed opportunity to educate themselves about how retail condominiums could work more effectively in the city.

City officials adamantly denied any claims of bias underlying their various studies or regulations. When I broached the topic with Fremont's former planning director Jeff Schwob, he clarified the difference between the regulations' effect and city officials' intent. "We didn't regulate just Asian malls, we regulated condos," he pointed out. "That may have been a form that happened to be maybe Asian-based, I don't know. But that wasn't the intent. It's really around the condo. It's not who is in it."[49] While the intent might not have been to control Asian malls, the impact clearly fell most heavily on them. Moreover, based on the various city council sessions about the ordinance and my various discussions with city officials about the issue, it appeared that many council members and planners clearly understood this. Such disparate impact did not, however, raise debate in the city council about the fairness of regulations.

It was also clear that what drove much of the debate over Asian malls was the many complaints, questions, and fears that these malls had generated across the city. When I asked Director Schwob why the city had decided to commission the report on Asian-themed retail in the city, he noted that the study was meant to address the complaints and questions that both city residents and officials had raised. "[T]here's fear in the unknown," he explained. "There's a desire to figure out at least what [Asian malls are]. What are the fears? How do we address those?"[50]

Would these questions have been raised by similarly structured projects owned by non–Asian American residents or businesses? What inspired the residents' and city officials' "fear" about these projects? How did these fears play into the reactions of residents and city officials to Asian malls? And how did they shape the discourse over Asian malls in the city? These questions were raised by many of the Asian mall developers with whom I spoke but were largely absent from public debate about these malls. Instead, race was a subtext of debates over the regulation of retail shopping centers in Fremont. However, absence of discussions about race does not mean that racially biased attitudes or the structures that support inequality based on race have gone away.[51] In Fremont, Asian malls clearly upset the presumed norms about retail development in the city that privileged a landscape whose rules were largely set in place before Asian Americans were a significant presence in the region. The pushback that these new shopping centers received by both city officials and non–Asian American residents revealed how Asian malls countered their assumptions about what a suburban shopping mall is, how it operates, who it is for, and what it should look like.

It was also clear that the city wanted to maintain its ability to control its retail form. The ability of well-to-do suburban communities such as Fremont to exercise rigid control over their form has long been an important part of reproducing race and class inequalities between cities and suburbs as well as among suburbs. While efforts to control the design and development of Asian malls in Fremont may not have been intended to exclude Asian Americans residents or businesses, the imposition of rigid standards of development, whether in the form of public regulations or private contracts such as CC&Rs, often have the effect of reproducing race and class inequalities.[52] In Fremont, the regulations may have discouraged some Asian American–owned businesses and new Asian malls from starting up in the city and signaled to those Asian mall developers, businesses owners, and customers that this form of retail is problematic if not altogether unwelcome. In the face of challenges to the city's existing retail form, officials used their power to reinforce the dominant standards of suburban commercial design but did not question the basis upon which the standards had been adopted in the first place or who they benefited most.

PUTTING ASIAN MALLS IN THEIR PLACE

While regulations and review processes have been used to control and perhaps at times restrict the growth of Asian shopping centers, the city's vision of desirable retail has also been an impediment to the growth of Asian malls in Fremont. This vision focuses on attracting retail establishments that are "typical" for a middle-income suburb. Despite Asian malls' apparent popularity and the critical social functions that they serve for the city's rapidly growing Asian American population, many city officials have not regarded them as being important to advancing Fremont's retail interests.

Race has long played a role in defining what is perceived as desirable development. Neighborhoods inhabited primarily by non-White residents tend to be deemed undesirable especially by Whites but also oftentimes by racial minorities. This is not just because of stereotypes about people of color but also because of the unique desirability of White American spaces. In suburbia, middle-class White Americans have long set the standard of both normality and desirability. In housing, such widespread perceptions have given an economic boost to White Americans who live in racially exclusive neighborhoods. In the commercial landscape, it has helped to bolster the premium often placed on the more mainstream retail establishments.

This is not to say, however, that Asian malls do not have a place in the suburban landscape. In Fremont, as the city struggled to define its own place within Silicon Valley's competitive commercial marketplace, officials used these shopping centers as a tool to better promote Fremont as an inclusive multicultural city that is open for business. This positioning of Asian malls underscores how culture and the places that seemingly represent it are commodified—products sold and marketed by cities in the service of profit and often at the expense of ethnic communities.[53] In Fremont, officials' efforts to use Asian malls to showcase the city's diversity did little to support Asian businesses. At the same time, their efforts ignored the struggles and tensions that Asian mall developers raised about these malls and instead aided the city in maintaining what Lisa Lowe calls "a consensus of inclusion."[54] Asian malls allowed officials to advertise Fremont as a global cosmopolitan city while failing to address the deep tensions that such rapid social and spatial change brought about.

Just a Normal Middle-Class Suburb

While Asian shopping centers have been the subject of much debate and regulation in Fremont, they have not been part of the city's strategic retail vision. Fremont's General Plan lays out a goal for attracting "quality and specialty retail" that can act as a catalyst for attracting "high-end retail."[55]

Nearly every city official and planner with whom I spoke about commercial development mentioned the city's consistent efforts to try to attract the kind of retail that they felt would appeal to a "typical" upper-middle-class consumer.[56] In a brochure I picked up from the city's planning department, the Fremont Office of Economic Development advertised that it was looking for "high-quality retail," including "more boutique shops, outdoor dining and cafés, and entertainment venues."[57] My conversations with many in the city revealed that it was not just high-end retailers that officials were after but also more mainstream retail establishments. As one economic development presentation on "targeted business recruitment" indicated, the city's efforts aimed at trying to attract major chains such as Whole Foods, Best Buy, Target, Home Goods, AMC Theatres, and McCormick and Schmick's Seafood Restaurant.

The city's efforts to attract these businesses were not as successful as hoped. "We are not getting the higher-end, traditional places," explained Mayor Bob Wasserman when we spoke in 2011. "We would like to get some nice, white tablecloth restaurant. We always have, and we've always gone after them."[58] Wasserman's comments brought with them a real sense of history. Having come to Fremont in 1976 as a newly hired police chief, Wasserman entered politics as a city council member in 1992 and was ending his second term as mayor when we spoke. "I'm only the link to the past," Wasserman joked in reference to how much the city had changed since he first began working there. The mayor, however, made clear that the city's desire for higher-end retail establishments was one of its few long-standing issues that remained in the face of a changing city.

Ironically, some city officials said that the main reason why Fremont has been unable to attract upscale retail establishments in a city with such a high median income was its large Asian American population. When I asked Mayor Wasserman what had hampered the city's recruitment efforts, he responded, "That has a lot to do with our demographics, unfortunately. Like Whole Foods. Whole Foods will never say it publicly, but the reason they're not here is because of our ethnicity."[59] Wasserman and other city officials argued that many large retailers make assumptions about what Asian Americans will and will not purchase. Economic development coordinator Angela Tsui explained that it can be difficult to bring in national chains that look at Fremont's demographics and say "I don't really think that your Asian population is really going to come and eat at a Claim Jumpers."[60] But she countered these stereotypes by pointing out that the popular California chain restaurant, which serves traditional American fare, is doing very well now in Fremont. Mayor Wasserman agreed that the city's stigma is unfounded. "I know that they're wrong, but how do you tell Whole Foods that they're wrong? You can't tell them they're wrong. They don't listen."[61]

The city's argument amounts to a claim of retail or commercial redlining, a discriminatory practice of denying service areas not based on their economics but instead on their racial or ethnic composition. This practice has long been noted in many predominantly African American communities, including several well-to-do suburban communities.[62] Many in the city envision their role as fighting against such inequities and getting the city up to par with the kind of development common for its middle-income demographic. This battle, however, also involves an implicit denial that the city is any different than any other typical middle- or upper-middle-income suburban community in terms of the desires of its residents for goods and services.

The Asian shopping center developers with whom I spoke were skeptical about whether the city's efforts were well placed, given that over half of the city's population was Asian American. "Fremont has been talking about Whole Foods for 20 years," explained John Luk. He argued that city officials were not able to make it happen because retail is market driven, and what is desired by the market are Asian shopping centers and stores.[63] Diana Li was also skeptical of the success of the city's strategy. "I'm not sure about it," she said. "Asians, they will spend money on housing, education. They will spend money for their kids to play, but, in turn, they [won't] spend money to dine at [a] fine tablecloth restaurant." While pulling on their own stereotypes about the needs and desires of Asian American consumers that enhanced the value of what they brought to the city, the developers critiqued the city as having ignored the needs of the vast majority of its population.

Asian mall developers also depicted city officials as being out of touch with or even dismissive of the dominant priorities of Asian Americans in the city. Charles Wang characterized the Fremont Planning Department as "basically a bunch of White males, middle-aged," whose vision of the city is "sort of a yuppified version of things." He saw the city as trying to conform and appeal to young White professionals who wanted the benefits of a cosmopolitan, urban lifestyle within the comforts of a quiet, well-to-do community.

Underlying such debates were broader economic concerns and questions about who was shaping the future vision of retail in the city. Asian mall developers clearly wanted to see their products promoted and prioritized and were frustrated by the city's willingness to do so. To them, the popularity of Asian malls in Silicon Valley spoke to the fact that the market was on their side. But this was a reality that they felt few in the city were willing to accept. Developers' discouragement bred tensions and charges of racism and xenophobia on the part of city officials.

While not denying that there was a market for Asian retail in the city, growing this market was admittedly not on the radar of many city officials. In fact, like many non–Asian American residents, city officials with whom I spoke often argued that the city already had enough Asian shopping centers or speculated that the market for these shopping centers in Fremont was built out. In describing the city's retail vision, one planner noted that "It's more about what we don't have than what we keep getting." What many in the city saw themselves as getting was more and more Asian businesses, restaurants, and shopping malls; what they saw themselves as missing was high-end mainstream retailers that were bypassing them for other middle-class suburbs.

The notion that the city had too many or enough Asian malls was also reflected in city officials' lack of attention to attracting Asian retailers. After Mayor Wasserman talked at length about his outreach efforts to more mainstream businesses, I asked him about the city's efforts to attract Asian businesses, especially high-end restaurants. He responded that the city does not have to "woo" Asian businesses because "they find us." The mayor spoke about his efforts to work with the Chinese Real Estate Association on particular deals but also noted that the majority of his time was spent trying to entice businesses that would "upgrade" Fremont's retail landscape.

Notably, however, the city's efforts ran counter to the findings of the *Fremont Market Analysis and Retail Strategy,* which concluded that "The predominance and growth of the Asian population suggests that specific strategies should be developed to assist Asian business owners and encourage Asian-oriented retail in order to create a more vibrant and successful retail environment."[64] Several Asian mall developers felt that the failure to heed this point had put the city at a disadvantage compared to other cities in the region. John Luk, for instance, argued that Fremont had still not managed to attract the type of quality Asian retail that a city of its size demands. Unlike Cupertino and Milpitas, which had comparably high percentages of Asian American populations but much larger and well-known Asian shopping centers, he explained, Fremont had missed out on the opportunity to bring large Asian banquet restaurants and other popular stores to the city.

One developer offered a striking example of how he believed the city's vision of desirable retail had affected the fate of Asian malls in Fremont. In the mid-2000s, a proposed Asian mall project was tied up in the Fremont Planning Department for nearly four years. The proposal included various small retail spaces and medical office condos on a site that was zoned for light industry. The project would require the approval of the city to change the zoning to neighborhood commercial in order to move forward. According to this developer, it was clear that the application had stalled because the city was not particularly keen on the Asian mall concept. The attitude among city officials, he said, was that "We're not really for that over here. We want to see an upscale supermarket."

In 2008, the developer approached the council with a proposal to shift the main anchor from an Asian supermarket to Berkeley Bowl, a well-known northern California organic food chain. "It is not an Asian market," the developer told the council. "This type of grocer crosses over to various cultures and to everybody."[65] The developer's proposal emphasized the pairing of an Asian mall with a more mainstream high-end grocer. The revised proposal received positive feedback from the council. In the end, the project faltered over the developer's inability to locate tenants during a harsh economic climate. But the main message that the story conveyed for the developer who related the story was that if you want something built in Fremont, it is best to align your project with the city's vision, not try to change it. Asian mall projects simply did not fit well with the vision.

This developer's account was no doubt different than what I would have received from city officials I did not talk to about the specifics of this project. Many Asian mall developers, however, had come to similar conclusions about what city officials wanted and did not want to see. Their perceptions raised doubts about how inclusive the city's vision of the future was and about Asian Americans' place within it. If Asian malls served as an indicator, many developers concluded, their place was clearly at the margins.

Diversity for Sale

While city officials may have been slow to embrace the market for Asian malls, they have recognized their value in promoting Fremont's diversity and attracting other types of investment to the city. Elsewhere, the marketing or branding of landscapes as culturally and ethnically diverse has also been shown to promote practices of racial and economic exclusion. In urban ethnic enclaves such as Chinatown in Washington, D.C., the symbols of once vibrant ethnic communities—Chinese-language signage, colorful gateways, and pagoda architecture—have emerged in the face of massive residential displacement.[66] Likewise, in the San Gabriel Valley a campaign to brand a commercial corridor as ethnically diverse justified the expulsion of many small businesses owned by Chinese immigrants.[67]

In Fremont, the rhetoric of multiculturalism has not been implicated in the direct displacement of Asian American–owned businesses or residents. It has, however, been employed to strategically position Asian malls in ways that reinforce the city's image as an inclusive cosmopolitan community. This logic has further marginalized Asian malls that do not fit into city officials' multicultural vision and acted as a convenient trope that allows city officials to dismiss the community tensions and issues of equity that these malls have raised. The reimagining of Fremont's landscape as a placid, multicultural meeting ground erases the sense that many developers hold of Asian malls as marginalized retail spaces.

Fremont's *Assessment of Asian-Themed Retail* provides recommendations to city officials about how to strategically leverage Asian malls. The study concludes that Asian malls should be positioned so as to showcase the city's diversity in its downtown:

> Asian retail would play a key role in Fremont's future International Street development to showcase its multicultural diversity. Given that the raw ingredients for a unique Downtown Fremont are being pursued along the freeway interchanges, the alternative opportunity to be a part of the "heart" of Fremont should be vigorously marketed to developers.[68]

Accordingly, as applications for Asian malls come to the city, the report suggests that planners ask "Would the proposed mix of retail be better suited to Downtown Fremont (such as the development proposal to showcase all Asian communities in its offering)?"[69] This strategy focuses on Asian malls' potential to attract new business and other investments by enabling the city to better bill itself as a diverse and inclusive community.

It was especially critical that the *Assessment of Asian-Themed Retail* suggested placing Asian malls at the heart of Fremont's Central Business District. For nearly 60 years, the city had tried to bring its five original towns together under a central downtown that could enhance and develop its civic identity. Plan after plan has been proposed over the years, but most officials recognized the city's failure to produce a vibrant downtown, relative to other Silicon Valley suburbs such as Mountain View and Palo Alto. As council member Suzanne Chan put it, Fremont did not seem to have much "there in the there."[70] The city's latest reincarnation of Fremont's *Downtown Community Plan and Design Guidelines* has among its main objectives to "reflect Fremont's cultural diversity."[71] While it does not appear that the city followed up on the report's recommendation to try to attract an Asian shopping center into the downtown area, the city made efforts to symbolically display diversity in the heart of its retail landscape and incorporate it as part of the city's identity.

Another example of how Fremont city officials have thought about how to best position diversity within its retail landscape was evidenced by their handling of the Globe Mall project. In 2005 Fremont received a proposal from the Imperial Investment and Development Company, a firm owned by John Wynn, whose family and partners owned several well-known Asian malls in Silicon Valley. The proposal called for "the first internationally-themed lifestyle center in the United States."[72] According to its marketing materials, the Globe Mall was to create "an environment that is inclusive of the different cultures of the world and to express them through the design of the architecture as well as the types of products and services offered."[73] The mall was to be a 700,000-square-foot project, one of the largest developments in Fremont. It included various retail, restaurant, and entertainment spaces representing 12 regions of the world at its various centers—Pacifica, Saigon Village, Little India, Europa, China Village, Little Tokyo, Korea Town, Australia, New Zealand, North America, South America, the Middle East, and Africa. "The Heart" of the project was where all its parts would come together to "celebrate cultural differences while at the same time promoting discovery of our commonalities" through art, music, dance, lectures, fashion shows, cooking competitions, and other community events.[74] The mall was to showcase and celebrate people and cultures from around the world. Its developers cited Fremont as the representation of such diversity.

The Globe Mall presented the city with the opportunity to display an ethnically "integrated" model of retail, which many believed Asian malls lacked. The *Assessment of Asian-Themed Retail*, for instance, recommended that "new Asian-themed development in Fremont should demonstrate a degree of cross-cultural appeal" and "a clear strategy to attract non–Asian Americans."[75] Moreover, "development proposals that cater to multiple closely linked Asian markets (such as Japanese and Korean or Chinese and Vietnamese) should be preferred to those that target a single group."[76] City officials I spoke to tended to agree with the report's conclusions. "The idea that you have a mall devoted to one culture, was not the Fremont way," Director Schwob pronounced in explaining the city's response to the conclusion of the report. "I think that they were hoping for more integration and diversity."[77]

Fremont city officials were excited by the Globe Mall's prospects, especially the three White members on the city council during the project's early phases. "My first reaction was, you're going to build an Epcot Center with upscale shopping in it," explained Mayor Wasserman at a 2006 council hearing. "It has such great potential for attracting people from all over the world, really. And will have features that will be unique to the whole West Coast, maybe the whole country."[78] Council member Dominic Dutra agreed: "The diversity component is a great, great theme."[79] Dutra came from a well-known Fremont political family, which included his father, who served on the council in the 1980s and went on to become a state senator, and his brother, John, who ran for the council unsuccessfully after Dominic's term ended. The Dutra family also owned one of the more successful residential and commercial real estate development companies in the region.

The two Asian American council members expressed more reservations about the project but were still supportive. Steve Cho, Fremont's first Chinese American council member, critiqued an early version of the project that did not include a section of the mall for Europe. Cho arrived in Silicon Valley from the East Coast, where he was born and raised, and had worked in high tech as a systems analyst before launching his own business. He was elected to the council in 2000 and served for eight years before running twice unsuccessfully for mayor. Anu Natarajan, the city's first Indian American council member, was the slowest to support the project. Born in Bangalore, India, Natarajan came to the United States to be educated, earning a double master's degree in urban design and planning. Having quickly worked her way from the planning department to an appointment on the planning commission and, two years later, to a seat on the city council, she was still fresh to the Fremont political scene. In fact, Natarajan's election in 2004, which made her the first Indian American female city council member in the state of California, occurred just one year after she was conferred U.S. citizenship. She lent a different perspective to the debate. For instance, when the developer showed pictures of the Taj Mahal as inspiration for some of the design elements, Natarajan expressed her concern that the architecture was presenting a "Disneyfied mockery of culture." When we met at a popular coffee shop in central Fremont, Natarajan expanded on her thoughts on the project:

I had a huge issue with The Globe, with its architecture, trying to mimic the different countries, like "What are you trying to build here? Disneyland?" I call it a "Disneyfied mockery of cultures," because that is what it was to me. I think there is a way of celebrating diversity; it's through food, through art in a various forms, and through people themselves coming together. I don't think it's the building itself [that] needs to be calling attention to the fact that it is diverse.[80]

Natarajan acknowledged that few of her fellow council members shared this position and found herself working directly with the developer to come up with a project that she could support. She noted, however, that she was never against the diversity theme of the project. "The idea was powerful," she explained, "but how they approached it was tacky."[81] The reelections of council members Cho and Natarajan relied on appealing to both their own ethnic communities and a broad cross-section of Fremont voters, neither of which could fault them for supporting a project that celebrated the diversity of the city.

The emphasis of additional comments surrounding the plan suggested that the multicultural appeal of the mall was critical to its popularity among Fremont council members. Perhaps sensing the concerns of council members about the perception of Asian malls as racially segregated spaces, when introducing the project to the council in 2006 city planners explained that they had already begun to think about how to make the project "appeal to a broad audience and not just one ethnic or cultural group."[82] Council member Cho stressed the importance of this aspect of the project in terms of public perception. "Although the predominant businesses that are shown on the map are Asian, the idea that we need to get across is that this is international," he explained. "I think that [it is] important to portray that image to the public."[83]

An exchange at a 2007 city council meeting between council member Natarajan and Roger Shanks, former Fremont planning director and at the time a consultant to the project developer, exemplified the desire to distance the Globe Mall from the image of ethnically exclusionary retail space. Natarajan reminded the developer to heed the city's requirements that signage be predominantly in English.[84] "Reiterate that this is not an Asian center but a global village," she suggested. In response, Shanks reassured her that indeed it was not an Asian center but rather an international center. "We are looking at everybody from European to Asian," he explained. "We want it to be inclusionary not exclusionary."[85]

The council assured the developers that it would work with them to "make sure the project happens as quickly as possible."[86] And indeed, the council did. While the project was proposed in January 2005, by March 2006 the Fremont City Council had unanimously voted to rezone the property from industrial to high-volume retail, the critical step that gave the developer the go-ahead for the plan. This occurred in spite of the fact that the plan included retail condominiums in the initial section of the development, about which the council expressed reservations. To address this issue, the council directed the developer to work with planners on the details of the condo plans to ensure that, in council member Natarajan's words, the "maintenance level and the quality is consistent and high."[87]

Yet the hope that the city had invested in the Globe Mall soon faded. In 2009 with only one section of the mall complete and only a few tenants in place, Saigon Village, LLC, the owners of the mall, filed for Chapter 11 bankruptcy. In explaining the failure of the project, city officials offered various explanations. It was a combination of bad economic times and an inexperienced developer with big aspirations, explained a city planner who had worked on the project. "Their business model wasn't sound," said council member Suzanne Chan, who replaced Cho as the second Chinese American on the council and voted to approve the project.[88]

The daughter of a Chinese "paper son," Chan grew up in the American Midwest. She settled in Silicon Valley in the 1980s, where her husband founded his dentistry practice, and quickly found herself involved in local politics. Shortly after receiving an appointment on the planning commission, she threw her hat into the ring when Cho termed out of his position on the council. "If not me, than there would not be a Chinese American on the council," she explained. Active in Asian Pacific Islander issues at the state level, Chan was not insensitive to the issue facing Asian shopping centers in Fremont. For her, however, the Globe Mall offered something than other Asian malls in the city different. "Asians have plenty of places to shop and eat," she noted, but the Globe Mall brought amenities such as an entertainment complex that were well needed in the community.

Several of the Asian shopping center developers I spoke to saw the failure of the Globe Mall in a different way. Disappointed with the city's lack of attention to their own projects, many saw a city that was so eager to put aside the perception of Asian shopping malls as exclusionary retail space that they rushed to support a project that better fit with many residents' and city officials' ideas about inclusion. This vision, some asserted, blurred the city's assessment of the Globe Mall as a doable project. While the reasons for the mall's failure were likely far more complex than either city officials or developers realized, including the blistering impacts of the Great Recession, the perceptions of developers showed how frustrated they had become with city officials' various visions of what and who this community was.

Ironically, however, the end product of the Globe Mall was essentially an Asian mall. Before filing for bankruptcy, the only section of the site that was built was Saigon Village, and its only tenants were oriented to Asian American consumers. After emerging from bankruptcy in 2011, the company reorganized its plans to focus on only a few key sections—Pacifica, Indus, Sino, Siam, Nippon, Europa, and "The Heart."[89] Outside of Europa, the cultures represented in the new mall were exclusively Asian. One planner who had worked on the project observed that the initial reaction to the Globe Mall proposal by many in the city was "Oh, it's just another Asian mall." Skeptical about whether the project was going to realize the multicultural vision that the developer had set forth, some speculated that the mall was not going to turn out as diverse as it appeared. After its reorganization, this fear "turned out to be partially true," the planner noted. His assessment was not that the developer intended the project to be as such but that somewhere along the way he recognized that "[Asian malls] are the most marketable properties here in Fremont." While the Globe Mall held the possibility of concretizing the multicultural vision that the city wanted to project, it instead came to represent the opposite—"just another Asian mall" (Figure 13).

"It appears that Fremont is facing significant challenges in overcoming its historic development patterns to create a more vibrant, retail environment for the community," concluded the *Fremont Market Analysis and Retail Strategy*. City officials have been actively trying to locate new retail opportunities, but their appeal has been limited largely to mainstream middle-class establishments that may not be addressing the needs of the city's predominantly Asian American patrons. Asian malls, while often viewed by city officials as an opportunity to improve the visibility of diversity in the city, are not well integrated into the city's retail vision or its plans.

. . .

Asian malls demonstrate the many aspirations that Asian Americans have brought with them in their migration to the suburbs and how they have reshaped the Silicon Valley landscape and, in turn, been reshaped by it. Throughout the valley, Asian malls have emerged at the critical intersections of Asian American suburban communities. These shopping centers have

FIGURE 13. The Globe Mall filed for Chapter 11 bankruptcy in 2009, turning many politicians' and planners' multicultural dreams into a nightmare. At the time, the only section of the mall that was built was Saigon Village, and its only tenants were Asian-owned businesses. Photo by author.

become the meeting grounds for Asian American suburbanites from all parts of the region and the globe. Within them, diverse groups have built a public culture that affirms their needs, desires, and identities. There, Asian Americans gather among old friends, family members, and colleagues as well as meet new ones; they celebrate their cultural roots and traditions while also encountering novel practices that reconfigure their identities and cultural practices; and they come together with their local communities while simultaneously engaging with translocal and global communities that reshape their sense of home and community. As different groups gather in Asian malls, they bring their old suburban dreams and build upon them.

The remolding of the suburban commercial landscape in ways that reflect Asian Americans' emergent and varied sense of home, community, and public life has, however, generated heated debates. The differences that set Asian malls apart from traditional American suburban shopping centers have become the basis upon which critiques have been leveled and regulations adopted. The shopping centers are regularly questioned by city officials and non–Asian American residents for the "nontraditional" and "foreign" elements they introduce and have often been perceived as out of place in an otherwise standardized commercial landscape. When viewed from the outside, these malls are rarely painted as the rich and diverse places they appear to be from the inside. Their important social and cultural functions fade away, and their departure from the traditional American suburban landscape is amplified but not affirmed. They have often been judged more for what they fail to provide to those who do not even use them or understand their value rather than for those for whom Asian malls are a critical part of their everyday lives and identities.

These shopping centers have been racialized both by the ways they have been imagined as not fitting into their given landscapes and the ways they have been. The former include the ways in which city officials and non–Asian American residents often view Asian malls as too strange, chaotic, messy, or segregated to fit into a middle-class suburban community. The latter includes the limited value often assigned to these places by municipal leaders in representing difference in the suburban landscape. Economic development strategies that focus on the strategic placement and design of Asian malls are little different than the brochures that paint urban Chinatowns and Little Saigons as exotic destinations wherein tourists can encounter the cultural "other." They market an illusion of authentic culture for profit while also denying these spaces' contested politics of difference, identity, and representation. In neither of these visions, however, are the diverse array of social and cultural values, meanings, and desires that Asian Americans express through their everyday use of Asian malls respected.

City planning policies and processes have emboldened city officials and planners to act as brokers with the power to judge what are and are not acceptable representations of the city's civic identity and commercial interests. As in many places, Fremont city officials tended to frame culture and its expression in the landscape as a thing to be observed, vicariously experienced, and sold like any other mall product.[90] At the same time, they tended to read the proliferation of such cultural expression outside of its presumed context as problematic and a challenge to the city's otherwise neat and orderly landscape. City regulations and policies have been used to manage the expression of difference in ways that make them more acceptable to mainstream audiences and outside business interests. Such policies marginalize already marginalized groups by claiming a narrow space in which they belong and attempting to craft the message that these places display to the outside world. Rather than taking on those who tend to stereotype and critique these malls' differences from the mainstream, they bolster their arguments and enable these groups to better shape the landscape in ways that are acceptable to them.

Given that both shopping malls and schools are part of the suburban public or pseudopublic sphere, it is perhaps not altogether unexpected that the changes that Asian Americans have introduced have generated fiery public deliberations. The next chapter shows how Asian Americans are inspiring new forms of the single-family home. And yet, even in this relatively private domain there is little indication that the intensity of local debate has waned. Debates over the design of suburban homes continue to show limits of Asian Americans to alter suburbia's customary form, enter the political fray, and change the dynamics at play.

FOUR

That "Monster House" Is My Home

> The hearing adjourns and one has a feeling of incompleteness, of missing information. There is more here than an issue of housing sizes. On the surface the old and young quarrel over lifestyles, while underneath the silent stream of distrust cuts chasms between races and cultures, between generations.
>
> DAVID LEY

"LET ME TELL YOU A VERY sad story," began Paul Chen in his statement before the Fremont City Council in 2008.[1] "My family needed more space. We decided to add a second story to our house [in] Mission Ranch two years ago. The city approved my permit," he explained. He went on to recount how after his neighbors became aware of his plans he and his wife began to receive harassing e-mails and were reported to the school system for allegedly falsifying their address. "We felt completely alone, as we were targeted and made to feel that we were somehow going to hurt the neighborhood by doing what others had done, which is simply to add on to their home," Paul told the council.[2] Feeling frustrated and humiliated, the Chens abandoned their remodeling plans and moved out of the Mission Ranch neighborhood to a two-story home nearby.

The neighborhood effort to stop the Chens' building plans marked the beginning of a four-year battle over the practice of tearing down or significantly remodeling existing homes to build much larger homes (oftentimes derisively referred to as McMansions, monster homes, or teardowns) in Fremont.[3] Between 2006 and 2010, a coalition primarily made up of established White residents led a virulent campaign against these homes that were built and occupied by mostly Chinese immigrants such as the Chens. The battle was mediated by Fremont planners and policy makers in a public debate that ended with the adoption of a new citywide design review process and guidelines for all new two-story homes and second-story additions. New development standards and design guidelines were also established specifically for Mission Ranch and Glenmoor Gardens, the two neighborhoods whose residents led the fight against these homes.

Fremont is not a unique case of large home debates or their regulation in the United States. In response to growing opposition over the teardown trend that has affected as many as 500 communities nationwide, numerous cities have adopted planning and design policies to control the construction of large homes.[4] Jack Nasar, Jennifer Evans-Cowley, and Vicente Mantero found that 57% of the 103 cities they surveyed adopted new or utilized established policies to regulate the construction of large homes in existing neighborhoods, commonly through building height limits, design reviews, reduced floor-to-area ratios, and bulk and mass controls.[5] To develop their new guidelines and standards, Fremont city officials reviewed the large home policies of at least 8 other cities in Silicon Valley. Amid this growing regulatory climate, however, few scholars have questioned the particular value of these homes to their occupants or the potentially disparate impact of their regulation.

Many of the arguments for the strict regulation of these building practices rely on the views of various writings about their form and environmental and neighborhood impacts. The term "McMansion" itself implies a critique of a home as being generic and of low quality. Scholars and the media alike have tended to describe these homes as reflections of developer greed and Americans' ever-increasing penchant for bigger homes—or what urban planner and architect Mark Hinshaw calls Americans' *nouveau riche* excess."[6] Critics claim that these homes often lack quality craftsmanship, appropriate scale, and contextual features and that they diminish a neighborhood's sense of character, identity, history, and community—"the epitome of public rudeness," according to Hinshaw.[7] Urban studies scholar Paul Knox called large homes the "nurseries of . . . neoliberalism"—places that put property rights and individual consumption above public amenities and civic infrastructure.[8] Some have argued that McMansions promote gentrification and the displacement of low-income residents by increasing the value of neighboring properties.[9] Many associate these homes, more broadly, with the ills of suburbia. Knox argued that like McMansions, suburbia—or what he calls "Vulgeria"—has become characterized by "bigness and bling," "conspicuous construction," and *nouveau riche* tackiness on an unprecedented scale."[10] Historian Robert Bruegmann concluded that "McMansions are the newest culprit of taste critiques against suburbs, judged as excessive in size and stylistic pretension."[11]

But there is a different and often untold story about these much-maligned homes. This chapter looks at the emergence of large homes in established neighborhoods against a background of Fremont's rapidly increasing Asian American population. Fremont's teardown and large home development trends coincided with the dot-com boom and an influx of Asian immigration in the region. And while the regional economic forces may have played a large role in driving these trends, Asian Americans also had a significant stake in the new homes that were being built. To many entering the city at a time of unprecedented growth and prosperity, the availability of new large homes was welcomed and highly sought after. These properties were not so-called McMansions to the residents who lived in them and many who could not afford to—they were homes, and desirable ones at that.

For their residents, these homes carried meaning for the kind of suburban lifestyles they aspired to and the ways in which they thought about home and community in Silicon Valley. Large homes were valued as places that helped residents gain wealth and stability in a new place, access desirable schools, support their multigenerational households, enable their busy lifestyles, reflect their aesthetic sensibilities, and affirm their affections for new and modern houses.

Like the changing culture of schools and Asian shopping malls, however, this particular marker of Asian Americans' presence in the valley has been the subject of significant social and political contest. Established residents have questioned the particular form of these homes, the values and forces that drive their development, and their impacts on existing neighborhoods. And as with schools and Asian malls, new regulatory policies have been adopted to help resolve the tensions that the changing form of single-family homes has generated.

Despite the ostensibly mechanistic neutrality of design reviews, guide-lines, and standards adopted to address these conflicts, this chapter shows how Fremont's new home policies reinforced dominant social and cultural norms about good and appropriate design. They tended to privilege extant suburban landscapes and their embedded ideals while also naturalizing and normalizing older, typically White residents' sense of place. At the same time, they disparately impacted Silicon Valley newcomers who did not share the same norms of housing and landscape design. While many exclusionary policies tend to discourage poor and working-class minorities from purchas-ing homes in suburban neighborhoods, the regulations adopted to deal with large homes in Fremont expose the ways that planning and design professionals, processes, and regulations marginalize even affluent suburbanites.

These debates challenge planning practitioners, policy makers, and scholars to look beyond issues of housing size and aesthetics to the social meaning of these homes and how issues of difference and change are dealt with in housing policy. Suburban homes have never simply been expressions of developers' interests but are also expressions of their occupants' values and identities. In attempting to understand what suburbia means to its newest residents, scholars must be willing to look beyond the "bigness and bling" to understand more about the people who live in these homes and think more critically about the impact of their regulation.

MCMANSION REGULATION AND THE PERPETUATION OF SUBURBAN INEQUALITY

Critics of teardowns and large home construction in established neighborhoods have generated wide support for their cause in contemporary policy circles. The National Trust for Historic Preservation (NTHP), for example, serves as an ambassador, advocate, and resource for local communities combating teardowns. Their writings epitomize the alarmist tone about these homes. They ask how homeowners can stop this "teardown epidemic" in which developers "roam their streets, looking for their next teardown target."[12] And further, how can neighborhoods avoid the fate of others that have "passed the point of no return" and are now filled with "jumbled oversized homes sitting uncomfortably next to forlorn-looking older homes waiting for the wrecking ball?"[13] NTHP president Richard Moe argued that teardowns were the "most serious threat to the character of neighborhoods since urban renewal."[14]

While this depiction of the teardowns creates one narrative about their drivers and impacts, scholars have also underscored the race and class dynamics that are sometimes intertwined with these practices and their politics. In Vancouver, Canada, for instance, the rebuilding of homes in middle- and upper-middle-class suburbs in the 1980s by recent Hong Kong immigrants generated a scholarly debate about how race and class factored into residents' support of or opposition to what many called "monster homes." Some claimed that Euro-Canadians' objection to new development was an expression of their racist fears over the "Hong Kongization" of their neighborhood.[15] Others suggested that their concerns were more based on class antagonisms brought about by the threat of a new global elite.[16] And still others argued that both race and class played decisive roles in Euro-Canadians' fears and anxieties over neighborhood change that, at their base, were efforts to preserve their own economic, social, and political power and reinforce their class status.[17] Particularly revealing was geographer Katharyne Mitchell's argument that the traditional design patterns of Euro-Canadians' homes and yards were the basis upon which established residents sought to normalize and naturalize their social positions vis-à-vis Hong Kong immigrants.[18] She pointed out that established residents' position was bolstered by the existing form of the land-scape, which had been modeled on the very values and aesthetics that they proclaimed. In trying to contest these values, Hong Kong immigrants had to battle long-held assumptions about suburbia's spatial design and social meaning.

Likewise, suburban homes and landscapes in the United States often naturalize the dominant meanings and ideals of White Americans. Architectural historian Diane Harris showed how the "little white houses" constructed in the post–World War II era helped to shape White Americans identities as linked to homeownership and privatization and naturalize their place within suburbia.[19] White Americans' association with suburbia and the single-family home in particular has since become so commonplace that few question the structural, social, and cultural forces that continue to support this association. Landscapes have the power to the turn the "social into the natural," wrote geographer Donald Mitchell.[20] In suburbia, the long-held connection between Whiteness, the single-family home, and the pastoral landscape often hide the work that goes into creating these privileged places.[21] This association also shapes the norms regarding proper suburban landscape aesthetics, form, and use in ways that favor White Americans.

Urban planning and design processes and policies also do the work of normalizing and reproducing dominant social and cultural ideas about sub-urban homes and neighborhoods. By establishing design standards, guide-lines, and review processes that reinforce hegemonic norms about housing's proper form and function, regulations can signal to newcomers that their values and preferences are not welcome. Denise Lawrence-Zúñiga character-ized the imposition of design guidelines in four cities in San Gabriel Valley as a kind of "aesthetic governmentality" that was embedded with certain epistemologies, identities, and ethos that have made it difficult for new Asian immigrants to contest the given spatial order.[22]

Like many other contemporary exclusive suburban policies and practices, the tools used to control the redevelopment of homes in existing neighborhoods can disparately impact racial and ethnic minorities as well as poor and working-class groups by raising the cost of homeownership through an insistence on certain design standards.[23] But as this chapter shows, such regulations can also disparately impact minorities of means living in some of suburbia's most exclusive neighborhoods, shedding light on how White privilege is engaged through residents' power to shape the landscape and its meanings through institutionalized planning policies and processes. The rebuilding of homes in Silicon Valley has been an important way in which Asian Americans have expressed different ideas about the suburban American Dream but has also been an arena in which their place in suburbia has been widely questioned and critiqued.

SILICON VALLEY IMMIGRATION AND THE RISE OF MCMANSIONIZATION

The size and bulk of new homes across the United States expanded rapidly during the last decade of the 20th century. Between 1990 and 2000, the average size of new single-family homes increased by nearly 20%, from less than 2,100 square feet to about 2,500 square feet.[24] This bump in housing size nationally corresponded to one of the peak periods of housing development in Silicon Valley during the dot-com boom (1995–2000). While in 1995 the valley had fewer than 6,000 new housing starts, four years later nearly 16,000 units of new housing had been approved.[25]

During this period of extraordinary growth, many neighborhoods began to see old homes being torn down to make way for larger homes. In Fremont, working-class neighborhoods such as Irvington saw a fair number of homes in established neighborhoods torn down during the period. But little public controversy emerged about home-building practices in these neighborhoods. Instead, protest emerged in Mission Ranch and Glenmoor Gardens, two of Fremont's oldest and traditionally most elite neighborhoods.

Completed in 1961 and 1966, respectively, Mission Ranch and Glenmoor Gardens were among the first neighborhoods built in Fremont following its incorporation in 1956. Both included ranch-style, single-story, two- to four-bedroom homes (318 in Mission Ranch and 1,624 in Glenmoor Gardens) averaging around 1,700 square feet on generous lots of around 7,000 square feet.

Like most postwar middle- and upper-middle-income suburban neighborhoods in the United States, part of what defined the elite character of these neighborhoods was their pastoral landscapes that were enforced through strict planning and design controls (Figure 14).

These neighborhoods were among the early beneficiaries of Fremont's exclusionary zoning regime in which large areas of farmland were set aside for large-lot single-family homes. Such zoning was made possible by incorporation, which I showed in Chapter 1 was primarily a defensive act against working-class and minority encroachment from Hayward and inner-city Oakland. Even more, both neighborhoods initially employed strict covenants, codes, and restrictions (CC&Rs) that dictated minimum house sizes, costs, setbacks, heights, and landscaping.

Another characteristic that defined the elite status of these neighborhoods was their racial and ethnic homogeneity. In 1990, for example, Mission Ranch was over 90% White, compared to around 70% for the city as a whole. But as land prices began to swell and immigration reached new heights, even elite neighborhoods such as Mission Ranch began to change. Between 1990 and 2010, Mission Ranch's White population decreased from just over 90% to less than 28%, while its Asian American population grew from around 7% to 67% (see table 3).[26] Ava Johnson, who lived in the neighborhood since the early 1980s, recalled how quickly the faces of the children changed at Chadbourne, Mission Ranch's local elementary school. She estimated that between 1995 and 2000, her daughter's class went from having just a few Asian Americans to her daughter being the only White student. A city directory of Mission Ranch residents showed that about 50% of residents had Chinese last names in 2006—the year that the neighborhood's large home controversy exploded.

Alongside Asian immigration came feverish development and dramatic changes in housing sizes and styles. In Fremont, the Mission San Jose area, with its scenic landscape, views, and highly rated schools, was among the city's most popular neighborhoods for high-end development. As new subdivisions were built in former greenfields, many established residents became uneasy. Those who could recall that these areas had only years before been filled with strawberry fields, apricot groves, and cow pastures often objected to the pace, density, and character of new development.[27] One observer compared Mission San Jose's densely packed new residential developments filled with "tasteless monster homes" to its older homes that "proudly display

FIGURE 14. Mission Ranch and Glenmoor Gardens were two of the earliest subdivisions built in Fremont, whose residents led the citywide debate over large home development. These early neighborhood advertisements emphasize that the elite character of both neighborhoods was defined by their highly planned pastoral landscapes, which were upset by new large home development. Images published in City of Fremont (2009b, 2009c).

FIGURE 15. The large homes being built in Mission San Jose's hillside communities have provoked a sense of unease among many longtime residents. Photo by author.

beautifully mature gardens and palm-lined streets."[28] Despite these criticisms, Fremont's progrowth city council, which was eager to attract new Silicon Valley wealth into its fold, allowed this kind of "greenfield McMansionization" to continue largely unabated (Figure 15).[29]

During the dot-com era, however, the region's new housing supply was not able to meet its demand. Competition for new houses was stiff, and home prices soared. Existing neighborhoods, especially those with relatively small and affordable homes on large lots such as Mission Ranch and Glenmoor Gardens, offered prospective home buyers the opportunity to expand or rebuild a small house, often for less than the cost of purchasing a new or existing home in a subdivision with larger homes. Across the nation, the redevelopment of existing neighborhoods has largely favored areas such as Mission Ranch and Glenmoor Gardens with high property values before expanding into less affluent neighborhoods.[30]

With its popular schools and high land values, Mission San Jose was the epicenter of these redevelopment trends within Fremont. Directly adjacent to Mission High, Mission Ranch was among Mission San Jose's most

FIGURE 16. Mission Ranch became ground zero for Fremont's large home debates. Highlighted above are two large homes built before the neighborhood's new design guidelines and development standards were passed in 2010. These homes are shown with their ranch-style neighbors. Photos adapted from Google Maps.

visibly impacted neighborhoods. By 2006, two existing single-story homes had been torn down in the neighborhood to make way for new 4,000- and 5,000-square-foot homes. Three other homes soon followed suit (Figure 16).

Four out of the five of these controversial new homes were built and occupied by Chinese immigrants.[31] According to a Fremont planner who had composed a database of all those seeking building permits in Mission Ranch and Glenmoor Gardens for the planning department during the period, the names of most permit seekers "certainly sounded Asian."

While not large in number, both the scale and design of new homes raised immediate concerns among many established residents. While older homes had low-pitched roofs, rustic exteriors, patios, porches, picture windows, large lawns, and lush landscaping, newer homes had none of these familiar features. For instance, a house that was built on Covington Street in Mission Ranch, which many in the neighborhood called "ground zero" for the large home controversy, sported palatial Italianate doors framed by an arched grand entryway and a Mediterranean red tile roof and was finished in pink stucco. A high wooden fence secured the entire perimeter of the property, and its small sparsely landscaped lawn featured a triple-tiered cascading fountain and an elaborate stone path (Figure 17).

FIGURE 17. The house on the right in Mission Ranch became a rallying point for neighborhood opposition to large homes in existing neighborhoods in Fremont. The captions compare the size, configurations, and tax-assessed values of this home and its neighboring property. Note that the tax-assessed value of the ranch-style home is not a reflection of its market value, as Proposition 13 significantly limited property tax increases on long-term homeowners in California. Photo adapted from Google Maps.

Though considered an eyesore by many established residents, these homes were permitted under existing zoning in both Mission Ranch and Glenmoor Gardens. And while both neighborhoods had initially adopted CC&Rs that could have restricted such large-scale redevelopment from occurring, their private protections fell short. Mission Ranch had disbanded its homeowners' association (HOA) soon after it was started, citing the lack of leadership needed to maintain it and enforce its CC&Rs. Glenmoor Gardens maintained an active HOA, but its officials spoke publicly about their distaste of the 1.5-story limit contained in their existing CC&Rs, which they claimed was inadequate to prevent the redevelopment trends happening in their neighborhood. Thus, as the practice of tearing down or significantly remodeling existing homes to build homes of twice or even three times the original house size generated backlash from established residents, they appealed to city officials and planners for help.

MCMANSION SUPPORTERS AND THEIR DISCONTENTS

Two years before Paul Chen gave his emotional testimony before the Fremont City Council, he had set off a firestorm in his own neighborhood. In 2006, the Chens approached their neighbors about plans to demolish their ranch-style house in Mission Ranch and replace it with a new 4,200-square-foot home. One of the Chens' neighbors, Amir Mehta, who was born in the United States but grew up in India, opposed the changes. At the refusal of the Chens to change their plans, Mehta began to rouse his neighbors in opposition to their proposed development. He and other residents began a letter-writing campaign to the owners and petitioned the Fremont Planning Department to intervene. When the department refused to do so, noting that the home was being constructed in accordance with citywide regulations, the neighbors appealed to the city council to change the regulations. In December 2006 members of the newly formed organization, Preserve Mission Ranch, presented a petition to the city council calling for a moratorium on the construction of all new two-story homes in the neighborhood.

Over the next four years, both supporters and opponents of large home development engaged in heated public debates. Both sides aligned largely, though not exclusively, along racial and ethnic lines. By most accounts, members of Preserve Mission Ranch and other opponents of large homes were mostly older White long-term residents. Among the 30 residents who spoke out against these developments publicly, about three-fourths had European last names, and many reported that they had lived in Mission Ranch or Fremont for many years. In contrast, supporters were largely Chinese Americans. Of the 23 members who publicly spoke in support of large home development, more than three-fourths had Chinese last names. Among those I interviewed, all were recent immigrants.

The lines that divided supporters and opponents within the debates were not hard and fast. Among the opposition, there were those such as Amir Mehta, the Indian American who cofounded Preserve Mission Ranch, and other Indian Americans, Japanese Americans, and Chinese Americans who were a part of the coalition or otherwise supported its efforts. Mary Walker, an Indian American who lived in the neighborhood adjoining Mission Ranch, never spoke out publicly on the issue but agreed with opponents' position. Although Mary speculated that homes in her neighborhood were being rebuilt primarily by Asian immigrants like herself, she vehemently opposed the practice. While driving to pick up her son from Mission High, she made a detour to take me by a house that she found particularly distasteful. "Look at that," she pointed out. "That house shouldn't look so out of place, but look at how out of place it looks." Likewise, I encountered long-term White residents who took a more laissez-faire stance on these homes. Standing at the window of her expansive Mission San Jose home, Alice

Mitchell looked out over a hillside dotted with newly remodeled homes. "I'm great with the teardown," she noted, pointing to one house that had been recently rebuilt as a second home by an established Fremont family. "It doesn't really look like it belongs in the neighborhood. But I've gotten used it." Teasing her husband who had just managed a two-year renovation of their deck, Alice joked that "People might accuse us of a McMansion." Like Mary and many others with whom I spoke, Alice's views on the issue were complex, including considerations such as existing neighborhood design, property values, and property rights. Their statements underscored the diversity among advocates on both sides of the issue as well as among those who were engaged in such practices.

But Mary and Alice were the exception, not the rule. In Fremont, the widely held perception was that Chinese and Indian immigrants were most responsible for the rush of large new homes in Fremont. Further, the face of the public debate that ensued about these homes showed a clear distinction between residents on different sides of the issue. Thus, like schools and Asian malls, the rebuilding of homes in established neighborhoods became yet another issue that divided Whites and Asian Americans and stoked racial tensions in the city.

The differences between opponents and supporters of these building practices were not only demographic but also ideological. As the debates played out in public forums, with largely Chinese immigrants on one side and established White residents on the other side, their different ideas about their homes and communities became more apparent. In particular, the debate highlighted important differences between opponents and supporters on issues related to neighborhood character, housing size, historic preservation, aesthetics, privacy, outdoor space, and sense of community.

Respecting and Retaining a Neighborhood's Existing Character

Opponents of these building practices emphasized the primacy of existing development patterns. They complained that cheap, modern, and "out-of-scale" homes failed to "blend in" and "fit in" with the rest of the neighborhood. Karen Miller charged that a neighboring large home was "over-the-top" and "looks like it belongs in Malibu" rather than her "quaint little neighborhood" of Mission Ranch.[32] "People that live in Mission Ranch want it to stay Mission Ranch and not let it become Mission Mish-Mosh," argued longtime resident Carol Parker.[33] Likewise, Mission Ranch resident George Baker commented that new large homes created "an eclectic neighborhood and that's just not *our* neighborhood."[34] Opponents of new homes laid claim to a particular set of spatial features that defined the Mission Ranch neighborhood. Their assertions led to a clear sense about what belonged in *their* neighborhood and what did not.

Supporters of new home development, however, did not feel that conforming to the existing styles of development enhanced the value of their properties or the neighborhood. Instead, they argued that modern additions and improvements were raising their property values and those of the entire neighborhood. Edward Wang claimed that large remodeled homes represented the "organic growth" of the Mission Ranch neighborhood that made it and the entire city a more attractive place to live.[35] Attempting to freeze Fremont's neighborhoods in time and refusing to allow them to change according to the demands of new residents and market conditions, he charged, would hurt the city's bottom line and that of its residents.

Moreover, many argued that the main value of Mission Ranch's homes was not in their ranch-style design but rather in their location in one of the nation's best school districts. Mei-Zhen Lowe noted that she had looked at over 100 houses throughout the San Francisco Bay Area before settling in Mission Ranch.[36] "We did not move into our house because we wanted a one-story ranch. I moved in here because I wanted to give my children the best education in the best home that I could afford," Lowe explained to the city council, urging its members not to pass a ban on second-story additions in the neighborhood. When I spoke with Amir Mehta, one of the primary opponents to residential redevelopment in the Mission Ranch neighborhood, he admitted that like many other Indian Americans, his primary goal when looking for a house in Fremont was to find a neighborhood with good schools.

The location of Mission Ranch within the Mission High School attendance area was key to the rebuilding practices that took shape within it. According to one city planner, when the city mapped out where it had granted building permits for such homes, by far the largest concentration was within the Mission San Jose High School attendance area. Among the many new Mission Ranch families were a number who had moved out of the Weibel neighborhood after the attendance boundaries were redrawn in 2000. With its proximity to Mission High, many figured that the neighborhood would be safe from future attendance boundary changes. Randy Zeng moved in just after the boundary decision, followed by three related families who had all lived next door to each other in Weibel. Among them were his sister-in-law, who after uncovering issues with electrical and plumbing systems in the new home decided to rebuild it before moving in. Her house was among those that catalyzed the citywide debate. Recognizing the value of the schools for other families, both Randy and his sister-in-law later also purchased rental homes in Mission Ranch. In their neighborhood, the primary value was its popularity among those like themselves, whose housing decisions were largely driven by the quality of the neighborhood schools.

The Value of Small Single-Family Homes

Critics of new homes in Fremont also complained about the height and bulk of new homes. In Mission Ranch and Glenmoor Gardens, many argued that new homes were out of scale with their existing small single-story homes. There were plenty of other neighborhoods where one could purchase two-story homes, they argued. "If you want a McMansion, move up on the hill," wrote one Mission Ranch resident in response to a planning questionnaire about the new regulations.[37] Neighborhoods that were originally built with single-story homes should be required to remain that way to protect the "integrity" of the neighborhood, others argued. Few could see the logic in the size of new homes beyond the desire of residents to show off their newfound wealth. Luke Johnson claimed that the building practices were "showpieces" for wealthy new homeowners who did not want "little comfortable ranch houses" like his. His wife Ava agreed. While their ranch-style home communicated a sense of modesty, bigger homes being built in the neighborhood, she said, conveyed the message that "I don't care about you. We want status and we want to show that we have money."

Those who supported the rights of owners to rebuild their homes countered that the increased size of homes served several purposes. Many felt that their home was first and foremost an investment—both in their children's future (giving them access to Mission San Jose schools) and in their own financial futures. Building homes to the maximum allowable size and with the most modern features quite simply maximized their resale value.

Supporters also claimed that larger homes accommodated greater household densities. Asian immigrants commonly respect joint family systems customary of their native countries and invite parents and other extended relatives to live with them. According to the 2010 U.S. census, about 10% of Fremont's Asian American–headed households included three or more generations, compared to fewer than 4% of non-Hispanic Whites. These percentages are likely low, given that many of the Asian American residents with whom I spoke said that their parents and other relatives live with them for only part of the year, for periods as short as a few weeks to as long as 10 months out of the year, because they are only able to obtain temporary visitor visas. Jin Huang lamented that if he was not able to build a second story onto his existing home in Mission Ranch, he might have to send his parents to a senior home.[38] "We are not looking to build a fancy house," Huang told the city council, "we just need a functional house [where] we can take care of each other at home. A home carries hope and happiness. We want [the] ability and options to create a better home the way we need it to be." Several residents explained that two-story homes were particularly important for a very practical reason. They allowed for two master suites—one for their parents on the first floor and another for themselves on the second floor.

In addition, supporters claimed that the size of new homes reflected the modern middle-class standard. In 2007 Anthony Lai, an immigrant from Taiwan who had built one of the controversial homes in Mission Ranch, presented studies to the city council showing that the typical size of new homes in the San Francisco Bay Area were between 2,200 and 3,700 square feet. Homes built in the 1950s and 1960s to accommodate small nuclear families, Anthony argued, were simply too small to support today's professional families who required space for home offices, gyms, guest bedrooms, and children's playrooms.[39]

Undoubtedly, the newfound wealth of Asian American families in Silicon Valley and in Mission San Jose in particular enabled their pursuit of their large new homes. But their version of the American Dream was not so different than that of the generation who had moved into the neighborhood before them, many of whom had also built onto their homes. Discussing the neighborhood debate over lemonade on her backyard patio, Elizabeth Hill, one of the fiercest opponents of these building practices in Mission Ranch, pointed out the additions that she had made to her 2,000-square-foot house. They included the addition of a master bath, a master bedroom, and a half bath. Adding onto homes, she noted, was relatively common among people who, like herself, had moved into the neighborhood in the 1980s. But as we sat in the shadows of a 5,000-square-foot home that had recently been rebuilt next door, Elizabeth noted a distinct difference between her decisions and those of her neighbor. While she and others of her generation had built onto their homes without changing the character of their neighborhoods, newer residents had not. If she could add onto her home in a way that maintained the "integrity" of the neighborhood, why couldn't newer residents do the same, she asked.

Preserving Historic and Unique Neighborhood Elements

Opponents of large home development also placed great emphasis on preserving the "unique" elements of their neighborhoods. "Mission Ranch is a unique and treasured neighborhood, and we want to preserve its integrity, its ambiance, and the quality of our life here," read the Preserve Mission Ranch website.[40] Luke and Ava Johnson described how Mission Ranch's large backyards, quiet tree-lined streets, and friendly neighbors, which were similar to the middle-class suburbs in which they had grown up, drew them to the neighborhood. As one of the neighborhood's most outspoken opponents, Ava explained that "We were just trying to keep our neighborhood the way that we thought people wanted it to be when they moved here." "Leave it to Beaver Style Forever!" wrote one resident in response to a neighborhood survey about the new guidelines and standards.[41] For some, it seemed that architectural preservation was entangled with a way of life that they enjoyed and that large new homes threatened. For others, architectural preservation was simply a tool to maintain the existing character of the neighborhood.

Many large home supporters, however, did not consider older homes particularly valuable. Instead, they described old homes as headaches—prone to multiple problems that cost them valuable time and money. For immigrant professionals who often worked late into the evening or whose H-1B visa required them to maintain employment for residency in the United States, taking time off to do home repairs was considered very costly. As we sat in the dining room of his newly rebuilt home, Anthony Lai said that the primary reason he and his wife chose to tear down their old ranch-style home was because of its age. He explained that his wife "hated the house from day one" and never liked dealing with the problems common to older homes. When the couple decided that they needed more space, Anthony tried working through several plans to renovate the existing house or expand onto it.

But in the end, he decided that it would be more cost-effective to tear it down and build the home they really wanted.

While his plans for the old house did not work out, Anthony threw everything he had into making the new one into his dream home. He became an amateur architect, learning everything he could about roofing materials, structures, electrical, and plumbing. He customized his ceilings and shelving, had a balcony built especially for his Christmas tree (which he said always fit awkwardly in his old home), designed his own foyer shoe closet, waited three months for a drawer big enough for the pans in his wok kitchen, installed a piece of stained glass his wife made during their time in Los Angeles, and crowned his achievement with a large crystal chandelier, which he imported from China, that took him and his two daughters a full day to assemble. It was so important to Anthony that the house be exactly as he desired that his family of four lived in his office for the three years that it took to finish the project, when they could have been in the house much sooner.

Like Anthony, many supporters expressed a desire for modern new homes. "One thing you need to understand about the Chinese is we prefer to live in new homes," explained one Fremont resident.[42] While certainly not true of all Asian Americans, those I spoke to in Mission San Jose who were generally high-income immigrants tended to agree. Both Chinese and Indian immigrants commonly described new homes as a practical means of creating wealth and stability in a new place. Many claimed that new homes gained in value quicker than old homes, required less maintenance, and were better suited or could be customized to suit their modern lifestyles and multigenerational households.[43] These residents tended to view opponents as attempting to freeze their neighborhoods in time and refusing to embrace the current times and modern design values.

Aesthetic Critiques of Large Homes

Opponents often described the large homes being built in their neighborhoods as being in poor taste and tacky. Jennifer Alvin, a 19-year Mission Ranch resident, explained that one of the reasons she had chosen her neighborhood was because of its "beautiful landscaping." With the new homes built in the neighborhood, she told the Fremont Planning Commission, she now had to hold her breath out of fear that she would be "visually assaulted by some horrible, large mansion."[44]

Supporters, however, said that they preferred the modern style of new homes in Fremont. "We strongly welcome more new homes to be built," they wrote in a group letter to the city council, "so that we can live in modern and more beautiful communities."[45] In China and Taiwan, such modern and ironically European-inspired housing styles are commonly associated with the rising middle and upper classes and are widely regarded as attractive.[46]

The contrasting views of supporters and opponents underscore James Duncan and Nancy Duncan's point that "There is no such thing as 'mere aesthetics.' There is always a politics of aesthetics, and an aestheticization of politics."[47] Historian John Archer adds that homes are an extension of their occupants' aesthetic ideal:

> Just as homeowners who have bought uniform tract houses and those living in stringently regulated master-planned communities have not regarded them as oppressive of their own senses of taste and beauty, those who make individualized alterations do not see their homes as sore thumbs or affronts to their neighborhood's spatial cohesion. Rather, a given house with its sometimes idiosyncratic improvements not only suits the family's practical needs but, because it is the product of the owners' endeavors, becomes an extension of the residents' aesthetic conventions.[48]

While homes express individual aesthetic ideals, the ability of different groups to embed their ideas in the landscape are important symbols of their social power and privilege. In southern California's ethnoburbs, the building of similarly styled homes led scholars to conclude that many wealthy Asian immigrants adopted the aesthetic conventions of Anglo-Americans to assert their inclusion within suburban "landscapes of privilege."[49] In Fremont, there was also nothing particularly Asian about the design of these homes. And while Asian Americans' adoption of Anglicized housing designs was one way for residents to reassert their class privilege, this did not lead to a sense of inclusion in their neighborhoods. Rather, their design choices became the basis of critique. Their attempts were seen by opponents as overdone, unsophisticated, and not in keeping with the aesthetic conventions of their neighbors.

A Man's Home is his Castle

Privacy concerns were paramount to large home opponents. Some spoke of their privacy as an inherent right of homeownership. Many complained about new homes' security cameras and second-story additions providing views into their backyards. "We want to maintain the privacy afforded [to] us by the single-story homes that surround us. This privacy, that we value highly, is destroyed by a two-story home or addition," read the Preserve Mission Ranch website.[50] After pointing out all the work that they put into their backyard over the years, Luke and Ava Johnson told me that they could not imagine giving up the privacy they had come to enjoy there, as some in their neighborhood had to do because of large homes that were built nearby.

Supporters, however, claimed that privacy was much less important, whereas their rights as property owners were paramount. They argued that like all previous owners, they should be able to build what they wanted as long as it fell within existing regulations. Mission Ranch resident He-Ping Zhang argued that the restrictions constituted "a fundamental violation of the constitutional rights of individual freedom."[51] Others argued that imposing strict regulations and standards on some neighborhoods and not others placed an unfair and disproportionate burden of time and money on new residents. "Taking away the right to add additional living space with two-story homes," wrote Anthony Lai in a letter to the city council, "simply violates the basic rights for others as part of the American Dream."[52]

In fact, both privacy and property rights have been intertwined tenets that have long shaped suburbia's exclusive form and character.[53] Such values have been used, for instance, to justify the increasing privatization of suburban space with everything from private roads and parks to CC&Rs and gated communities. In Mission Ranch, however, the introduction of residents with different design ideas upset whatever consensus had been established about where the balance between privacy and property rights should be drawn.

The Value of the Great Outdoors

Opponents argued that outdoor space is intrinsically valued and valuable. They complained that large homes cast shadows over their existing properties, impaired views to the bay and the hills, and reduced their access to sun. Preserve Mission Ranch's website contrasted the value placed on the outdoors in newer and older homes:

> [W]ith more space and amenities inside, and smaller yards outside, the entire "value" of newer homes is inside the home. Significant amount of value for ranch style homes is outside the home—in the large, private backyards,

and the openness and warmth of the neighborhood. And that is what goes away when you put 4000+ sf homes on relatively small (about quarter acre or less) lots.[54]

Among opponents with whom I spoke, many counted themselves as environmentally conscious and enjoyed gardening and spending time outdoors. Such arguments had traction among others outside Mission Ranch such as Mary Walker, who worried about the environmental impact of heating and cooling large new homes. "It's a huge carbon footprint," she noted. Opponents asked that the original neighborhood designs' emphasis on outdoor space be respected by new residents.

Supporters pointed out that large homes and environmental consciousness were not necessarily opposing values. Anthony Lai argued that newer homes that were well insulated with new windows, upgraded systems, and small yards might be just as energy efficient as older homes. While living in a large home, he and his wife recycled, composted, had a garden, and were extremely water conscious. As we walked through his 4,946-square-foot five-bedroom home, he pointed out with pride all the ways in which its custom-built design efficiently used both space and energy. Pulling on stereotypes of other Asian Americans, Anthony claimed that "the Asian way" was often to let their lawns die because of the time and expense required to maintain them, but he added that this practice was more "environmentally friendly."

Supporters and large home opponents, however, seemed to agree on at least one point—many new residents did not spend as much time outside as inside their homes. Several noted that neither they nor their children use outdoor space as intensively as their White neighbors. More important than lawns, landscaping, or views was their desire for playrooms, home offices, and guest rooms. This was not necessarily culturally driven, as Anthony suggested, but was instead simply a reflection of their busy lifestyles, which did not leave much time for outdoor activities that were so central to community life in earlier generations. He disagreed that some intrinsic value should be placed on outdoor as opposed to indoor space.

Though not raised in the Fremont debates, during the "monster home" controversies in Vancouver, Chinese immigrants argued that feng shui was an important reason for limiting green space and cutting trees that obstructed their *qi* (or life force according to Taoist beliefs).[55] Shenglin Chang also found that feng shui was an important factor in home selection and design among Taiwanese immigrants in Silicon Valley.[56]

A Deteriorating Sense of Community

Several opponents raised concerns that the new large homes threatened their sense of community. Many Mission Ranch residents feared that speculative investors, rather than "real" residents, were developing new homes. As we sat at the kitchen table of their 1950s ranch-style home in Mission Ranch, Luke Johnson characterized the debate as a classic battle between "the development realtors" and the "family neighborhood." Meanwhile, Ava shuffled through a stack of papers before landing on what she considered to be evidence of the primary drivers behind the teardown trend. "A vision to bring custom homes to the City of Fremont," read the brochure she had unearthed from a real estate company that advertised to prospective home buyers the opportunity to build their dream homes in the "finest locations to keep you and your family close to school, shopping, and recreation." For Ava, this showed that there was an industry scouting out neighborhoods such as hers to make a quick profit.

It was not only the existence of real estate speculators that opponents balked at; it was also the perceived motivations and values of the residents who chose to purchase these homes. "I guess from my perspective a house is what I live in. It's where I live," explained Luke Johnson. "It's not my income." In her testimony before the city council, Ava argued that the new homes being built in the neighborhood violated the time-honored principles of good neighboring. A neighborhood, she reflected, is made up of people who will "watch your house and animals when you go on vacation" and "neighbors who will store your food and medicine in the refrigerator on the hottest time in three decades [and] will help your children grow into responsible adults." Those coming from outside the neighborhood to buy homes, fix them up, and sell them, she said, "take away from us what's precious; makes our neighborhoods special—our vistas and our friendliness—our neighborhood."[57] Raised in Glenmoor Gardens but now a resident of Mission San Jose, Sam Phillips argued that "they built McMansions because their lives were contained in those homes, whereas we all had small houses and our lives were more outside." Newer residents, he said, often "simply built their McMansions and shut the doors." For some, new development was experienced as a sense of loss over the shared values that once held their neighborhoods together. While many could remember a time when kids rode their bikes freely in the streets and when neighborhood block parties, Fourth of July barbeques, and trick-or-treating were the norm, they associated large home development with the loss of this way of life.

Supporters found the assertion that they and their homes were responsible for a declining sense of community troubling. In contrast to many opponents' claims about speculative investors, Fred Jiang, a Chinese immigrant, described the families who built large homes in Mission Ranch as "down-to-earth nice families [who] want to live in this nice neighborhood, start up their family. They're very simple. They're all new immigrants. They work very hard." While no one denied that there were developers looking for opportunities in the neighborhood and that these homes were important financial investments, most of the families who had rebuilt their homes in Mission Ranch occupied them as their primary residences. It was unrealistic and unfair, supporters argued, to expect working parents, who had limited English-language proficiency and spent their evenings and weekends shuttling their children around to various activities, to engage with their neighbors in the same way that families did in the 1960s and 1970s. Neither immigrant families nor many others for that matter define their community today primarily or solely within the boundary of a neighborhood. For many, the homes into which they welcomed their friends and families and connected with those overseas were spaces just as important if not more so for creating and fostering their sense of community.

Fremont's debates over large homes in established neighborhoods provided a lens into the politics of development in neighborhoods impacted by the global economy and immigration. While opponents claimed that respectful neighboring included conformity to the existing form and character of development, supporters claimed a right to different priorities, uses, values, and meanings of their homes. While opponents spoke about the value and beauty of their small homes designed for single-family nuclear households, supporters argued about the value of large homes to accommodate multigenerational households and provide access to Mission San Jose's esteemed schools. While opponents spoke of the importance of their historically rooted design practices, supporters claimed the need and desire for new and modern housing and its aesthetic. And in contrast to many opponents' ideal of a community in which the value of privacy and green space were commonly held, supporters claimed that a neighborhood should respect their private property rights and different uses and meanings of open space.

A Neighborhood Divided

The public hearings in which these issues were debated were heated. Attendants recalled several meetings in which shouting, cheering, and name-calling were commonplace. "Both sides came out in full force at planning commission and city council meetings," recalled one city staff planner who noted that the extenuated battle took a substantial emotional toll on those who were involved and drained city resources. In reference those who spoke in opposition to large homes at city council meetings, Mayor Wasserman recalled that "There were people coming to council meetings in their 80s coming up to the podium with tears in their eyes [saying] 'This was the home I've known all my life' and then 'why are you doing this to me?'"[58]

Tensions spilled over into the neighborhoods, where tempers flared and debates became tinged with racial rhetoric. Lawsuits were threatened between neighbors as building permits were approved in the neighborhood. One flier circulated by supporters to rally others to oppose a proposed ban on two-story homes in Mission Ranch brought to a head what many had long seen as the racial undertones of the debate:

> "Privacy issues," "the preservation of the neighborhood's character" and "obstruction of the view" were arguments used by the proponents of the ban. We believe the real reason that they are pushing for the ban is one of envy. There is also an underlying reason for the ban as a way to reduce the influx of Asian families, as many two story additions were done by Asian families.

Supporters speculated about the racist motives that drove the actions of their neighbors. The flier even got personal, arguing that the campaign was being driven by a "small group of neighbors" who were "selfishly working to steal your property rights."

Opponents were livid about the flier, which they turned over to the police department, arguing that it represented a direct threat. "There was a time that we felt under siege. We felt like it was war," recalled Luke Johnson, who counted himself among the "small group" that the flier denounced. The fights even embroiled the local elementary school, where a teacher who was active in organizing for the opposition was accused of talking to her students about the issue. A group of parents subsequently called for her resignation.

The debates attracted the attention of the media. The issue was featured in local and regional newspapers, on television, and in the *World Journal,* the largest Chinese-language newspaper in the United States. Such reports further inflamed neighborhood tensions. "It was really awful," Ava Johnson recalled. Amid the media blitz, Ava admitted that she began to feel sorry for neighbors whose large homes were swarmed by television vans and news crews. But while sympathies were evoked, the two sides continued to line up on different sides of the aisle at the various public meetings, forcing the issue to be resolved by politicians and public policy rather than among neighbors.

THE POLITICS OF RESIDENTIAL DESIGN CONTROLS

The city's large home debates led to the adoption of two new policies. The first emerged out of city officials' attempts to find an "interim solution" to the problem. The planning department suggested a citywide design review process and design guidelines for all new two-story single-family homes, second-story additions, and any project that involves "substantial expansions," which the city council unanimously approved in 2007. City officials then directed their attention to resolving the issues raised in Mission Ranch and Glenmoor Gardens directly. In September 2008, the council imposed a moratorium on construction permits for all new two-story homes in these two neighborhoods. In April 2009 the council adopted neighborhood-based design guidelines and development standards on a trial basis, and in July 2010 both the Fremont Planning Commission and the city council unanimously voted to make them permanent. The design guidelines provide planners with a sense of what they should consider when approving building or remodeling plans in Mission Ranch and Glenmoor Gardens. The development standards changed the neighborhoods' zoning designations, maximum permissible floor-to-area ratios, setbacks, and height limits.

Many city officials proclaimed the new guidelines and standards as a compromise and a fair resolution to the debate. Many who fought hard against such regulations, however, felt otherwise. In 2010 just before the passage of the Mission Ranch and Glenmoor Gardens design guidelines and standards, a petition with over 100 signatures opposing the new guidelines was submitted to the council, about 85% of which were from residents with Chinese last names.

On their face, the new regulations established a set of neutral policies and principles to promote good design. These regulations, however, also made various normative claims about the proper and appropriate uses, values, and meanings of suburban homes and landscape design. Their assertions regarding neighborhood character, housing size, historic preservation, aesthetics, privacy, and outdoor space largely favored the positions expressed by estab-

Avoid
Encourage

FIGURE 18. These images appear in the Mission Ranch design guidelines as illustrative examples of housing and landscape elements that residents should "avoid" and planners to "encourage." Images published in City of Fremont (2009b, 2009c).

lished residents in the debate while giving far less credence to those expressed by many of their new Asian American neighbors.

The new design guidelines and processes put particular emphasis on maintaining the neighborhoods' existing character. The citywide design review process was adopted explicitly to consider the design of new two-story homes and proposed additions "in the context of the surrounding neighborhood."[59] Likewise, Mission Ranch's design guidelines explain that maintaining a visual fit among properties ensures that a building's or site's character not be "irreversibly damaged or diminished" by introducing "inappropriate" materials or "unrelated" features or removing or changing its elements.[60] The neighborhood's "character defining features," the guidelines state, are *the* primary contributors to its "enhanced value and special standing" among Fremont neighborhoods.[61] Accordingly, all alterations and additions to existing properties should be "compatible" both in size and architecture with established neighborhood design.

To achieve compatibility, the guidelines establish specific design and landscape elements that planners should "encourage" and those that residents should "avoid." Designs that are encouraged reflect traditional ranch-style architecture and landscape design. Enhanced by illustrative sketches of ranch-style homes, the guidelines specify desirable features such as facades and roofing materials, trim patterns, garage door styles, and window treatments. In contrast, sketches of large new homes provide examples of design elements to avoid. These include wrought iron fencing, "grand entries," and Victorian, Italianate, or other "ornamental" front doors that are "unrelated to prevailing materials and character-defining features of the neighborhood" (Figure 18).[62]

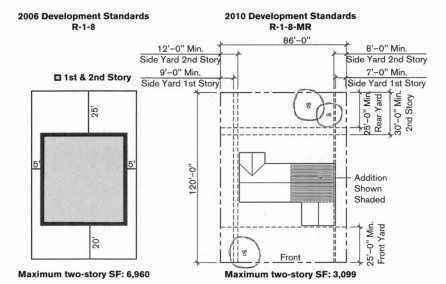

2006 Development Standards
R-1-8

2010 Development Standards
R-1-8-MR

□ 1st & 2nd Story

12'-0" Min.
Side Yard 2nd Story

9'-0" Min.
Side Yard 1st Story

8'-0" Min.
Side Yard 2nd Story

7'-0" Min.
Side Yard 1st Story

86'-0"

25'

5'   5'

20'

120'-0"

25'-0" Min. Rear Yard

30'-0" Min. 2nd Story

Addition
Shown
Shaded

25'-0" Min. Front Yard

Front

Maximum two-story SF: 6,960

Maximum two-story SF: 3,099

FIGURE 19. Under Mission Ranch's new R-1-8-MR zoning designation, development stand-ards reduced the build out for two-story homes by more than 50 percent, from 6,950 to 3,100 square feet. The new standards increased setbacks and reduced height limits and floor-to-area ratios, especially for two-story homes. Right image published in City of Fremont, Community Development Department (2006). Left image published in City of Fremont (2009c).

Another central aim of the new regulations was to control the size and bulk of new homes. In Mission Ranch and Glenmoor Gardens, this was accomplished through the adoption of special neighborhood zoning stand-ards, R-1-8-MR (for Mission Ranch) and R-1-6-GG (for Glenmoor Gardens). These standards increased the front-, rear-, and side-yard setbacks and reduced permissible building heights and floor-to-area ratios (FARs). In Glenmoor Gardens, the standards forbade the construction of any new two-story homes—a restriction favored by Glenmoor Gardens' HOA officials. In Mission Ranch two-story homes were permitted, but their maximum FAR of 0.3 was 40% less than the citywide standard and 10% less than for one-story homes to encourage residents to expand out rather than up. Taken together, these new standards reduced the maximum allowable square foot-age of Mission Ranch homes from around 7,000 to 3,100 square feet for two-story homes and to 4,100 square feet for one-story homes; in Glenmoor Gardens, the maximum allowed went from around 5,600 to 3,600 square feet (Figure 19).[63]

Residents were permitted to add onto their homes but only in ways that were thought be compatible in size with existing homes and enhanced the single-story character of the neighborhoods. In Mission Ranch, the new regulations made two-story homes virtually impossible, permitting instead what some residents referred to as "submarine homes," where the bulk of the house is on the first floor and only a small room is permitted on the second floor.

One of the more contested aspects of the new design guidelines and standards was their application only within the two Fremont neighborhoods whose residents were most vocal and active in opposing large home development. City officials defended their selectivity based on the need to preserve the "historic" and "unique" features of these "treasured" Fremont neighborhoods. Comparing Fremont to Palo Alto, which had adopted similar design guidelines to protect postwar homes built by renowned architect Joseph Eichler, council member Anu Natarajan argued that "Although we don't have Eichlers, some of our ranch-style homes are as symbolic and need to be preserved."[64] The design guidelines for Mission Ranch and Glenmoor Gardens placed great emphasis on defining and preserving these neighborhoods' historic elements.

The city's emphasis on the preservation of existing neighborhood character was also influenced by the consultants they hired to draw up the design guidelines, which included a historical architect, an architectural historian, and an urban designer. Among them was Alex Wilson, who previously worked for the city on the photographic recordation of homes in another neighborhood that was undergoing significant redevelopment. A self-described modernist with a love of the international style and early postwar architecture, Alex told me that he appreciated the style of Mission Ranch homes and the existing qualities of the neighborhood, which would be among his top choices of neighborhoods in Fremont. While not insensitive to the arguments made by newer residents, Alex was passionate about the need to retain the neighborhoods' unique qualities. He saw the financial interests of many newer residents overriding core neighborhood principles such as "continuity" and "stability." "They're not interested in stability," he charged of newer residents. "They are interested in one single thing and it's called the Almighty Dollar." Like many established residents, Alex believed that new residents were primarily driven by profit and greed, values that he felt should not be allowed to outweigh the interests of existing residents or the existing neighborhood fabric.

Fremont's new regulations also placed great emphasis on housing and landscape aesthetics. The new citywide design guidelines stress aesthetics in various elements, including a homes' massing, articulation, and materials. The guidelines, for instance, warn against square or "blocky" homes with minimal architectural detail and the "relentless, dull, and overwhelming appearance" created by the use of a single material.[65] The design guidelines in Mission Ranch and Glenmoor Gardens suggest that aesthetic quality should be measured by how well a property fits with its existing surroundings. The guidelines, for instance, recommend traditional ranch-style home practices such as painting front doors in signature colors. At the same time, they caution against homes that may attract "undue attention" with elements such as copper gutters and simulated stone roofing, which they note are commonly found in new homes but appear "coarse" and "conspicuous" and "lack subtlety."[66] The planning commission report urging the city council to adopt the neighborhood guidelines argued that regulation was necessary to address the negative impacts of large homes on opponents' "aesthetic sensibilities."[67]

The new regulations also reflected opponents' concerns about privacy. According to new citywide guidelines, "back yards are typically private and more personalized. These should be designed for privacy from neighbors."[68] They suggest plantings in front of windows and, in Mission Ranch and Glenmoor Gardens, locating windows "to minimize visual intrusion into adjacent properties."[69] Visual distance is further established by increasing the required setbacks in Mission Ranch to adjacent properties from 5 to 9 feet on the first floor and from 5 to 12 feet on the second floor.

Fremont's new design guidelines and standards also responded to the concerns of large home opponents about outdoor space. The new citywide design guidelines state that "independent of the setbacks required by each zoning district," each lot shall be provided with a "reasonable flat usable rear yard area" no less than 15 by 20 feet.[70] In addition to the increased setbacks, the design guidelines for Mission Ranch suggest that second stories be located and configured to retain existing views to and of the hills, which "add to the value and enjoyment of each property and contribute to the neighborhood's very distinctive sense of place."[71]

Finally, the new guidelines make implicit claims about the value of a neighborhood-based sense of community. Fences are discouraged, as the guidelines state that they reduce a neighborhood's sense of "openness" and "friendliness."[72] Instead, the guidelines emphasize maintaining traditional ranch-style elements such as their "informal but inviting front doors" that "beckon, shelter, and welcome visitors and connect the interiors—and the owners—to the street and to the neighborhood."[73]

The new development standards and design guidelines were touted by many city officials as a compromise, because despite a reduction in the allowable square footage, they still permitted new residents to add onto their existing homes. However, the city's new guidelines and standards institutionalized principles of design that reaffirmed the existing home and neighborhood character. In doing so, the city disavowed many of the claims made by large home supporters about the importance of these homes.

PLANNING PROCESSES AND MARGINALIZED MINORITY VOICES

Why were established residents so successful in influencing the outcomes of the debate? Various scholars have written about the ways in which planning processes and professionals marginalize minority voices and discourage their participation.[74] Building on the work of these scholars, I argue that city officials, planners, and the public process gave established residents the upper hand in the debate for two principle reasons. First, planners and policy makers tended to share established residents' view that "good design" was grounded in spatially homogenous and relatively static and stable neighborhoods. And second, the public process favored organized and vocal residents who understood the importance of and easily worked within the established system.

Unlike most residential home design issues in Fremont that are handled by the planning commission and the city's planning staff, the issue of large homes was taken up by the city council and largely directed from the top. Throughout the four-year process, the city council played a heavy-handed role in directing the actions of the planning staff, often bypassing the traditional role played by the planning commission. Many speculated that one of the reasons for this was because the debate became so highly visible and heated that council members felt compelled to take a stand. Others charged that council members were sensitive to the issue from the very beginning largely because they agreed with the arguments made by the opposition.

The city council at the time consisted of mainly established Fremont residents. Three out of five members on the 2010 city council, which fought hard for regulations, were White and had lived in the city for at least 35 years. These members expressed their support of opponents early on. In 2006, for example, Mayor Bob Wasserman explained that his support for new regulations rested on the principle that "people should be allowed to do things that fit the neighborhood, and they shouldn't be allowed to do things that distort the neighborhood."[75] Sitting down with me in his office several years later, he continued to reflect on his position:

> People were coming in and just building these horrible looking things that virtually ruin the neighborhood. I was very sympathetic. I'm usually pretty liberal on what I'd allow to build, but that was terrible what they were doing architecturally and even culturally. I mean, people, they were miserable. They didn't want to go out of their homes because look what they have to look at, all of [a] sudden. I mean, after living there for 30, 40 years.

Wasserman indicated that he clearly understood the issue as one that divided new residents from long-term residents but one that he nonetheless felt passionately about. Instead of letting new residents "ruin the neighborhood" with their "horrible looking" homes, he felt that the city council had to intervene. Council member Bill Harrison, who succeeded Wasserman as Fremont mayor in 2012, had grown up in Glenmoor Gardens and reportedly used his early support of regulations on large home development in established neighborhoods in his bid for city council reelection in 2010.

Regardless of their racial and ethnic backgrounds or residential histories, however, city council members and planners were almost uniformly opposed to these building practices. In large part, their opposition seemed to stem from these homes' departure from professional planning and design norms regarding maintaining a neighborhood's existing character. Council member Anu Natarajan, who was trained as an urban designer and planner, stated that her support for the regulations rested on the premise that "if it does not fit, do not permit"—a common urban planning maxim.[76] When I asked council member Suzanne Chan about her position on the issue, she stated that the council's main concerns were to ensure that the new homes "honor the character of the neighborhood" and "maintain the feel of the ranch style" but also that the regulations did not infringe on residents' right to adapt their properties.[77] Although Chan underscored the council's multiple goals, the guidelines emphasized neighborhood character as the principle concern.

Similar comments pervaded the opinions expressed by those on the planning commission, which was often described as an extension of or ladder onto the city council, as its members were appointed by the council. In 2010 at the time when the regulations were passed, the commission included four White long-term residents, one Chinese American, and two Indian American representatives. In a direct response to a question about the extent to which the commission should address the issue of multigenerational families, Rakesh Sharma, an Indian American commissioner, sharply dismissed the claim, stating that "The issue is whether someone can go into the established neighborhoods and destroy their character because of their economic decision."[78]

Within the planning department, there was also widespread cynicism about these homes. Planning director Jeff Schwob argued that the basic principle underlying new design guidelines and standards ought to be "to make sure that everything we build fits in the neighborhood."[79] In discussing comments that she had overheard among planning staff when reviewing permits about these homes, one staff planner noted that although the staff held mixed feelings, there were many, including herself, who largely objected to the practice:

> I would say that there were some mixed feelings about these large homes, just as [there were] personal sort of comments being made about [them], based on the staff's own sort of taste in homes and aesthetics. Some of us have our own concerns about changing the neighborhood too. So if something came in and it was completely different from what was already in neighborhood, we already felt, "Oh, here is another one, here is another one."

She recalled articles being circulated among planners about large homes being built in other established neighborhoods and a distinct sense of disdain for the practice among many of her colleagues. Policy makers' and planners' race and ethnicity did not seem to matter nearly as much as professional planning norms in shaping what they considered to be a good or desirable housing and neighborhood form.

Regardless of the opinions of planning staff, the commission, or the city council, however, probably the largest factor swaying the outcome of the debate was the planning process. Opponents led a highly organized and sophisticated campaign that made use of their experience with and understanding of the public process. They established a website to distribute information about large homes in their neighborhood and upcoming public meetings, held regular neighborhood informational sessions, and met frequently with planning staff. Preserve Mission Ranch members monitored applications for new building permits in the neighborhood, contacted attorneys to discuss various options, researched the history of the neighborhood and policies adopted in other areas, and shared their findings with planning staff. They consistently showed up in large numbers at all the city council meetings held between 2006 and 2010 and sponsored several letter-writing campaigns. They prepared their members to speak in the two minutes allotted for individual public comments at city council and planning commission meetings and spoke clearly and eloquently about their position. As Ava Johnson noted, even with the support of most of the city council, opposition organizers such as herself understood the importance of continuing to show a united voice at public meetings. "They may agree with you," she explained of city council members, "but if you don't have all that support at the meetings . . . you can't get anywhere."

Opponents' sustained efforts were enabled by the fact that several of the regular public meeting attendees were retired and most were American-born, long-term residents who understood the public process. Opponents also seemed to hold more political clout because established older residents in Fremont, as elsewhere, are the most likely residents to attend public meetings and vote.

In contrast, supporters of large home development struggled to organize residents to attend public meetings. For the first two years of the debate, Anthony Lai was the lone voice at public meetings opposing the city's plans. It was not until 2008, when city officials began to push for a single-story zoning overlay, that Anthony was finally able to organize other supporters to speak out. He estimated that between 100 and 130 residents showed up to one public meeting in which city council members decided to reject the single-story zoning overlay in favor of new design guidelines and development standards. But such efforts were short-lived. By 2010 when the final guidelines and standards passed, Anthony had left his lead organizing role, and the movement struggled to maintain its momentum. Not a single supporter was present at the final city council meeting to adopt the Mission Ranch and Glenmoor Gardens guidelines and standards, even though a petition signed by 100 residents declaring their opposition was submitted to the city council for consideration.

Anthony and others said that they faced several barriers to organizing residents. First, the majority of residents opposing the regulations were Chinese immigrants who were oftentimes unfamiliar with the public process and afraid to speak publicly. One supporter told me that she supported the cause financially but never spoke at a hearing because she was too shy. For others, language was a significant barrier. While Anthony said that he tried to prepare residents to speak at the hearings, the transcripts showed that supporters were far less articulate and organized in their comments than opponents. Several opponents I spoke with characterized supporters' comments as being "angry" or "off-handed," whereas opponents focused on being "nice" to city representatives and "focused" in their comments.

Time and access to information were also significant barriers. Many large home supporters were Silicon Valley professionals who struggled to find the time to participate in the campaign in any sustained way. Organizers also complained that it was difficult to find information about the hearings and that the city did a poor job of notifying residents about the meetings. According to Anthony, only those who had been to previous meetings received written announcements about subsequent meetings, which privileged the continued participation of opponents. As required by law, all meetings notifications were posted in English in the local newspaper.

In effect, large home supporters entered the debate with the odds stacked against them. They lacked the time, political influence, and sophisticated knowledge about the planning process of opponents. Further, unlike schools, which have been a lightning-rod issue in Asian American politics in many suburban communities, the issue of large homes was generally perceived as affecting a much smaller population and was met with less enthusiasm from Asian Americans both inside and outside affected neighborhoods. Supporters also faced politicians and planning policies that suggested that they held the burden of conforming to the established spatial norms and practices of the neighborhoods into which they moved.

Supporters, however, questioned whether such respect needed to be reciprocated. They asked why they were being asked to give due regard to their neighborhoods' existing form and character as well as established residents' rooted design practices and sense of community when they themselves did not feel that they were getting the same treatment. Should established residents not also be called on to acknowledge their desire for new modern homes that accommodated their multigenerational households and provided access to Mission San Jose's esteemed schools as well as their property rights and different uses and meanings of open space? Asian Americans struggled to find a place in the debate in which their positions were heard and validated.

.   .   .

Fremont's peak of housing redevelopment in established neighborhoods occurred during the housing boom of the early 2000s, a period that closely tracked trends in teardowns across the nation.[80] After the Fremont City Council passed new regulations and the demand for new homes fell precipitously during the Great Recession, the issue of large homes died down in the city. Yet, looking back at the debates offers many lessons about the ways Asian Americans have helped sculpt the suburban landscape and how issues of difference are dealt with through planning and design policy.

Fremont showed that the large homes that many deride as McMansions are not solely about bigness and bling or developer greed. These homes, like all homes, express and embody important place identities and are spaces through which ideals about homes and communities are materially constructed and imagined. With so much focus on critique and regulation, scholars have often overlooked the value and meaning that residents have invested in these homes.

For many Asian Americans who arrived in Silicon Valley in the late 1990s and mid-2000s, these homes became a common landscape through which they expressed their ideas about the value of schools, multigenerational households, and new and modern housing. These homes were an important site through which Asian American newcomers sought to secure their financial stability, express their accomplishments, and build their sense of community, just as a generation before them had done in their ranch-style homes. But unlike previous generations, Asian Americans did not, on the whole, find their sense of home and community closely tied to the neighborhoods in which they settled. Instead, many looked beyond their neighborhoods—to schools that provided the kind of education they wanted for their children, to the shopping centers that served familiar products and connected them to diverse people around the region and the world, and to the coethnic friends, colleagues, and family members who regularly gathered within their large homes. While they were not opposed to socializing with their neighbors, many also did not share the same ideas and practices that had drawn these neighborhoods together a half century ago—ideas that were reflected in the design of the ranch-style home.

The issue of large home development in Fremont became more than just about the size or style of new homes. It became a contest over the ideas that were embedded in the design of homes and communities and whose ideas mattered most. Established residents were not necessarily being racist when they stated their desires to protect the "way of life" and the landscape that they had come to enjoy in their neighborhoods. But they also failed to acknowledge how their way of life and what they considered to be "inappropriate" or "incompatible" with their existing neighborhood had long been supported by policies of residential race and class exclusion.

The suburban residential landscape and norms that shaped the postwar period have largely remained intact in the United States. Thus, it does not take racist intent of established communities to continue the kinds of policies and processes that have historically protected White privilege in suburban America. It only takes the assertion of principles such as the preservation of neighborhoods' "stability," "character," and "integrity." Such terms have long been used as euphemisms for racial segregation and excluding groups that may threaten property values.[81] In Fremont, it became clear that such terms can be used as a means of protecting neighborhoods from unwanted changes of many kinds, including those that threaten established residents' sense of belonging and control.

Public policies often come to the aid of established residents. In other contexts, antidevelopment and managed-growth campaigns that emerged in the face of new immigration have been read as expressions of long-term residents' anxiety over geographic and economic displacement and their own sense of place.[82] In Fremont, the same anxiety could be sensed in the comments made by established residents that their "way of life" and sense of community were threatened during a period of rapid demographic change in Silicon Valley. Just down the road from Fremont, the city of Cupertino had its own battles over teardowns and "White flight" in the schools. In response, a Taiwanese American resident argued that many established residents used Asian immigrants as a scapegoat for the sense of loss they feel in the midst of rapid neighborhood change. "They think, 'You come here driving a Mercedes. You live in big houses, we live in small houses. You get all the sunshine, we get all the shadows,'" he explained.[83] Such anxieties play out acutely in neighborhoods such as Mission San Jose, where change is all too evident in the landscape—be it the size of new homes, the Chinese signage on new shopping malls, or the changing academic culture of schools.

It is not only the resistance of residents to change but also institutional processes and practices that enable older, established, and most often White residents to dictate the norms that shape suburban form. Policy makers and planners must be critical of the presumed neutrality of design guidelines and standards and actively question the normative presumptions behind their regulations and whom they benefit. Instead of simply giving in to the efforts of established residents to curb development and neighborhood change, policy makers need to carefully consider the impacts of regulations on vulnerable groups, including their needs for different uses and ideas about their homes and a sense of place and belonging in their neighborhoods. Bending to the will of the loudest and most well-organized and vocal groups or even relying on their own sense of what is acceptable may lead politicians and planners to decisions that sustain and naturalize White privilege.

Instead, planners and policy makers must create spaces in which the voices of different communities can be heard and can affect the shape of the landscapes they occupy. To do so requires addressing many of the barriers that prevented Asian Americans from fully participating in and being heard in the large home debates in Fremont, including issues of language, cultures of participation, and diverse forums and formats of participation. The need to expand participatory planning through strategies such as those aimed at greater outreach and engagement with underrepresented communities, the creation of more open and flexible forums for democratic decision making, and opportunities for more diverse representation on planning bodies is well established in scholarly literature.[84] However, what is needed to build equitable communities in which residents feel a deep sense of connection and belonging goes well beyond participatory planning. It includes attention to the processes, policies, and ideas about place making and citizenship that shape landscapes. It is toward a vision of suburban spatial justice to which I now turn.

FIVE

Charting New Suburban Storylines

[H]ow can "we" (all of us), in all of our differences, be "at home"
in the multicultural and multiethnic cities of the 21st century?

LEONIE SANDERCOCK

LIKE OTHER REGIONS IN THE United States, Silicon Valley is constantly
being reshaped by migrants from all parts of the globe who arrive, carrying
with them the many cultures and communities they left behind and an unwa-
vering determination to create better futures. Back in 2007 my exit off I-880
led to my long engagement with a small slice of this story, as I became engrossed
in Fremont's rich history, dynamic growth, eclectic landscape, and contested
development politics. But I could have just as easily stopped a little north in
Union City, headed south another 10 miles to Milpitas, or taken a turn onto
I-280 toward Cupertino and found similar tales of new migrants transforming
the culture and character of the region. Had I spent more time in Santa Clara,
Hayward, or San Jose, this book might have been about Latino or Vietnamese
Americans and how their evolving sense of place changed their chosen com-
munities.[1] Had I ventured farther from the valley's core, my lens might have
shifted to the confluence of Southeast Asians, Latinos, and African Americans,
pushed to the margins by rising real estate values that remade the rural landscapes of exurban working-class towns.[2] More time spent in northern Fremont's
Centerville neighborhood would have revealed stories about how the largest
Afghan population outside of Afghanistan turned its main street into "Little
Kabul" with mosques, halal markets, Persian restaurants, Farsi-language
schools, and refugee-serving social services.

Here and elsewhere, dramatic demographic shifts have shocked the consciousness of suburbia. Perhaps in San Francisco or Oakland, no one would
have taken so much notice. Central cities have, after all, long been upheld as
the citadels of cosmopolitanism and the intersection of America's cultural
crosswinds—segregated, to be sure, but still a meeting ground for many
different racial and ethnic groups. Suburbs, on the other hand, while long

maintaining a diversity of forms, lifestyles, family structures, religious practices, and linguistic groups, have little reference point for the pace and character of change they are now experiencing.

Half a century of massive immigration and racial integration has fundamentally reshaped suburbia's spatial form and social makeup. It has introduced various shades of gray into a metropolitan landscape once predominantly characterized by chocolate cities and vanilla suburbs.[3] It is a tide that shows little signs of slowing. Between 2000 and 2010, nearly half of the 100 largest metropolitan areas in the United States saw increases in their foreign-born populations of at least 50%.[4] Further, by 2010, over half of all immigrants lived in the suburbs of these metropolitan areas, 22 of which were already majority-minority.[5] "Fremont [is] the city that other cities will become," predicted one Fremont city official. "We're just at the leading edge of what other cities will be."

If immigration laws continue to favor highly skilled migrants, these stories of suburban transformation will be especially robust in high-tech job centers such as Silicon Valley. Similar processes and politics are at play, for instance, in the Research Triangle Park region of North Carolina. In the small town of Morrisville, dubbed by one local paper as "Little India," residents reelected their first Indian American member of the town council in 2013, warehouses and old churches were made into Hindu or Buddhist temples, parks changed to cricket fields, and the town opened the area's first Asian mall, "NC Chinatown," a name that itself exposed just how new immigration was in the region.[6] Alongside these changes came new debates about growth, local jobs, housing, and education. In Chapel Hill, a boundary debate took a surprising turn in late 2012 when a group of largely Chinese immigrants became highly vocal and organized. Citing racial targeting of their neighborhood as well as the high test scores of their children among the reasons for a proposed lawsuit against the district, the issues were surprisingly similar to those I observed in Silicon Valley.

Creative-class and other global migrants are spreading out and moving to new places. Whether these new destinations are in the American South or the global South, the American Heartland or the New Sun Belt, communities continue to wrestle with tough questions about how to make room for their fast-growing and ever more diverse populations.[7] The reaction so far has been mixed. Some suburbs are actively welcoming immigrants into their fold with new facilities, social services, and public policies to accommodate their needs.[8] Others are more conservative, exposing the less savory realities of ongoing social, spatial, and economic inequality and exclusion.[9] And many, such as Fremont, are a mixed bag. Yet these hyperlocal, seemingly sleepy suburbs are some of the most interesting places in which the global politics of immigration, diversity, and difference, spatial or otherwise, are playing out. They are places where globalization and its many flows—of people, finance, technology, media, and ideas—hit home.[10]

In this splintered spatial order, migrants act as their own cultural ambassadors.[11] They bring memories of familiar places and people, important customs and beliefs, and treasured items and heirlooms. As they settle in new places, they create landscapes that become the storehouses of their complex identities and concepts of home. They are places that remind them of where they came from and embody their aspirations for their new homelands.[12] Straddling and moving among national and cultural borders, both real and imagined, their landscapes are a bricolage of memory and desire.

This is not only the case for immigrants. One need only think of the iconic Eichler homes in Palo Alto or the classic postwar suburb of Levittown to understand how other groups have similarly fashioned their own visions and values in the landscape. White middle-class suburbanites did not simply accept the mass-produced homes and neighborhoods they were sold. They molded them over time, customizing the spaces in the community to their personal needs and tastes, and gave them new meaning through their uses.[13] In Levittown, they built onto their homes, adding garage apartments, sunrooms, playrooms, and new home offices; they covered their crabgrass with patios, work sheds, and basketball courts; and they revitalized underused open spaces with community gardens and new playgrounds. There is nothing new in the reformulation of the suburban built environment. It has always served as a mirror reflecting the ideas and ideals of its developers, inhabitants, and the politics of their times.

In today's suburbs, seemingly natural processes of landscape change are fraught by conflict not only because of the complexity of the identities and values at play but also because of the hidden privileges and powers embedded in their form. In the not-so-distant past, various property regulations explicitly shielded many suburban neighborhoods from unwanted changes—declining property values and undesirable neighbors that threatened residents' social and economic status. Today, the suburban landscape and the regulations that govern it continue to police its borders in far more subtle ways. Battles over suburbia's built form, growth, and development are among the many outlets for communities' unresolved and emergent tensions and fears over increasing immigration and racial and ethnic integration.[14] Globalization has unsettled the predictability and stability of places, creating ever more "unhomely" moments of encounter at the local level.[15]

However, if the design of the built environment has played a significant role in creating long-held social problems, it must also be seen as a site for their redress.[16] As suburbia becomes increasingly the focus of designers', planners', and policy makers' efforts to create more economically and environmentally sustainable places, raising questions about its responsiveness to the needs and sensibilities of different groups is important to ensuring that these places are also equitable.[17]

A more just suburbia requires new and more inclusive ideas about suburban citizenship. David Harvey defines the "right to the city" as the right to change and reinvent the city according to our hearts' desire.[18] He claims that all groups, however defined, must have power over the processes that shape cities. For this power to be fully realized, the ideas and values that different groups bring to the table must be recognized. Various theories of social justice highlight the right to express one's differences without exclusion, otherizing, or questioning of one's humanity as a core value.[19] In urban spaces, this implies places in which, as Leonie Sandercock writes, "difference, otherness, fragmentation, splintering, multiplicity, heterogeneity, diversity, and plurality prevail."[20] Key to this idea is a fundamental respect for the multiple and sometimes conflicting ways that people occupy space and express themselves in and through it.

In Fremont and many other cities and suburbs across the globe, the seeds of such radical claims are being sown. As Henri Lefebvre noted, the ritualistic terrain of everyday life is often at the center of the politics of difference and where they are most bitterly fought.[21] For American minorities and new immigrants, these places are more and more suburban. In schools, parking lots, shopping centers, and sometimes plush single-family homes, many are pushing back against antiquated ideas and policies; they are charting their own storylines and demanding respect for them. They are part of what John Archer has called "suburban counter publics," who fight the constant norming of patriarchy, heteronormativity, White privilege, and many other dominant ideologies that suburbia not only often represents but also reifies.[22]

Suburban newcomers are demanding a larger voice in shaping their communities, a more just distribution of metropolitan resources, and a more diverse built environment that supports who they are and what they want. They are unwilling to lose their cultures and community ties and assimilate into the mainstream in their move to the suburbs, as generations before them were often forced to do. Instead, they are searching for other pathways to opportunity and ways of "remaking the mainstream" to include their American Dream.[23]

Such a right to difference and the politics needed to sustain it implies a radical rethinking of suburban planning policy and practice. First and foremost, it requires a critical examination of planning and design values and norms as well as where they come from and what they support. Scholars have long documented the conservative underpinnings of suburban policies regarding slow growth, low taxes, privatization, and property rights and their negative impact on communities of color and the poor.[24] I have shown how values such as history, context, order, conformity, stability, and cohesion embedded in policies promoting "good suburban form" similarly tend to privilege and naturalize the way things are, resist spatial change, and frame those who do not fit with existing norms as outsiders, interlopers, or indeed, even trespassers. While many planners, designers, and policy makers may deride suburbia's standardized landscape as ugly, boring, or exclusive, they also regularly pass policies that uphold its core tenants.

Even with the current popularity of tools to promote mixed-use and mixed-income suburban development, these values continue to hold sway. New Urbanist design principles and many municipalities' current fascination with form-based codes are prime examples.[25] These policies often dictate design to such an extent that vernacular expressions of difference are virtually impossible except in their most prescribed forms. Their designer-knows-best aesthetics prize uniformity and neat, orderly environments. While they claim to actively support and welcome diverse incomes and ethnicities, they also send a message to new occupants that "you may live here, but only if you can conform to our rules and standards." It is, then, perhaps not so surprising that many New Urbanist communities' efforts to attract diverse racial and economic groups have been found lacking.[26]

Such principles must be replaced by new planning and design values that put difference first. Diversity that is hung on street banners, celebrated in parades, and marketed in economic development brochures is shallow and fragile. It does not bestow on communities a badge of tolerance or inclusivity. As one developer argued, "as much as Fremont or the politicians and people love to say it, because it sounds so politically correct, just because you have a lot of different ethnicities does not necessarily make it a melting pot." A respect for difference is the hallmark of a community's commitment to substantive and sustainable diversity. It requires neighbors to learn about each other, have hard conversations, listen openly, and make compromises.

Respect for difference also requires an aesthetic sensibility attuned to difference.[27] This includes respect and tolerance for places that, to some, may appear messy, incoherent, or even unattractive. It is through a dominant cultural frame calling for order and neatness in the highly manicured landscapes that places with a diversity of functions and material perspectives are deemed undesirable. In changing the frames through which they are viewed, such landscapes may also be seen as beautiful.[28]

A diverse society requires neighborhoods that look different, schools that meet different needs and expectations, and a variety of environments for worship, work, and play. Our built environments and the policies that shape them must allow for diverse expressions and actively encourage occupants to co-opt them and participate in their construction. We need flexible, open, and "loose" spaces that are complex, contain layers of meaning, express multiple points of view, and offer users different kinds of experiences.[29] When people are able to express their identities in places, they feel more connected to them.[30] The landscapes of our everyday lives are our labors of love. Participating in the act of creating places, whether in their planning, management, design, or construction, turns residents into stakeholders.[31]

Suburbia's landscape should be flexible and open enough to support and enable its new occupants' objectives and endeavors. It should be a place where everyone, whether new or old, can grow roots, celebrate and consecrate their most sacred and mundane moments, and live out their lives in ways that are meaningful to them. To do so, they must be given opportunities to craft the landscape and put their own mark on it. Newcomers cannot simply fit into someone else's shoes. They must be empowered to chart their own futures and claim space for their own purposes.

Inclusive processes translate these values into practical policies and plans and ensure that places remain open to new residents as well as their different uses and needs. Antagonistic planning and design politics are also critical to building a community's tolerance and respect for differences.[32] They help residents face and address their fears and provide healthy venues to express divergent interests and values. Communities can move toward solutions without necessarily resolving all conflicts or settling on a unified vision or identity of a place. They can learn to respect each other's differences by simply allowing them to coexist.

Such inclusive processes are unlikely to emerge in communities segregated by race, class, ethnicity, or otherwise and are more likely to occur in communities that confront difference in their own backyards. More often than not, however, issues of difference drive communities apart. Groups that leave, be they well-off Whites or Asian Americans, often take their economic power and racial privilege with them and secure them in ever more tightly bounded and securitized zones. These processes have time and time again crafted the American metropolis as an increasingly fragmented and segregated landscape.[33]

Policy makers need to continue to plug the many loopholes that reward communities for turning their backs on the less privileged in the name of better schools, public amenities, and safer, more comfortable neighborhoods. Regional planning has long been an uphill battle but one well worth fighting for. Our "metropolitics" must be able to bridge municipal boundaries to find cross-jurisdictional solutions to tough affordable housing, transportation, and environmental issues that require regional cooperation.[34] Communities also need to stop allowing fragmentation and segregation to occur within their own borders. Indeed, in Fremont it was not only debates about school curriculum and culture that shaped the boundary disputes that took place in Mission San Jose but also the unequal land-use policies that had for generations allowed wealthy neighborhoods such as Mission San Jose to exist in such stark contrast to working-class neighborhoods such as Irvington.

Asian Americans have benefited from the unequal distribution of resources across geographic space. Compared to other poor and working-class groups who have never managed to break through the suburban wall or have become isolated in the many pockets of poverty now emerging within suburbia, the residents I have profiled are indeed privileged and have used their racial and economic power to further secure that privilege for themselves and their children. At the same time, however, they are also carving out spaces within these places for landscapes of difference to emerge and grow.

Suburbia is fertile ground for new beginnings that can rewrite its own narrative of social exclusion. Though it has been known as the birthplace of the new American Right and neoliberal politics, suburbia is now a global meeting ground that may allow for new ways of thinking about building inclusive and equitable communities.[35] This will be accomplished not by denying the differences that exist within communities but instead by disrupting the spaces that affirm and promote the unequal treatment of people based on these differences. It will be through chipping away at the invisible lines that keep different groups from moving into and out of such spaces freely and openly as well as undoing the subtle ways in which spaces communicate, both through their design and regulation, who belongs and who does not.

My time in Fremont taught me the value of affirming landscapes of difference as an important part of every community and how radical expressions of difference in urban space can be. Landscapes of difference challenge existing social hierarchies and positionalities and make room for new spatial meanings, identities, and forms as well as new ideas of civic and social belonging. Nowadays when I pass through the side streets of my neighborhood or any number of other places, I am more attentive to the subtle stories that landscapes tell about the diverse people, contested politics, and complex processes that produce them. I gain inspiration from kitschy lawn figurines, odd house colors, and other idiosyncratic design decisions that seem to have something to say about the people who live there. I am looking not for window dressings but instead for genuine expressions of an occupant's identity that I read as bold claims for a set of precious rights that have receded in tandem with suburban growth. While many may not welcome these statements of difference, such conflicts force hard but needed conversations between neighbors and entire communities. What I have attempted to sketch in this book are not prescriptive policies or formulas. They are ways of understanding the conflicts and tensions inherent to our ever-changing global metropolis and the processes, ethics, and efforts needed to meet them.

Change is an inescapable urban condition. Our built environments will continue to act as revolving doors for innumerable groups that occupy them over time. In Fremont alone, homes have turned over from Portuguese settlers to Japanese, Mexican, and Filipino farmworkers to White middle-class commuters and today to Chinese American and Indian American high-tech workers. Like rings on a tree, landscapes accumulate layers that speak of the many people who have lived on or passed over them. We need places that are able to absorb all of these stories. They need not erase or venerate any among them. Each ring must grow to tell its own tale about the people who lived there.

We are all constantly charting storylines through the landscapes of our lives as we travel back and forth through new places and old. My father still lives in the West Virginia farmhouse where I was born and raised. When I visit, I often find myself wandering into the woods to the place where some of the best moments of my childhood are stored. It is a small hill at the intersection of two narrow creeks. Nothing exceptional marks this place. But in my mind's eye, it is the most remarkable spot on Earth. Standing near the top, I recall feeling that the world was brimming with hope and possibility as I swung from a woody vine and dropped into a soft patch of moss and ferns below, just missing the creek by a few feet every time. In town, I regularly pass the house where I lived throughout most of my elementary school years. It now stands in a state of disrepair—paint peeling, windows cracked, and the lawn overgrown in parts and eroded or browning in others. Just outside etched into the sidewalk are my initials "WL" that I wrote there with my own finger over 20 years ago. Time has not washed them away, but neither has time stood still. I am a part of all the places that I have been—places that have touched my heart and shaped who I am. That I made my mark on these places matters. All of us want to sketch our names in the landscapes of our lives in some way. The untamed vines, patchy moss, and fading letters in the sidewalk tell my story. While others who pass by these places may never know or understand them in similar ways, we are woven together through these land-scapes and must resolve to make peace with our differences.

Afterword

KEEPING THE DREAM ALIVE IN TROUBLED TIMES

In January 2017 as I pored over the final edits to this book, my attention was continuously drawn to the immigration debates that were rocking the nation. After the election of Donald J. Trump as the 45th president of the United States, hate crimes against immigrants, Muslims, people of color, women, and the LGBT community spiked. Within his first week in office, Trump issued a series of executive orders that were widely criticized as being anti-immigrant and anti-Muslim. One denied federal funds to so-called sanctuary cities that refused to use local authorities to enforce federal immigration laws and established new criteria to prioritize more undocumented immigrants for deportation. Another directed the construction of a wall along the U.S.-Mexican border and boosted the number of border patrol and immigration enforcement officers. A third ordered a four-month ban on all refugees from entering the United States, a permanent ban on all Syrian refugees, and a 90-day stay on immigrants from seven majority-Muslim nations while also signaling that more countries would be added to the list.

Cities across the nation erupted in protest. People took to the streets and gathered at airport terminals and around legislative office buildings in San Jose, Oakland, San Francisco, and many other cities around the United States and the world. In Fremont, rising threats toward and fear among Muslim Americans, including immigrants from Afghanistan, Pakistan, and India, prompted city officials to issue an open letter reaffirming their commitment to diversity and inclusion. While various cities and counties across Silicon Valley had declared themselves immigrant sanctuaries before the election, in response to Trump's orders California lawmakers moved to prevent state law enforcement from complying with the new law and to reposition itself to withstand cuts in federal funding. The top executives of high-tech giants such as Google, Apple, Facebook, Microsoft, and Tesla, whose corporate headquarters are located in the former General Motors plant in Fremont, signed a joint letter to the president opposing the immigrant and refugee ban, noting that diverse immigrants were key to their success and continued growth. Citing the 1965 Immigration and Nationality Act that barred discrimination against immigrants on the basis of national origin, organizations such as the American Civil Liberties Union and several cities and states filed lawsuits against the new administration. As a result, a restraining order was issued on the ban that was later upheld by the U.S. Ninth Circuit Court of Appeals.

In the face of rising intolerance, xenophobia, and extreme nationalism, an unprecedented number of communities in Silicon Valley and elsewhere stood up to declare themselves welcome to immigrants and other marginalized groups. This book has shown that breaking down the barriers that keep residents of different backgrounds out of privileged spaces, be they neighborhoods or countries, and establishing the social and spatial infrastructure that allows diverse values, practices, and aspirations to thrive takes the sustained efforts of those beyond the halls of Congress and the White House. Particularly as federal protections wane, states, regions, and especially localities are increasingly powerful places in which to sow the seeds of social inclusion. Whether urban, suburban, or rural, communities can act as spaces of resistance and transformation by ensuring that their borders are open and that their everyday spaces engender a sense of belonging and solidarity among people of different backgrounds and beliefs. City councils, neighborhood associations, businesses, school boards, and planning commissions can insist that new migrants be provided with the space and tools to help shape the life and culture of their new homes—be it by building a mosque or a badminton court; through opening a restaurant or an after-school program. The ways that communities make space for difference is a test of the strength and resilience of the nation's democratic ideals and of the American Dream.

APPENDIX

Methods for Revealing Hidden Suburban Narratives

Urban scholars have long had a fraught relationship with suburbia. At the turn of the 20th century, many observers hailed suburbs as the antidote to America's deteriorating, crowded, and unsanitary cities. But by the 1960s, the love affair was over. As historian Becky Nicolaides observed, "Suburbs were no longer the city's benevolent partners but their destroyers."[1] By and large, urban scholars of the period critiqued suburbia's social and spatial environment as unhealthy and unsustainable, as many continue to do so today.[2]

Ideas about suburbia, however, are changing. Ongoing efforts to document suburbia's shifting demographics, multiple spatial uses and structures, and diverse cultures and meanings have helped scholars rethink its seemingly static and homogenous character. While not blind to the challenges its form and politics pose to social and environmental sustainability, especially in addressing issues of metropolitan inequality, there is a well-recognized need to inform practices of suburban redevelopment with deeper understandings of the forces that shape its diverse character and identity.[3]

To tell this side of the story requires tools that allow scholars to investigate suburbia from the ground up. My methods have been influenced by Herbert Gans, D. J. Waldie, Sarah Mahler, Bruce Haynes, Setha Low, Mary Pattillo-McCoy, and others who have written about the suburbs from the perspective of its occupants.[4] Their sensitive portraits have compelled readers to confront widely held stereotypes about suburbanites (albeit largely White and middle class) and their homes, communities, and values. I have also been inspired by suburban landscape and architectural studies such as those of Ann-Marie Adams, Margaret Crawford, Diane Harris, and James Rojas.[5] Their deep interrogations of mundane and often overlooked spaces provide novel insights into the processes, people, and politics that have produced suburbia's built environment and continue to shape it today. My research drew upon techniques common to these fields, including in-depth interviewing, participant observation, site analysis, and content analysis of secondary data.

Between 2008 and 2012, I conducted 74 in-depth interviews with key Fremont politicians, planners, developers, business owners, community leaders, and local residents. These took place in coffee shops and participants' living rooms, kitchens, offices, and backyards—places that were personal and meaningful to them. My conversations included a series of open-ended questions about the social and spatial dynamics at work in a rapidly changing city and region, beginning with questions about participants' histories to inform the largely unwritten story of Asian American migration to and within the region. Each participant was also asked about the histories, regulations, and common uses of as well as debates over specific places under study. I sought out some participants for their expertise about particular places, but most came from referrals from earlier interviews, forming a robust snowball sample. With the permission of participants, most interviews were audio recorded. These interviews were transcribed, coded, read, reread, and analyzed to develop connected themes and issues around each of the central topics of the chapters. Although many participants graciously allowed their names to be used for this project, in most cases I have used pseudonyms to protect their identities. As is customary in social science research, actual names and citations appear for all interviews with public officials.

The chapter on Fremont schools was based on my discussions with 5 high-ranking Mission San Jose High School staff, 4 teachers, a Fremont Unified School Board member, 22 current and former Mission High parents, and 12 students. Among parents, 14 were Chinese immigrants, 2 were Indian immigrants, and 6 were native-born White Americans. Among the students, 11 were American-born, and 1 was foreign-born but raised in the United States. Three students identified as White, 3 identified as Chinese American, 2 identified as Indian American, 1 identified as Japanese American, 1 identified as Korean American, and 2 identified as having mixed ancestry (Caucasian and Afghani and Caucasian and Chinese). For the chapter on Asian malls, I spoke with 7 mall managers, developers, owners, and brokers. In addition, I conducted 65 brief semistructured interviews with store owners, employees, and customers during visits to local Asian shopping malls. For insights into the city's large home debates, I spoke with Fremont's former director of planning, 2 staff members involved in drafting the new large home policies, 3 city council members who presided over the debates, the urban design consultant for the design guidelines and development standards, and 20 neighborhood residents. Among residents, 9 lived in Mission Ranch and were involved in the debates, either through neighborhood activism or their appearance at public meetings (5 were against large home development, and 4 supported it). Eleven residents lived in Glenmoor Gardens or Mission San Jose, the larger neighborhood in which Mission Ranch sits, but they were not personally active in the debates.

The interview process challenged me to reflect upon my own identity as a researcher. Being American-born and of both African American and Chinese heritage, I sometimes struggled to find ways to establish rapport with long-term White residents as well as recent Asian immigrants. While I found that sometimes my ethnicity or nationality distanced me from my subjects, in most cases it worked to my benefit.[6] For many Chinese immigrants, my ability to speak Chinese (albeit limited) and my racial and ethnic identity helped to build trust. Many inquired about my father's immigration history and my experiences growing up in the United States, which provided a nice launching point for our conversations about Asian immigration in the region, especially the experiences of second-generation youths. With others, my racial and ethnic ambiguity was a source of frequent discussion. As people were generally unable to make assumptions about my ethnicity, they often asked. My complicated answers on the matter served to open up otherwise difficult discussions about race, ethnicity, nationality, and immigration.

I also regularly spent time observing the physical qualities of the Silicon Valley landscape and its users. At Mission San Jose High, the principal and teachers invited me to sit in on several classes and otherwise informally observe students in their daily lives. My observations on Asian shopping centers were informed by visits to 35 malls in 11 cities throughout the valley as well as the regular trips I took alone and with family and friends to my local Asian shopping mall during the research period. Over the course of this study, I conducted windshield surveys of all the most controversial large homes in the Mission Ranch neighborhood and was given tours of both old and new homes by several neighborhood residents. During visits to all of these places and many more, I copiously photographed and noted what I was seeing and hearing. My field notes included observations about architecture and urban form, cultural and neighborhood conflicts, patterns of use, and residents' alterations to the landscape.

No study like this is complete without secondary data. To better understand Fremont's history, I consulted archives held at Fremont and Silicon

Valley historical societies and local libraries. For additional insights on Mission High's changing academic and social culture, I reviewed copies of the student newspaper, the *Smoke Signal,* dating back to 1974. On the school boundary debate, I analyzed local, regional, and national newspaper coverage of the issue as well as relevant transcripts and video recordings of local school board and county and state board of education meetings. For Asian shopping centers, I referenced design and development data that I obtained from developers, the Fremont Planning Department, local newspapers, and transcripts from city planning and council debates. On Fremont's large home debates, I analyzed publicly available city council and planning commission transcripts from the meetings held about large home development, media reports, resident correspondence with city officials, Fremont Planning Department reports, community meeting notes, resident surveys, and documents shared with me by residents about their homes, neighborhood mobilization efforts, and the planning process. I also reviewed publicly available subdivision maps, real estate tax assessments, and sales data on Mission Ranch's most controversial homes.

I analyzed the region's demographics by looking at U.S. census data, including those compiled by the Bay Area Census, dating back to 1960 for the city and the region. This data was also mapped using Geographic Information Systems software to understand Asian Americans' changing social geographies. For Mission High, I also consulted demographic data from the California Department of Education and the Mission High administration.

My mixed methods generated many contradictions, competing accounts, and conflicting opinions. In real-world settings, especially in places as diverse and dynamic as Silicon Valley, this simply reflects the richness and complexity of everyday life.[7] Making sense of such diverse claims is, however, never an easy or perfect process. In doing so, I have tried to find what Todd Jick calls a "plausible framework," or logical pattern, through which to tell the stories of Asian American migration, place making, and politics in Silicon Valley suburbia.[8] My focus has been on honoring and giving voice to the stories of those who so generously shared their lives with me while also casting a critical lens on the larger social and structural issues at play.

NOTES

INTRODUCTION

The epigraph is from Hughes (1951/1990, p. 221).

1. Naz8 Cinemas (2009).

2. Fremont Gurdwara (n.d.).

3. On the back-to-the-city movement among millennials and baby boomers, see Ehrenhalt (2012) and Gallagher (2013). On the diversity of contemporary suburbs, see Frey (2011) and Wilson & Singer (2011).

4. Frey (2001) and Orfield & Luce (2013).

5. See, for instance, Harris (1999); Harris & Larkham (1999); Kruse & Sugrue (2006); Lasner (2014, 2015); Lewis (2004); McManus & Ethington (2007); Nicolaides (2002); Nicolaides & Wiese (2006, 2016); Retzloff (2015); Walker & Lewis (2001); Wiese (2004).

6. On the racial and ethnic diversity of contemporary suburbs, see Alba, Logan, Stults, Marzan, & Zhang (1999); Alba, Logan, Stults, & Zhang (1999); Berube, Katz, & Lang (2004); Frey (2011); Hanlon (2010); Hanlon, Short, & Vicino (2009); Hanlon, Vicino, & Short (2006); Katz & Lang (2004); Orfield & Luce (2013); Singer (2004); Wilson & Singer (2011). On the suburban poverty and its consequences, see Anacker (2015); Hanlon (2010); Kneebone & Berube (2013); Kneebone & Garr (2010); Lucy & Phillips (2000); Roth & Allard (2015); Short, Hanlon, & Vicino (2007); Vicino (2008).

7. Frey (2014).

8. Kotkin & Cox (2015).

9. Li (1998, 2009).

10. On ethnoburbs in New York, see Chen (1992); Kwong (1996); Zhou & Logan (1991). On Los Angeles, see Cheng (2013); Fong (1994); Horton (1995); Li (1998, 2006, 2009); Saito (1998). On both cities, see Logan, Zhang, & Alba (2002).

11. For writings about Asian American suburbanization in some of these places, see Alba, Logan, & Leung (1994); Kalita (2005); Kuk (2010); Park (1993); Park & Li

(2006); Skop (2002, 2012); Skop & Li (2005). For a more general overview of Asian American high-tech suburbanization, see Li & Lo (2009, 2012).

12. Florida (2002) and Kotkin & Cox (2015).

13. Park & Li (2006).

14. On Asian immigrants in high-tech occupations, see Saxenian (1994, 1999) and Saxenian, Motoyama, & Quan (2002). On Asian Americans in the low-wage labor sector, see Pellow & Park (2002); Pitti (2003); Smith, Sonnenfeld, & Pellow (2006).

15. The term "places of their own" comes from Andrew Wiese's seminal history on African American suburbanites. See Wiese (2004).

16. For an analysis of social power and spatial belonging, see Cresswell (1996).

17. For an articulation of the argument about Asian Americans as the "new Whites" as it relates to education, see Sue, Bucceri, Lin, Nadal, & Torino (2007). For a counterargument, see Park & Liu (2014) and Zhou (2004).

18. My thinking about insurgent practices of place making has been influenced by the writings of James Holston on "insurgent citizenship" and Margaret Crawford's writings about how practices of insurgency in the everyday landscape can generate new forms of urban citizenship and belonging. See Holston (1998) and Crawford (1999, 2008).

19. Kalita (2005); Rojas (2003); Wiese (2004).

20. For more on the politics of neighborhood change in gentrifying urban neighborhoods, see Freeman (2011) and Hyra & Prince (2015).

21. Foucault (1975/1995); Harvey (2008); Lefebvre (1974/1991).

22. Laguerre (1999, p. 4).

23. Schein (2006, p. 4). For other writings about race in the landscape, see Lipsitz (2007) and Schein (2006).

24. Anderson (1991).

25. Lowe (1996).

26. Harris (2013).

27. The term "community builders" comes from Weiss (2002). On the postwar history of race and class exclusion in suburbia, see Harris (2006); Hirsch (1983); Jackson (1985); Lassiter (2006); Self (2003); Sugrue (1996).

28. Nicolaides & Wiese (2006, p. 6).

29. On the naturalization of White privilege in the landscape, see Duncan & Duncan (2004). On contemporary tools of suburban exclusion, see Blakely & Snyder (1997); Caldeira (2000); Duncan & Duncan (2004); Low (2004); McKenzie (1994); Sies (1997).

30. See, for instance, Haynes (2001); Kalita (2005); Mahler (1995); Pattillo-McCoy (2013); Straus (2014).

31. See, for instance, Cheng (2013); Fong (1994); Horton (1995); Li (2009); Saito (1998).

32. Various scholars have written about creating geographies of opportunity and promoting spatial justice through planning and public policy. See, for instance, Briggs (2005); Fainstein (2010); Marcuse (2009); Powell (1999); Soja (2010).

33. This argument is well illustrated in Sarah Mayorga-Gallo's (2014) investigation of the exercise of racial power and privilege in a multiethnic suburb in Durham, North Carolina.

34. Carter Taylor Seaton (2014) writes of the "hippie homesteader" movement that brought families such as mine to West Virginia in the early to mid-1970s.

35. Massey & Denton (1993).

36. The term and method of "taking the city apart" come from the writings of Edward Soja (1989) on postmodern urbanism.

37. This approach is rooted in the fields of environmental design and cultural landscape studies. For more on these methods, see Groth (1997). John Brinkerhoff Jackson (1984), a pioneer in the field of cultural landscape studies, wrote about the importance of scholars to "learn by seeing" (p. xii). Grady Clay (1973) and Allan Jacobs (1985) have also written extensively on the power of and methods for observation in urban landscape analysis.

38. For more on the methods used for this research, see the appendix.

39. Brooks (2009).

40. See, for example, Doan (2015) and Nusser & Anacker (2013) on the challenges of planning for LGBTQ communities. For an examination of the social support and infrastructure that meet the needs of vulnerable groups in the suburbs, see Lo, Preston, Anisef, Basu, & Wang (2015) and Roth & Allard (2015).

41. Basso (1996).

42. I have adopted the term "migrant metropolis" from the conference by the same name sponsored by the Center for the History of the New America at the University of Maryland on March 13–14, 2014.

43. Briggs (2005, p. 320).

1. THE NEW GOLD MOUNTAIN

The epigraph is from Tobias (1985, p. 250).

1. Pseudonyms are used throughout the book in reference to most interviewees. If a pseudonym has been used, a reference to the interview is not provided. If interviewees' real names are used, a reference to the interview is provided. Additional details on the use of interviewees' names can be found in the appendix.

2. Fong (1994).

3. Pellow & Park (2002).

4. For more on how postwar suburbanization helped shape the American Dream for many White working- and middle-class Americans, see Cohen (2003).

5. See, for instance, Berlin (2005); Castells (1994); English-Lueck (2002); O'Mara (2005, 2006); Richards (2000); Smith (2010); Williams (1998).

6. See, for instance, Wong (1998, 2005) and the various writings by AnnaLee Saxenian on Asian Americans immigrant entrepreneurs in Silicon Valley, including Saxenian (1999, 2006). On diversity and creative-class cities, see also Florida (2002).

7. Malone (1985).

8. Corbett (2011).

9. For more on the history of Asian exclusion and laws impacting Asian immigration, see Fong (2008); Ngai (2014); Takaki (2012).

10. Frey (2014).

11. Chinese Historical and Cultural Project, Gong-Guy, & Wong (2007).

12. Cavin (2012, 2013) and Pitti (2003).

13. For further discussion about racial zoning in the prewar period and its impact on Asian Americans, see Brooks (2009).

14. Lukes & Okihiro (1985)

15. Country Club of Washington Township, Research Committee, & Bendel (1965, p. 25).

16. Brooks (2009).

17. Ibid., p. 140.

18. For more on postwar growth in the western Sunbelt, particularly California, see Abbott (1995); Findlay (1992); Hise (1997).

19. Vance (1964).

20. Ibid.

21. Heiman (2015, p. 58).

22. Lee (2004) and Ma (2013).

23. Fogelson (2005).

24. On the history of racial and ethnic exclusion in suburbia especially during the postwar period, see Fishman (1987); Fogelson (2005); Hayden (2009). Jackson (1985) provides an especially poignant analysis of the important role played by federal policy.

25. Self (2003). On the consequences of suburban incorporation for minorities and the poor, see also Orfield (1997).

26. Oral History Associates & Mission Peak Heritage Foundation (1989).

27. Qtd. in Bartels (1959, p. 31).

28. Ibid., p. 72.

29. Smith (1959, p. 2).

30. Qtd. in Bartels (1959, p. 99).

31. Brooks (2009) and Ngai (2014).

32. Little has been written about the postwar battles over racial integration that took place *within* suburbs. For an account in Levittown, Pennsylvania, see Harris (2010); for Seaside, California, see McKibben (2011); and for Newark, New Jersey, see Cohen (2003). For an alternative account of interracial coalition building in a California suburb during the period, see Sanchez (2004). For contemporary accounts of suburban social justice activism, see Carpio, Irazábal, & Pulido (2011) and Niedt (2013).

33. On the postwar urban crises and its causes, see Hirsch (1983) and Sugrue (1996).

34. Brooks (2009); Lee (2004); Saito (1998).

35. Ma (2014) and Rhomberg (2004).

36. Hirsch (1983); Kirp, Dwyer, & Rosenthal (1997); Sugrue (1996); Wilson (1987).

37. General Motors (1964).

38. For more on GM's early employment policies in Fremont, see International Socialists (n.d.). On racial segregation and integration in the United Automobile Workers union, see Sugrue (1996) and Wiese (2004). For a similar perspective on Silicon Valley, see Ruffin (2009, 2014).

39. On Asian Americans' participation in the urban race riots and militant Asian American groups, see Maeda (2005) and Ogbar (2001).

40. This act was later effectively nullified by the passing of Proposition 14 in California a year later. It was reaffirmed by a California Supreme Court ruling in 1967 (HoSang, 2010).

41. McKenzie (1994).

42. For a comparative perspective on the experience of the first African American family to integrate Levittown, Pennsylvania, in the late 1950s, see Harris (2010) and Kushner (2009).

43. Hirsch (1983). For more on African American history in Silicon Valley, including neighborhoods in which African Americans rented and purchased homes in the prewar and immediate postwar periods, see Ruffin (2014).

44. Freund (2007).

45. Brooks (2009).

46. Brooks (2009). See also Cheng (2013).

47. South Bay Chinese Club (n.d.).

48. Gillmor (2004).

49. For histories about the emergence of Silicon Valley in the South Bay, see Findlay (1992) and O'Mara (2005, 2006).

50. Saxenian (2006).

51. On the design and history of Silicon Valley office parks and corporate campuses, see Mozingo (2011) and O'Mara (2005). On the Silicon Valley dreamscape, see Richards (2000).

52. The Immigration and Naturalization Act allocated all countries an equal quota of 20,000 visas per year and set up a preference system whereby 74% of visas were granted for family reunification, 20% for skilled labor and professionals, and 6% for political refugees.

53. As quoted in Kammer (2015, p. 9).

54. Singer, Hardwick, & Brettell (2009).

55. Regarding racial and class segregation in the early Silicon Valley labor force, see Hossfield (1988) and Park (1993).

56. For a brief history of the push and pull factors affecting Chinese immigrants in the San Francisco Bay Area, see Wong (1998). For Filipinos, see Vergara (2008).

57. For accounts of Vietnamese refugees' settlement in San Jose, see Freeman (1989).

58. For a discussion of the working conditions of low-wage immigrants and women in Silicon Valley, see Matthews (2003); Pellow & Park (2002); Pitti (2003).

59. Trounstine & Christensen (1982).

60. For a discussion of the geography of race and class in early Silicon Valley, see Rogers & Larsen (1986).

61. Filipino Americans were far less concentrated in San Jose than were Vietnamese Americans. While disproportionately located in San Jose, Filipinos also had a significant presence in many other working- and middle-class suburbs, including Union City, Milpitas, and Daly City.

62. Findlay (1992, p. 156).

63. Saxenian (1985) and Trounstine & Christensen (1982).

64. Thomas (1989).

65. Johnson (2000).

66. Oral History Associates & Mission Peak Heritage Foundation (1989).

67. Dennis (2011).

68. City of Fremont (1991).

69. Thomas (1989).

70. Researchers have long understood the importance of social and family networks on the migration patterns and social geographies of recently arrived immigrants. See, for example, Alba & Nee (2003).

71. I. Shah, interview with author, July 1, 2012.

72. Kalita (2005, p. 3).

73. Ibid., p. 12.

74. Zhou (1992).

75. Of these, 10,000 were set aside for a new visa category known as EB-3 "employment creation," which applied to immigrants who established commercial enterprises worth $1 million or more and created at least 10 jobs. David Ley (2010) has characterized this new category of immigrants as "millionaire migrants."

76. In 1998 the American Competitiveness and Workforce Improvement Act was passed, significantly increasing the number of visas for skilled workers.

77. Editorial (2000).

78. For more on the Silicon Valley lobby, see Kvamme (2000).

79. Saxenian (2006).

80. Lowell (2000).

81. Saxenian (1999).

82. Peri, Shih, & Sparber (2014). Comparatively, in 1989 Indians had received less than 9% of all visas. See Lowell (2000).

83. Peri, Shih, & Sparber (2014).

84. Saxenian (2006).

85. Wadhwa, Saxenian, Rissing, & Gereffi (2007).

86. Saxenian (2006).

87. Several exemptions to the law have allowed for the extension of additional visas. These include exemptions for applicants with master's level or higher degrees, all university or government employees, and foreign-born students graduating from American universities.

88. Saxenian (2006).

89. Lowe (1996, p. 7).

90. Youngdahl (2009).

91. Saxenian, Motoyama, & Quan (2002). Such fluid relationships among national borders has led scholars to conclude that the old model of global migration, characterized by high-tech "brain drain" from the global South to the global North, is today more appropriately characterized as "brain circulation" or even "reverse brain drain." See Ley (2010); Saxenian et al. (2002); Wadhwa (2009).

92. China developed returnee incentive programs and underwent its own technology bubble in the 1990s that created many jobs for returnees. India had fewer returnees, who largely operated in isolation rather than being incentivized by national policy or the economy (Saxenian, 2006).

93. Ong (2003).

94. Chang (2002, 2006) and Chang & Lung-Amam (2010).

95. Li (2009, p. 39).

96. Cross-border connections are also being forged among cities. In 1993 Fremont adopted Jaipur, India, as its sister city and has since welcomed international delegations from India, China, and Taiwan.

97. This finding was confirmed by several interviewees in this study.

98. Lang & LeFurgy (2007).

99. Fremont also appeared on Edward Glaeser and Jesse Shapiro's list of "high fliers," those cities in the United States with a population of 100,000 or more that grew by more than 10% in the 1990s, which they note tend to be western cities with high human and financial capital. See Glaeser & Shapiro (2003).

100. The latter finding is based on analysis of census data conducted by Gade (2014).

101. This estimate is drawn from the 2014 American Community Survey five-year data. Various scholars have pointed to practices that commonly exploit the vulnerabilities of high-skilled laborers in Silicon Valley and elsewhere. The practice of "body shopping," whereby companies lease out high-tech labor on short-term contracts, was especially popular during the dot-com era among immigrants from India (Kalita, 2005). Aiwah Ong (2003) refers to the practice as a kind of "illegal immigration of skilled work" that produces "glamorized indentured servants" (p. 164). The H-1B visa program has been critiqued as producing a class of "high-tech coolies" who are paid less than American workers and do not have the same legal protections as citizens (Kalita, 2005; Matloff, 2003). H-1B recipients often face significant barriers to promotion and feel forced into positions of employee loyalty, as the fate of migrants' green cards depends on maintaining employment (Matloff, 2003).

102. Home price data comes from an estimate of home values in the "Vineyard-Avalon neighborhoods" of Fremont between June 2015 and May 2016. See Zillow (n.d.).

103. Johnson (2000).

104. B. Wasserman, interview with author, June 15, 2011.

105. Akizuki (1999).

106. Henricks (2012).

107. O'Mara (2005, p. 225).

108. Saxenian (2006).

109. For more on the "bamboo ceiling," see Hyun (2005).

110. Wei Li (2009) notes that immigrants in ethnoburbs are much less likely to feel the same pressure as previous generations to assimilate during the process of suburbanization. According to a *San Jose Mercury News* poll, 85% of immigrants in Santa Clara County do not feel any pressure to give up their ethnic identities (Cha, 1999). Nationwide, Asian Americans were the highest-income, best-educated, and fastest-growing racial group in the United States in 2010. Among all racial minority groups, they were far more likely than others to live in racially mixed neighborhoods (Pew Research Center, 2013).

111. Brooks (2009, p. 236).

2. A QUALITY EDUCATION FOR WHOM?

The epigraph is from Jones-Correa (2008, p. 313).

1. Portions of this chapter have been adapted or reprinted from Lung-Amam (2013a). Reproduced by permission of Taylor and Francis Group, LLC, a division of Informa plc.

2. These schools with high percentages of Asian American students include Gretchen Whitney High (70%), Oxford Academy (59%), Lowell High (66%), Mission San Jose (83%), and Monta Vista High (75%). With the exception of Lowell High in San Francisco, these schools are all located in suburban areas.

3. See, for instance, Lee & Zhou (2015); Ng, Lee, & Pak (2007); Pearce (2006); Zhou (2000); Zhou & Li (2003).

4. See, for instance, Avila (2004); Kruse (2005); Lassiter (2006); Massey & Denton (1993); Orfield (2001); Wells & Crain (1997).

5. In 2000, 51% of Mission San Jose's Chinese American residents were born in Taiwan. By 2010, that figure dropped to 39%. These numbers are based on U.S. census data for the 94539 zip code.

6. For a discussion about how selective migration boosts Asian American academic achievement, see Lee & Zhou (2015).

7. U.S. Census Bureau, American Community Survey, five-year data.

8. Figures on Mission San Jose home values were retrieved from Zillow (n.d.).

9. Silicon Valley has one of the most expensive real estate markets in the country. Richard Florida (2014) found that 10% of zip codes in the San Jose metro area had a median home value of more than $2 million.

10. Zillow (n.d.).

11. Butcher (2004); Collins (2006); Ley (2010); Ong (1999, 2003); Waters (2005).

12. Chang & Lung-Amam (2010).

13. See also similar findings in Lee & Zhou (2015).

14. S. Prairie, interview with author, February 23, 2011.

15. See, for instance, Hum (2004); Li (2009); Zhou (2009). For studies related to Silicon Valley, see Chang & Lung-Amam (2010) and Saxenian (2006).

16. Bartley & Spoonley (2008); Ley (2010); Waters (2005).

17. Kalita (2005) and Shankar (2008).

18. Biyani (2004).

19. Coloma (2006) and Ng, Lee, & Pak (2007).

20. For more on the model minority myth as it relates to Asian Americans in education, see Lee (2004); Shankar (2008); Lee & Zhou (2015).

21. Dang (2000).

22. Charney, Yeoh, & Tong (2003).

23. Sanchez (2004a).

24. Hull (2000a).

25. Heiman (2015).

26. Alba & Nee (2003).

27. Chang & Lung-Amam (2010); Ley (2010); Louie (2001); Ong (1999); Waters (2005, 2006). American degrees are so highly sought after in Asia that immigrant students are easily exploited. Ley (2010) found that many fake institutions have been established to take advantage of Asian students seeking Western degrees. Waters (2006) showed how school districts in Vancouver used private agencies to recruit students in Asia and strategically place them within undersubscribed schools in the district.

28. Ong (2003, p. 160).

29. Louie (2001).

30. Ong (1999).

31. Ley (2010) and Waters (2005).

32. Li (1998). The Taiwanese government requires 2 years of military service for all males at the age of 18. However, if an eligible military enrollee attends a university, he is given the option of waving the mandatory inscription.

33. Marech (2002).

34. Akizuki (2000).

35. Staff Writers (1974).

36. Walter (1987).

37. Prairie, interview with author.

38. Aboumrad (2005).

39. Prairie, interview with author.

40. J. Frydendahl, interview with author, March 22, 2010.

41. These "ethnic systems" of supplementary education have been found to boost Asian American achievement but also reproduce inequalities between Asian Americans and other groups as well as among Asian Americans. On the benefits of supplementary education for Asian Americans, see Zhou (2008); Zhou & Kim (2006); Zhou (2009). On its costs, see Ochoa (2013).

42. Amos (1976).

43. Rosen (1978).

44. Somashekhar (2003).

45. Aratani (2007).

46. Noguchi (2009).

47. Hopkins (2011).

48. Aiyer & Ricci (2003).

49. Chua (2011).

50. Noguchi (2009).

51. Lee & Zhou (2015).

52. A 2013 Pew Research Center study provides additional evidence of Asian Americans' views toward parenting. The study found that 39% of Asian American adults agreed that Asian American parents from respondents' countries of origin put too much pressure on their children to do well in school. Only 9% said the same about all American parents. Asian American college graduates were more likely than those who have not attended college to endorse the approach taken by parents from their own country of origin. Among college graduates, 51% said that parents from their country of origin put about the right amount of pressure on their children to do well in school, compared to about 43% of those with no college experience. Surprisingly, foreign-born residents were less likely to agree with the statement, compared to native-born Asian Americans, 46% compared to 56%, respectively (Pew Research Center, 2013).

53. Lin & Kao (2002).

54. Nguyen (2007). Many students at Mission High contested the way that they were portrayed by the report. One *Smoke Signal* editorial argued that the report reinforced the model minority myth and the "misconception of the typical MSJ student as a parent-dependent, textbook regurgitating drone." See Editorial Board (2007).

55. Zhou & Li (2003, pp. 67–68).

56. Melony (pseudonym), e-mail correspondence, March 23, 2006.

57. Gao (2009).

58. R. Gao, interview with author, March 18, 2011.

59. See, for instance, Cheng (2013); Jiménez & Horowitz (2013); Ochoa (2013).

60. Lee & Zhou (2015).

61. Bernstein, Dhawan, Jafarnia, & Yuan (2010).

62. Shankar (2008).

63. Kao (2005).

64. Brown (2001).

65. Farr (2002).

66. Lee & Zhou (2015) and Ochoa (2013).

67. For a more in-depth analysis of the ways that the ethno-racial divide has impacted Asian American and White students' relations, see Lung-Amam (2013a).

68. The findings from this section are similar to those of Tomás Jiménez & Adam Horowitz (2013), based on their research of Asian American and White students in Cupertino schools.

69. In contrast, much of the literature on suburban segregation has stressed Asian Americans' remarkably low rates of segregation compared to other racial and ethnic groups. See, for instance, Logan (2003).

70. Hwang (2005). This is not the same phenomenon described by William Frey (1994) as "the new White flight," which references poor Whites leaving communities in which minority immigrants are settling.

71. See, for instance, Chen (2005); Chien (2006); Gokhale (2007).

72. Gokhale (2007).

73. Ibid.

74. In 2000, Whites in Pleasanton, Livermore, and Sunol constituted 76%, 74%, and 86% of the population, respectively, compared to 41% in Fremont. In 2010, API scores for Pleasanton high schools were 888 for Foothill High, 883 for Amador Valley High, and 531 for Village High, compared to 953 for Mission San Jose High.

75. Gokhale (2007).

76. Overcrowding and the declining facilities at Mission High are a perpetual problem, brought on by the popularity of Mission San Jose schools and state cutbacks in educational funding. Mission High San Jose also shares its relatively high-income tax base with the large and economically diverse Fremont Unified School District.

77. On the different educational views among various racial and class groups and immigrants, see Ochoa (2013).

78. Lipsitz (2006, p. 1).

79. Prairie, interview with author.

80. See, for instance, Briggs (2005); Chetty, Hendren, Kline, & Saez (2014); Oliver & Shapiro (2006); Pastor (2001); Squires & Kubrin (2005).

81. Lipsitz (2006).

82. In the 1999–2000 school year, Mission High had an API score of 910 compared to Irvington High's 692. Irvington's student population was 54% White, 20% Asian American, 15% Latino, and 4% African American. At Irvington High, 15% of students received free or reduced lunch, compared to Mission High's 3%. In 2000, the year that the boundary changes took effect, Weibel was 250 students over capacity, Mission High was 600 students over capacity, and Irvington maintained room for another 450 to 500 students. See Dang (2000).

83. Hull (1999).

84. Rockstroh (1999).

85. Sanchez (2004b).

86. Hull (2001).

87. Newman (1993).

88. Suzanne Chan, the vice mayor of Fremont and the first Chinese American to hold her position, credited Anna Muh with making a place for her and other Asian Americans in Fremont politics. She said that the school board has since served as an important stepping-stone for many Asian American political candidates. S. Chan, interview with author, July 1, 2011. Wei Li (2006) notes that Asian Americans often start with schools, especially school boards, as their entry into politics. Mayor Bob Wasserman argued that the election of Muh was important for getting Chinese Americans registered to vote for the first time. "There was not a better thing to get them registered than 'our school,'" explained Wasserman. "That really made them active in politics." Wasserman, interview with author.

89. Hull (2000c).

90. Reang & Akizuki (2000).

91. Hull (2000a).

92. The real estate market showed the effects of the desirability of Mission San Jose schools to Weibel homes. According to several people with whom I spoke, at the height of the dot-com boom, Weibel homes stayed on the market for inordinately long periods of time during the boundary debates. Alice Mitchell, who moved into the Weibel attendance area in 1999 right before the boundary decision, bought a home that had been on the market for three or four months. "It was a stale property because it was currently, at the time, it was in the Mission District. And it was known that it might not be," she explained. The uncertainly regarding the boundary decision gave her negotiating power and reportedly a great deal.

93. Hull (2000b).

94. Jones (2000).

95. Staff Report (2000).

96. Sanchez (2004b).

97. Prairie, interview with author.

98. On how low-performing schools shape neighborhood racial geographies, see Straus (2014).

99. Frey (2015) and Massey & Denton (1993).

100. Cheng (2013).

101. Lipsitz (2007, p. 12).

102. Jiménez & Horowitz (2013).

103. On Asian Americans and school policy in the age of color-blind, neoliberal education policy, see Robles (2013).

104. Sandercock (2000).

3. MAINSTREAMING THE ASIAN MALL

1. Asia Mall (n.d.).

2. Lung-Amam (2015).

3. Various scholars have studied the form of Asian shopping centers. Lai (2000, 2009), Lai et al. (2001), Lo (2006), Preston & Lo (2000), and Qadeer (1998) have analyzed their architectural styles, tenant compositions, and other defining characteristics.

4. 99 Ranch Market (also known as Ranch 99 and Tawa Supermarket) is the largest ethnic supermarket chain in the United States. Other popular supermarket anchors in Silicon Valley include Lion Supermarket and Marina Foods. Large banquet restaurants such as Asian Pearl, King Wah, ABC, and the 10,000-square-foot Mayflower restaurant at Milpitas Square serve as popular secondary anchors.

5. P. Su, interview with author, November 29, 2012.

6. A provision of the 1990 Immigration and Naturalization Act grants visas to business owners who employ up to 10 people.

7. Kaplan & Li (2006); Li (1992); Lo (2006); Wang (1999).

8. Conrad (2010).

9. Lung-Amam (2015).

10. According to John Luk, the low price of goods at many Asian supermarkets means that Asian shopping center owners make little profit from their main anchor and have to charge high rents to other tenants. J. Luk, interview with author, September 29, 2011. Shenglin Chang (2006) notes that the high rent strategy pursued by many Asian shopping centers can also serve as a purposive deterrent to non-Asian businesses that can find lower rents elsewhere. Ranch 99, Lion Foods, and several other Asian supermarkets have been at the center of labor controversies because of their refusal to hire unionized labor. Luk argued that the slim profit margins of Asian supermarkets indicate that they cannot afford to hire union labor. But labor union leaders accuse Asian supermarkets of attempting to keep profits high by using a divide-and-conquer strategy, which uses language barriers to keep immigrant laborers from organizing for higher wages or other benefits. See Hukill (1999).

11. Wood (2006) and Allen-Kim (2014).
12. Patrick L. (2006).
13. Luk, interview with author.
14. Chang (2006, p. 105).
15. Chang & Lung-Amam (2010).
16. DuBois (1903).
17. Amin (2002) and Anderson (2011).
18. Su, interview with author.
19. Drew (2001, p. 22).
20. Brown (2003).
21. City of Fremont (2005, p. 10).
22. Lyons (1996).
23. Chang (2006).
24. Nahm (n.d.).
25. Chang (2002).
26. Brown (2003).
27. Nahm (n.d.).
28. Brown (2003).
29. Wong (n.d.).
30. Fong (2010, pp. 53–54).
31. Brown (2003).

32. For case studies of contested neighborhood and city politics surrounding Asian shopping centers in Canadian suburbs, see Edgington, Goldberg, & Hutton (2006); Lai (2000); Preston & Lo (2000).

33. See, for instance, Kim (2004); Lee (2004); Lowe (1996).
34. Artz (2011).
35. I am using the pen names of those who posted comments to the website.
36. Ochoa (2013).
37. City of Fremont (2005).
38. Ibid., p. 1.
39. Ibid., p. 33.
40. City of Fremont (2008).

41. Ibid., p. 68.

42. A. Tsui, interview with author, May 4, 2010.

43. Duncan & Duncan (2004).

44. City of Fremont (2008).

45. City of Fremont (2009a, p. 4).

46. City of Fremont (2007a, p. 2).

47. J. Schwob, interview with author, August 8, 2011.

48. Ibid.

49. Ibid.

50. Ibid.

51. Bonilla-Silva (2006).

52. McKenzie (1994).

53. Greenberg (2009) and Zukin (1996).

54. Lowe (1996, p. 86).

55. City of Fremont (2011, chap. 6, p. 32)

56. The city's efforts to attract upscale retail dates back to at least the late 1980s. See McCloud (1987).

57. City of Fremont (n.d.).

58. Wasserman, interview with author.

59. Ibid.

60. Tsui, interview with author.

61. Wasserman, interview with author. Ironically, Whole Foods announced that it had found a suitable location and would be moving to Fremont in 2011.

62. See, for instance, Bullard (2007); Helling & Sawicki (2003); Kwate, Loh, White, & Saldana (2013).

63. Luk, interview with author.

64. City of Fremont (2008, p. 46).

65. Anonymous, testimony at City of Fremont Council meeting, Fremont, California, April 22, 2008.

66. See, for instance, Leeman & Modan (2010) and Shaw (2011).

67. Cheng (2010).

68. City of Fremont (2005, p. 31).

69. Ibid., p. 10.

70. Chan, interview with author.

71. City of Fremont (2014, p. 24).

72. Fernandez (2006).

73. Imperial Investment and Development Company (n.d.).

74. Ibid.

75. City of Fremont (2005, p. 30).

76. Ibid., p. 31.

77. Schwob, interview with author.

78. B. Wasserman, City of Fremont Council meeting, Fremont, California, March 7, 2006.

79. D. Dutra, City of Fremont Council meeting, Fremont, California, March 7, 2006.

80. A. Natarajan, interview with author, April 2, 2013.

81. Ibid.

82. S. Ruhland, testimony at City of Fremont Council meeting, Fremont, California, March 7, 2006.

83. S. Cho, City of Fremont Council meeting, Fremont, California, March 7, 2006.

84. As of 2015, Fremont sign ordinance does not, in fact, require English-language translations on commercial signage and instead "encourages" them. In other cities, such regulations have been applied to Asian shopping centers. See examples in Domae (1998); Li (2006); Smith & Logan (2006).

85. R. Shanks, testimony at City of Fremont Council meeting, Fremont, California, February 13, 2007.

86. A. Natarajan, City of Fremont Council meeting, Fremont, California, March 7, 2006.

87. A. Natarajan, City of Fremont Council meeting, Fremont, California, February 13, 2007.

88. Chan, interview with author.

89. Segall (2011).

90. On culture as a thing, see Mitchell (2000).

4. THAT "MONSTER HOUSE" IS MY HOME

The epigraph is from Ley (1995, p. 200).

1. An earlier version of this chapter appeared in Lung-Amam (2013b), published by Taylor and Francis (www.tandfonline.com).

2. P. Chen (pseudonym), testimony at Fremont City Council meeting, Fremont, California, September 23, 2008.

3. The term "McMansion" can refer to large homes built in subdivisions of similarly scaled properties or in existing neighborhoods (Nasar & Stamps 2009). The latter is the definition used is this chapter.

4. National Trust for Historic Preservation (2008).

5. Nasar, Evans-Cowley, & Mantero (2007).

6. Hinshaw (2002, p. 27). For other critiques of McMansions, see Devlin (2010); Fine & Lindberg (2002); Kendig (2004); Knack (1999); Weinberg (2001).

7. Hinshaw (2002, p. 27).

8. Knox (2008, p. 173).

9. Fine & Lindberg (2002) and Kendig (2004).

10. Knox (2008, p. 163).

11. Bruegmann (2005, p. 151). A few scholars have also acknowledged the potential benefits that teardowns may have for some residents and communities. They have pointed out, for example, that large homes can encourage neighborhood continuity and revitalization, increase property tax revenues, contribute to urban infill, and allow residents to age in place. See Danielsen, Lang, & Fulton (1999); Lang & Danielsen (2002); McMillen (2006); Szold (2005).

12. National Trust for Historic Preservation (2008).

13. Fine & Lindberg (2002, p. 6).

14. El Nassar (2006).

15. Mercer (1988) and Ray, Halseth, & Johnson (1997).

16. Gutstein (1988) and Wong & Netting (1992).

17. Ley (1995); Ley & Murphy (2001); Majury (1994); Mitchell (1998); Rose (2001).

18. Mitchell (1997).

19. Harris (2006, 2013).

20. Mitchell (2000, p. 256).

21. Duncan & Duncan (2004) and Harris (2006).

22. Lawrence-Zúñiga (2015).

23. On these different tools and their impacts, see Blakely & Snyder (1997); Fogelson (2005); Low (2004); McKenzie (1994); Self (2003, 2006).

24. Kiersz (2015).

25. Silicon Valley is defined here as including Santa Clara County as well as parts of San Mateo, Alameda, and Santa Cruz Counties. For 1995 housing starts and 1999 units approved, see Joint Venture (1997, 2005).

26. In 2010 the census block boundaries for the Mission Ranch neighborhood changed, making it difficult to compare 1990 and 2010 data. However, these figures are consistent with the larger Mission San Jose neighborhood.

27. Housing projects slated for open space have often been fiercely contested in Fremont. For example, as a result of neighborhood backlash, the developer of Avalon, a gated community built along the famed Mission Peak hillside (referred to in Chapter 1), was forced to set aside 1,500 acres of open space for the city. On the Avalon neighborhood protests, see Viloria (1996).

28. Loyd, Toxey, Farrell, Yee, & Cohen (2000).

29. The term "greenfield McMansionization" comes from Nasar & Stamps (2009).

30. Charles (2013).

31. The number of homes that were rebuilt in Mission Ranch were still small compared to the city as a whole. At a 2008 Fremont City Council meeting, Planning Director Jeff Schwob reported that the planning office had received about 98 applications in the last year and a half for second-story additions and major home remodels. J. Schwob, testimony at Fremont City Council meeting, Fremont, California, June 24, 2008.

32. K. Miller (pseudonym), e-mail correspondence with Fremont City Council, presented at the Fremont City Council Meeting, Fremont, California, June 10, 2010.

33. C. Parker (pseudonym), testimony at Fremont City Council meeting, Fremont, California, September 23, 2008.

34. G. Baker (pseudonym), testimony at Fremont Planning Commission meeting, Fremont, California, June 10, 2010 (my emphasis).

35. E. Wang (pseudonym), testimony at Fremont City Council meeting, Fremont, California, September 23, 2008.

36. M. Lowe (pseudonym), testimony at Fremont City Council meeting, Fremont, California, June 24, 2008.

37. Anonymous, Mission Ranch questionnaire, Fremont Planning Department, Fremont, California, May 17, 2010.

38. J. Huang (pseudonym), testimony at Fremont City Council meeting, Fremont, California, September 23, 2008.

39. A. Lai (pseudonym), testimony given at Fremont City Council meeting, Fremont, California, February 27, 2007.

40. Preserve Mission Ranch (2007).

41. Anonymous, Mission Ranch questionnaire.

42. DelVecchio & Pimentel (2001).

43. Preferences for new modern homes have also been noted among Chinese immigrants in Vancouver, Hong Kong, and Monterey Park, California. See Ho & Bedford (2006); Ley (2010); Li (2009); Lo (2006).

44. J. Alvin (pseudonym), testimony at Fremont Planning Commission meeting, Fremont, California, June 10, 2010.

45. Qtd. in De Benedetti (2007).

46. Chang (2006) and Zhang (2010).

47. Duncan & Duncan (1997, p. 170).

48. Archer (2005, p. 363).

49. Nicolaides & Zarsadiaz (2015).

50. Preserve Mission Ranch (2007).

51. Zhang, H. (pseudonym), e-mail correspondence with Fremont City Council, Fremont, California, June 22, 2010. Submitted as information correspondence to the city council meeting, July 27, 2010.

52. Qtd. in De Benedetti (2006).

53. Harris (2007).

54. Preserve Mission Ranch (2007).

55. Ley (1995).

56. Chang (2006).

57. A. Johnson (pseudonym), testimony at Fremont City Council meeting, Fremont, California, January 23, 2007.

58. Wasserman, interview with author.

59. City of Fremont (2009d).

60. City of Fremont (2009c, p. 16). Although most references to Fremont's neighborhood design guidelines and standards contained in this chapter refer to those for Mission Ranch, similar if not the exact same wording is also contained in the Glenmoor Gardens guidelines and standards. See City of Fremont (2009b).

61. City of Fremont (2009c, p. 18).

62. Ibid., p. 20.

63. In 2007, Fremont adopted a maximum citywide FAR of 0.7 for all residential properties. These numbers compare the maximum build out permitted in 2006, the year that the controversy began and before citywide FARs were imposed, and in 2010, the year that new development standards were passed.

64. A. Natarajan, Fremont City Council meeting, Fremont, California, December 19, 2006. Annmarie Adams (1995) provides a fascinating account of how largely middle-class and upper-middle-class White women altered the design of Eichler homes to suit their needs, desires, and lifestyles.

65. City of Fremont (2007b).

66. City of Fremont (2009a, p. 22).

67. City of Fremont (2010).

68. City of Fremont (2007b).

69. City of Fremont (2009c, p. 19).

70. City of Fremont (2007b).

71. City of Fremont (2009c, p. 21).

72. Ibid., p. 12.

73. Ibid., p. 14.

74. See, for example, Briggs (1998); Burayidi (2003); Qadeer (1997); Sandercock (2003).

75. B. Wasserman, Fremont City Council meeting, Fremont, California, December 19, 2006.

76. A. Natarajan, Fremont City Council meeting, Fremont, California, December 19, 2006.

77. Chan, interview with author.

78. R. Sharma, testimony at Fremont Planning Commission meeting, Fremont, California, June 10, 2010.

79. J. Schwob, testimony at Fremont City Council meeting, Fremont, California, April 28, 2009.

80. Charles (2013).

81. McKenzie (1994).

82. See, for example, Fong (1994); Li (2009); Ong (1999); Smith & Logan (2006).

83. Stocking (1999).

84. See, for example, Briggs (1998); Burayidi (2003); Qadeer (1997); Sandercock (2003).

5. CHARTING NEW SUBURBAN STORYLINES

The epigraph is from Sandercock (2003, p. 1).

1. Erica Allen-Kim provides accounts of Vietnamese place making and politics in the suburbs of Los Angeles and Houston. See Kim (2011) and Allen-Kim (2014).

2. Alex Schafran has written about the conditions within low-income exurban communities in the San Francisco Bay Area. See Schafran (2009, 2012).

3. Farley, Schuman, Bianchi, Colasanto, & Hatchett (1978).

4. Wilson & Singer (2011).

5. Frey (2014) and Wilson & Singer (2011).

6. Wallace (2013).

7. William Frey (2014) has defined the American "Heartland" and the "New Sun Belt" as regions that have some of highest rates of new immigrant settlement. On the globalization of suburbs, including many countries in the global South, see Herzog (2014) and Keil (2013). On the U.S. patterns of immigrant settlement, see Massey (2008).

8. On immigrant-friendly cities, see Harwood & Lee (2015).

9. On the politics of immigrant exclusion in suburbs, see Vicino (2012).

10. Appadurai (1996) discusses globalization in terms of these five global cultural flows.

11. Graham & Marvin (2001) popularized the term "splintering urbanism" in their account of the ways in which an increasingly fragmented and privatized network infrastructure contributes to global and local inequalities.

12. Laguerre (1999, p. 79).

13. On the remodeling of homes in Levittown, see Baxandall & Ewen (2000) and Kelly (1993). On Eichler homes in California, see Adams (1995).

14. Aiwah Ong (1999) argues that wealthy Asian immigrants sometimes induce a sense of displacement among groups who do not feel that they are benefiting from globalization to the same extent.

15. Bhabha (1994).

16. Talen (2008).

17. On the redevelopment or redesign of suburbia's built environment, see Blauvelt (2008); Dunham-Jones & Williamson (2011); Tachieva (2010); Williamson (2013).

18. Harvey (2012, p. 4). On the right to the city, see also Mitchell (2003).

19. Appiah (2006); Calhoun (2002); Young (1990).

20. Sandercock (2003, p. 1). On multiculturalism and interculturalism in urban planning and place making, see also Amin (2002); Burayidi (2000, 2003, 2015); Fincher & Iveson (2008); Hou (2013); Watson (2006).

21. Lefebvre (1974/1991).

22. Archer (2005).

23. Alba & Nee (2003). For a discussion about the many "mainstreams" into which new immigrants incorporate, see Vallejo (2012).

24. See, for instance, Avila (2004); Davis (1990); Harwood (2005); Hirsch (2006); Self (2003).

25. On New Urbanism design principles, see Duany, Plater-Zyberk, & Speck (2010).

26. Day (2003) and Southworth (2003).

27. Loukaitou-Sideris (1996, 2012).

28. Nassauer (1995).

29. For writings on "loose," temporary, and flexible spaces as well as tactical and do-it-yourself urbanism, see Bishop & Williams (2012); Finn (2014); Frank & Stevens (2007); Lydon & Garcia (2015).

30. There are various writings on place attachment that speak to this issue, including the classic writings on the subject by Altman & Low (1992). On the built environment as an expression for ethnic identity, see Hanhörster (2000).

31. Hester (1984, 2006).
32. Sandercock (2003).
33. Soja (2000).
34. Orfield (1997).
35. On suburbia as the home of the new American Right, see Lassiter (2006).

APPENDIX

1. Nicolaides (2006, p. 82).
2. For summaries of historical and contemporary suburban critiques, see Nicolaides (2006) and Bruegmann (2005).
3. Archer, Sandul, & Solomonson (2015).
4. See, for instance, Gans (1967); Haynes (2001); Low (2004); Mahler (1995); Pattillo-McCoy (2013); Waldie (2005).
5. See, for instance, Adams (1995); Crawford (1999, 2008); Harris (2006); Rojas (2003).
6. Dunbar, Rodriguez, & Parker (2002) note that building rapport can often be difficult when the researcher and participants are of different ethnic or cultural backgrounds.
7. Jick (1979).
8. Ibid.

BIBLIOGRAPHY

Abbott, C. (1995). *The metropolitan frontier: Cities in the modern American West.* Tucson: University of Arizona Press.

Aboumrad, A. (2005, February 11). AP Statistics at MSJ top in the world. *Smoke Signal, 15*(6), 1.

Adams, A. (1995). The Eichler home: Intention and experience in postwar suburbia. *Perspectives in Vernacular Architecture, 5,* 164–178.

Aiyer, V., & Ricci, M. (2003). Operation grade change: Abort. *Smoke Signal, 38*(7), 1.

Akizuki, D. (1999, August 1). Taiwan ties: Immigrants transform Fremont; Rapid influx is changing bedroom community to business hub. *San Jose Mercury News,* p. 1A.

Akizuki, D. (2000, January 27). Mission High shines: Fremont's schools ranking 5th best in the state. *San Jose Mercury News.*

Alba, R. D., Logan, J. R., & Leung, S.-Y. (1994). Asian immigrants in American suburbs: An analysis of the greater New York metropolitan area. *Research in Community Sociology, 4,* 43–67.

Alba, R. D., Logan, J. R., Stults, B. J., Marzan, G., & Zhang, W. (1999). Immigrant groups in the suburbs: A reexamination of suburbanization and spatial assimilation. *American Sociological Review, 64*(3), 446–460.

Alba, R. D., Logan, J. R., Stults, B. J., & Zhang, W. (1999). Strangers next door: Immigrant groups and suburbs in Los Angeles and New York. In P. Moen, D. Dempster-McClain, & H. A. Walker (Eds.), *A nation divided: Diversity, inequality, and community in American society* (pp. 108–132). Ithaca, NY: Cornell University Press.

Alba, R. D., & Nee, V. (2003). *Remaking the American mainstream: Assimilation and contemporary immigration.* Cambridge, MA: Harvard University Press.

Allen-Kim, E. S. (2014). Exile on the commercial strip: Vietnam War memorials in Little Saigon and the politics of commemoration. *Buildings & Landscapes: Journal of the Vernacular Architecture Forum, 21*(2), 31–56.

Altman, I., & Low, S. M. (Eds.). (1992). *Place attachment.* New York: Plenum.

Amin, A. (2002). Ethnicity and the multicultural city: Living with diversity. *Environment and Planning A, 34*(6), 959–980.

Amos, R. (1976). Campus turmoil kills morale. *Smoke Signal, 11*(4), 1.

Anacker, K. B. (2015). *The new American suburb: Poverty, race and the economic crisis.* Farnham, UK: Ashgate.

Anderson, E. (2011). *The cosmopolitan canopy: Race and civility in everyday life.* New York: Norton.

Anderson, K. J. (1991). *Vancouver's Chinatown: Racial discourse in Canada, 1875–1980.* Buffalo, NY: McGill-Queen's University Press.

Appadurai, A. (1996). *Modernity at large: Cultural dimensions of globalization.* Minneapolis: University of Minnesota Press.

Appiah, A. (2006). *Cosmopolitanism: Ethics in a world of strangers.* New York: Norton.

Aratani, L. (2007, November 4). Crash course: Experts at Stanford University have created a program to help stressed-out students gain perspective—before they collapse. *Washington Post Magazine,* W24.

Archer, J. (2005). *Architecture and suburbia: From English villa to American dream house, 1690–2000.* Minneapolis: University of Minnesota Press.

Archer, J., Sandul, P. J. P., & Solomonson, K. (2015). Introduction: Making performing, living suburbs. In J. Archer, P. J. P. Sandul, & K. Solomonson (Eds.), *Making suburbia: New histories of everyday America* (pp. vii–xxv). Minneapolis: University of Minnesota Press.

Artz, M. (2011, January 30). No Whole Foods quite yet. *Tri-City Beat.* Retrieved from http://www.ibabuzz.com/tricitybeat/(2011)/01/30/no-whole-foods-quite-yet/

Asia Mall. (n.d.). Retrieved on April 15, 2008, from www.asiamall.com

Avila, E. (2004). *Popular culture in the age of white flight: Fear and fantasy in suburban Los Angeles.* Berkeley: University of California Press.

Bartels, R. E. (1959). *The incorporation of the city of Fremont, California: An experiment in municipal government.* Unpublished PhD dissertation, University of California, Berkeley.

Bartley, A., & Spoonley, P. (2008). Intergenerational transnationalism: 1.5 generation Asian migrants in New Zealand. *International Migration, 46*(4), 63–84.

Basso, K. H. (1996). *Wisdom sits in places: Landscape and language among the western Apache.* Albuquerque: University of New Mexico Press.

Baxandall, R., & Ewen, E. (2000). *Picture windows: How the suburbs happened.* New York: Basic Books.

Berlin, L. (2005). *The man behind the microchip: Robert Noyce and the invention of Silicon Valley.* Oxford: Oxford University Press.

Bernstein, M., Dhawan, S., Jafarnia, N., & Yuan, S. (2010, June 11). Mission's melting pot: Celebrating MSJ's ethnic diversity. *Smoke Signal, 40*(9), 5.

Berube, A., Katz, B., & Lang, R. E. (Eds.). (2004). *Redefining urban and suburban America: Evidence from Census 2000.* Washington, DC: Brookings Institution Press.

Bhabha, H.K. (1994). *The location of culture*. New York: Routledge.

Bishop, P., & Williams, L. (2012). *The temporary city*. London: Routledge.

Biyani, G. (2004). Living out of bounds: Students illegally attending school at MSJ. *Smoke Signal, 39*(8).

Blakely, E.J., & Snyder, M.G. (1997). *Fortress America: Gated communities in the United States*. Washington, DC: Brookings Institution Press.

Blauvelt, A. (Ed.). (2008). *Worlds away: New suburban landscapes*. Minneapolis: Walker Art Center.

Bonilla-Silva, E. (2006). *Racism without racists: Color-blind racism and the persistence of racial inequality in America*. Lanham, MD: Rowman & Littlefield.

Briggs, X. de S. (1998). Doing democracy up-close: Culture, power, and communication in community building. *Journal of Planning Education and Research, 18*(1), 1–13.

Briggs, X. de S. (2005). *The geography of opportunity: Race and housing choice in metropolitan America*. Washington, DC: Brookings Institution Press.

Brooks, C. (2009). *Alien neighbors, foreign friends: Asian Americans, housing, and the transformation of urban California*. Chicago: University of Chicago Press.

Brown, P.L. (2003, March 24). The new Chinatown? Try the Asian mall. *New York Times*. Retrieved from http://www.nytimes.com/2003/03/24/us/the-new-china town-try-the-asian-mall.html

Brown, P.L. (2001, May 26). The new melting pot: With an Asian influx, a suburb finds itself transformed. *New York Times*, p. 1A.

Bruegmann, R. (2005). *Sprawl: A compact history*. Chicago: University of Chicago Press.

Bullard, R.D. (2007). Introduction: The significance of race and place. In R.D. Bullard (Ed.), *The Black metropolis in the twenty-first century: Race, power, and politics of place* (pp. 1–16). Lanham, MD: Rowman & Littlefield.

Burayidi, M.A. (2000). *Urban planning in a multicultural society*. Westport, CT: Praeger.

Burayidi, M.A. (2003). The multicultural city as planners' enigma. *Planning Theory & Practice, 4*(3), 259–273.

Burayidi, M.A. (Ed.). (2015). *Cities and the politics of difference: Multiculturalism and diversity in urban planning*. Toronto: University of Toronto Press.

Butcher, A.P. (2004). Educate, consolidate, immigrate: Educational immigration in Auckland, New Zealand. *Asia Pacific Viewpoint, 45*(2), 255–278.

Caldeira, T.P. (2000). *City of walls: Crime, segregation, and citizenship in São Paulo*. Berkeley: University of California Press.

Calhoun, C.J. (2002). The class consciousness of frequent travelers: Toward a critique of actually existing cosmopolitanism. *South Atlantic Quarterly, 101*(4), 869–897.

Carpio, G., Irazábal, C., & Pulido, L. (2011). Right to the suburb? Rethinking Lefebvre and immigrant activism. *Journal of Urban Affairs, 33*(2), 185–208.

Castells, M. (1994). *Technopoles of the world: The making of twenty-first-century industrial complexes*. London: Routledge.

Cavin, A. (2012). *The borders of citizenship: The politics and race of metropolitan space in the Silicon Valley*. Unpublished PhD dissertation, University of Michigan, Ann Arbor.

Cavin, A. (2013). Suburban expansion and the Mexican American struggle for Alviso, California. In C. Niedt (Ed.), *Social justice in diverse suburbs: History, politics, and prospects* (pp. 105–128). Philadelphia: Temple University Press.

Cha, A. E. (1999, April 15). Sorting out an identity: Newcomers find it possible to thrive without assimilating. *San Jose Mercury News*, p. 1A.

Chang, S. (2002). Transcultural home identity across the Pacific: A case study of high-tech Taiwanese transcultural communities in Hsinchu, Taiwan and Silicon Valley, USA. In A. Erdentug & F. Colombijn (Eds.), *Urban ethnic encounters: The spatial consequences* (pp. 142–159). New York: Routledge.

Chang, S. (2006). *The global Silicon Valley home: Lives and landscapes within Taiwanese American trans-Pacific culture*. Stanford, CA: Stanford University Press.

Chang, S. E., & Lung-Amam, W. (2010). Born glocal: Youth identity and suburban spaces in the U.S. and Taiwan. *Amerasia Journal, 36*(3), 29–52.

Charles, S. L. (2013). Understanding the determinants of single-family residential redevelopment in the inner-ring suburbs of Chicago. *Urban Studies, 50*(8), 1505–1522.

Charney, M. W., Yeoh, B., & Kiong, T. C. (Eds.). (2003). *Asian migrants and education: The tensions of education in immigrant societies and among migrant groups*. Norwell, MA: Kluwer Academic.

Chen, H.-S. (1992). *Chinatown no more: Taiwan immigrants in contemporary New York*. Ithaca, NY: Cornell University Press.

Chen, J. (2005, December 7). The new separate but equal. Retrieved from http://www.americanthinker.com/2005/12/the_new_separate_but_equal.html

Cheng, W. (2010). "Diversity" on Main Street? Branding race and place in the new "majority-minority" suburbs. *Identities: Global Studies in Culture and Power, 17*(5), 458–486.

Cheng, W. (2013). *The Changs next door to the Díazes: Remapping race in suburban California*. Minneapolis: University of Minnesota Press.

Chetty, R., Hendren, N., Kline, P., & Saez, E. (2014). Where is the land of opportunity? The geography of intergenerational mobility in the United States. *Quarterly Journal of Economics,* 1553–1623.

Chien, E. (2006, January 10). Backlash of *Wall Street Journal* story reverberates in Bay Area Chinese community. Retrieved from newamericamedia.org/news/view_article.html?article_id=061ea3b27e79e9ceaa77912a9e870e5f

Chinese Historical and Cultural Project, Gong-Guy, L., & Wong, G. (2007). *Chinese in San Jose and the Santa Clara Valley*. San Francisco: Arcadia.

Chua, A. (2011). *Battle hymn of the tiger mother*. New York: Penguin.

City of Fremont (n.d.). *Think retail, think Fremont!* [Brochure]. Fremont, CA: Office of Economic Development.

City of Fremont. (1991, May 7). *Fremont general plan*. Fremont, CA: Fremont Planning Department.

City of Fremont. (2005, July). *Assessment of Asian-themed retail: City of Fremont.* Fremont, CA: Thomas Consultants Development Strategies.

City of Fremont. (2007a). *Resolution No. 2007–73: A resolution of the City Council of the City of Fremont initiating proceedings to review regulations pertaining to the development of new commercial condominiums and the conversion of existing buildings to commercial condominiums including, but not limited to, those regulations set forth in Fremont municipal code section 8-22135.1.* Fremont, CA: City Council.

City of Fremont. (2007b, March 17). *An overview of City of Fremont planning policies and regulations relating to construction of new two-story homes and second-story additions to existing homes.* Fremont, CA: Community Development Department, Planning Division.

City of Fremont. (2008, September). *Fremont market analysis and retail strategy.* Fremont, CA: Strategic Economics.

City of Fremont. (2009a) *Ordinance No. XX-2009: An ordinance of the City of Fremont repealing and reenacting Fremont Municipal Code Title VIII, Chapter 2, Article 21.3, Section 8-22135.1 regarding commercial, industrial and non-residential condominiums* [Draft]. Fremont, CA: City Council.

City of Fremont. (2009b, May 12). *Design guidelines and standards for alteration and construction of single-family homes in Glenmoor Gardens.* A guide by T. R. Hardy, R. B. Anderson, & W. Minor. Fremont, CA: Planning Division, Community Development Department.

City of Fremont. (2009c, May 12). *Design guidelines and standards for alteration and construction of single-family homes in Mission Ranch.* A guide by T. R. Hardy, R. B. Anderson, & W. Minor. Fremont, CA: Planning Division, Community Development Department.

City of Fremont. (2009d, September). *Building permit with site plan and architectural review: Second story preliminary review.* Fremont, CA: Community Development Department, Planning Division.

City of Fremont. (2010, June 10). *Planning commission staff report: Prepared for the Fremont Planning Commission.* Fremont, CA: Community Development Department, Planning Division.

City of Fremont. (2011, December 13). *Fremont general plan.* Fremont, CA: Community Development Department, Planning Division.

City of Fremont. (2014, July 22). *Fremont downtown community plan and design guidelines.* Fremont, CA: HOK Planning Group.

City of Fremont, Community Development Department. (2006, December). *Consideration of large home policies.* Presented at the City Council work session, Fremont, CA.

Clay, G. (1973). *Close-up: How to read the American city.* New York: Praeger.

Cohen, L. (2003). *A consumers' republic: The politics of mass consumption in postwar America.* New York: Knopf.

Collins, F. L. (2006). Making Asian students, making students Asian: The racialization of export education in Auckland, New Zealand. *Asia Pacific Viewpoint, 47*(2), 217–234.

Coloma, R. S. (2006). Disorienting race and education: changing paradigms on the schooling of Asian Americans and Pacific Islanders. *Race Ethnicity and Education, 9*(1), 1–15.

Conrad, K. (2010, April 16). Broker thrives by straddling two worlds. *Silicon Valley Business Journal.*

Corbett, M. R. (2011, July 12). Historical resource record: Fremont-Beard property. Fremont, CA: Prepared for the City of Fremont.

Country Club of Washington Township, Research Committee, & Bendel, W. H. (1965). *History of Washington Township.* Stanford, CA: Stanford University Press.

Crawford, M. (1999). Blurring the boundaries: Public space and private life. In J. Chase, M. Crawford, & J. Kaliski (Eds.), *Everyday urbanism* (pp. 22–35). New York: Monacelli.

Crawford, M. (2008). Introduction. In M. Crawford, J. Kaliski, & J. Chase (Eds.), *Everyday urbanism* (pp. 6–12). New York: Monacelli.

Cresswell, T. (1996). *In place—out of place: Geography, ideology, and transgression.* Minneapolis: University of Minnesota Press.

Dang, J. (2000, March 22). Learning limits: How redrawn school boundaries are pitting Asian American parents against one East Bay school district. *AsianWeek* [San Francisco].

Danielsen, K., Lang, R., & Fulton, W. (1999). Retracting suburbia: Smart growth and the future of housing. *Housing Policy Debate, 10*(3), 513–540.

Davis, M. (1990). *City of quartz: Excavating the future in Los Angeles.* London: Verso.

Day, K. (2003). New Urbanism and the challenges of designing for diversity. *Journal of Planning Education and Research, 23*(1), 83–95.

De Benedetti, C. (2006, December 21). Fremont housing report: Size matters. *Inside Bay Area.*

De Benedetti, C. (2007, February 12). Megahome supporters fight back: Fremont residents say that houses will increase jobs, but opponents aren't sold on idea. *Inside Bay Area.*

DelVecchio, R., & Pimentel, B. (2001, March 26). Asians bring change to Fremont, Milpitas; Fremont, Milpitas ride immigration wave—Asian influx, technology create big changes in East Bay cities. *San Francisco Chronicle,* p. A1.

Dennis, R. (2011, December 30). Fremont mayor Bob Wasserman dead at 77. *San Jose Mercury News.*

Devlin, A. S. (2010). *What Americans build and why: Psychological perspectives.* Cambridge, MA: Cambridge University Press.

Doan, P. L. (2015). *Planning and LGBTQ communities: The need for inclusive queer spaces.* New York: Routledge.

Domae, L. K. (1998). *Multicultural planning: A study of inter-ethnic planning in Richmond, British Columbia.* Unpublished master's thesis, School of Urban and Regional Planning, Queen's University, Kingston, Ontario, Canada.

Drew, R. (2001). *Karaoke nights: An ethnographic rhapsody.* Walnut Creek, CA: Rowman and Littlefield.

Duany, A., Plater-Zyberk, E., & Speck, J. (2010). *Suburban nation: The rise of sprawl and the decline of the American Dream.* London: Macmillan.

DuBois, W.E.B. (1903) *The Souls of Black Folks.* Chicago: A.C. McClurg & Co.

Dunbar, C., Rodriguez, D., & Parker, L. (2002). Race, subjectivity, and the interview process. In J. F. Gubrium & J. A. Holstein (Eds.), *Handbook of interview research: Context and method* (pp. 279–298). Thousand Oaks, CA: Sage.

Duncan, J. S., & Duncan, N. G. (1997). Deep suburban irony: The perils of democracy in Westchester County, New York. In R. Silverstone (Ed.), *Visions of suburbia* (pp. 161–179). London: Routledge.

Duncan, N. G., & Duncan, J. S. (2004). *Landscapes of privilege: The politics of the Aesthetic in an American suburb.* New York: Routledge.

Dunham-Jones, E., & Williamson, J. (2011). *Retrofitting suburbia, updated edition: Urban design solutions for redesigning suburbs.* Hoboken, NJ: Wiley.

Edgington, D. W., Goldberg, M. A., & Hutton, T. A. (2006). Hong Kong business, money, and migration in Vancouver, Canada. In W. Li (Ed.), *From urban enclave to ethnic suburb: New Asian communities in Pacific Rim countries* (pp. 155–183). Honolulu: University of Hawai'i Press.

Editorial. (2000, August 7). Jobs vs. homes: Econ 101 explains the insane prices, but other cities besides San Jose need to work harder on new housing opportunities. *San Jose Mercury News,* p. 10B.

Editorial Board. (2007, June 11). Are Asian students smarter? *CNN* feature perpetuates stereotypes. *Smoke Signal, 42*(11), p. 4.

Ehrenhalt, A. (2012). *The great inversion and the future of the American city.* New York: Random House.

El Nassar, H. (2006, June 27). Teardowns have critics torn up. *USA Today.* Retrieved from http://www.usatoday.com/news/nation/2006-06-27-teardowns-preser vation_x.htm

English-Lueck, J. (2002). *Cultures @ SiliconValley.* Stanford, CA: Stanford University Press.

Fainstein, S. S. (2010). *The just city.* Ithaca, NY: Cornell University Press.

Farley, R., Schuman, H., Bianchi, S., Colasanto, D., & Hatchett, S. (1978). "Chocolate city, vanilla suburbs": Will the trend toward racially separate communities continue? *Social Science Research, 7*(4), 319–344.

Farr, A. (2002, September 25). Listen up, MSJ: Reverse racism. *Smoke Signal, 38*(2), 2.

Fernandez, L. (2006, March 15). Global vision guides new mall: Themed shopping center rising in Fremont. *San Jose Mercury News.*

Findlay, J. M. (1992). *Magic lands: Western cityscapes and American culture after 1940.* Berkeley: University of California Press.

Fincher, R., & Iveson, K. (2008). *Planning and diversity in the city: Redistribution, recognition and encounter.* New York: Palgrave Macmillan.

Fine, A. S., & Lindberg, J. (2002). *Protecting America's historic neighborhoods: Taming the teardown trend.* Washington, DC: National Trust for Historic Preservation.

Finn, D. (2014). DIY urbanism: implications for cities. *Journal of Urbanism: International Research on Placemaking and Urban Sustainability, 7*(4), 381–398.

Fishman, R. (1987). *Bourgeois utopias: The rise and fall of suburbia*. New York: Basic Books.

Florida, R. (2002). *The rise of the creative class: And how it's transforming work, leisure, community and everyday life*. New York: Basic Books.

Florida, R. (2014, July 3). ZIP codes of the super rich. Retrieved from http://www .citylab.com/housing/2014/07/zip-codes-of-the-super-rich/373013/

Fogelson, R. M. (2005). *Bourgeois nightmares: Suburbia, 1870–1930*. New Haven, CT: Yale University Press.

Fong, J. C. (2010). Globalized/localized Asian American banks in the twenty-first century. *Amerasia Journal, 36*(3), 53–82.

Fong, T. (1994). *The first suburban Chinatown: The remaking of Monterey Park, California*. Philadelphia: Temple University Press.

Fong, T. P. (2008). *The contemporary Asian American experience: Beyond the model minority*. Upper Saddle River, NJ: Pearson Prentice Hall.

Foucault, M. (1975/1995). *Discipline & punish: The birth of the prison*. A. Sheridan (Trans.). New York: Vintage Books.

Franck, K., & Stevens, Q. (2007). *Loose space: Possibility and diversity in urban life*. New York: Routledge.

Freeman, J. M. (1989). *Hearts of sorrow: Vietnamese-American lives*. Redwood City, CA: Stanford University Press.

Freeman, L. (2011). *There goes the 'hood: Views of gentrification from the ground up*. Philadelphia: Temple University Press.

Fremont Gurdwara. (n.d.). Retrieved August 30, 2016, from http://www.fremont gurdwara.org/

Freund, D. M. P. (2007). *Colored property: State policy and white racial politics in suburban America*. Chicago: University of Chicago Press.

Frey, W. H. (1994). The new White flight. *American Demographics, 16*(4), 40–44.

Frey, W. H. (2001). *Melting pot suburbs: A Census 2000 study of suburban diversity*. Washington, DC: Center on Urban and Metropolitan Policy, Brookings Institution.

Frey, W. H. (2011). *Melting pot cities and suburbs: Racial and ethnic change in metro America in the 2000s* (Paper No. 30). Washington, DC: Center on Urban and Metropolitan Policy, Brookings Institution.

Frey, W. H. (2014). *Diversity explosion: How new racial demographics are remaking America*. Washington, DC: Brookings Institution Press.

Gade, A. (2014). *Street spectacle: Fremont's Festival of India parade and the transformation of a Silicon Valley suburb*. Unpublished master's thesis, University of California, Berkeley.

Gallagher, L. (2013). *The end of the suburbs: Where the American dream is moving*. New York: Penguin.

Gans, H. J. (1967). *The Levittowners: Ways of life and politics in a new suburban community*. New York: Random House.

Gao, R. (2009, January 22). Don't blame race or parents; students push themselves at my school. *San Jose Mercury News*, p. 14A.

General Motors. (1964, March). Corporation commemorative brochure [Brochure]. Fremont, CA: General Motor's Assembly Plant.

Gillmor, C. S. (2004). *Fred Terman at Stanford: Building a discipline, a university, and Silicon Valley*. Stanford, CA: Stanford University Press.

Glaeser, E. L., & Shapiro, J. M. (2003). City growth: Which places grew and why. In A. Berube, B. Katz, & R. E. Lang (Eds.), *Redefining urban and suburban America: Evidence from Census 2000* (pp. 13–32). Washington, DC: Brookings Institution Press.

Gokhale, K. (2007, January 6). Percentages of White high school students decline in Silicon Valley. Retrieved from http://news.newamericamedia.org/news/view _article.html?article_id=374b95c244fe32eef88c9a48c306bbb2

Graham, S., & Marvin, S. (2001). *Splintering urbanism: Networked infrastructures, technological mobilities and the urban condition*. London: Routledge.

Greenberg, M. (2009). *Branding New York: How a city in crisis was sold to the world*. New York: Routledge.

Groth, P. (1997). Frameworks for cultural landscape study. In P. E. Groth & T. W. Bressi (Eds.), *Understanding ordinary landscapes* (pp. 1–24). New Haven, CT: Yale University Press.

Gutstein, D. (1988). Hong Kong money. *Vancouver, 21*(12), 39–48.

Hammond, W. L. (2003). *Remembering my life in Irvington, California, and other memories: 1931–1943*. Modesto, CA: The Author.

Hanhörster, H. (2000). Whose neighbourhood is it? Ethnic diversity in urban spaces in Germany. *GeoJournal, 51*(4), 329–338.

Hanlon, B. (2010). *Once the American Dream: Inner-ring suburbs of the metropolitan United States*. Philadelphia: Temple University Press.

Hanlon, B., Short, J. R., & Vicino, T. J. (2009). *Cities and suburbs: New metropolitan realities in the US*. New York: Routledge.

Hanlon, B., Vicino, T., & Short, J. R. (2006). The new metropolitan reality in the US: Rethinking the traditional model. *Urban Studies, 43*(12), 2129–2143.

Harris, D. (2006). Race, class, and privacy in the ordinary postwar house, 1945–60. In R. H. Schein (Ed.), *Landscape and race in the United States* (pp. 127–156). New York: Routledge.

Harris, D. (2007). Race, space, and the destabilization of practice. *Landscape Journal, 26*(1), 1–9.

Harris, D. (2010). *Second suburb: Levittown, Pennsylvania*. Pittsburgh: University of Pittsburgh Press.

Harris, D. (2013). *Little white houses: How the postwar home constructed race in America*. Minneapolis: University of Minnesota Press.

Harris, R. (1999). *Unplanned suburbs: Toronto's American tragedy, 1900 to 1950*. Baltimore: Johns Hopkins University Press.

Harris, R., & Larkham, P. (Eds.). (1999). *Changing suburbs: Foundation, form and function*. New York: Routledge.

Harvey, D. (2008). The right to the city. *New Left Review,* (53), 23–40.

Harvey, D. (2012). *Rebel cities: From the right to the city to the urban revolution*. New York: Verso.

Harwood, S.A. (2005). Struggling to embrace difference in land-use decision making in multicultural communities. *Planning Practice & Research, 20*(4), 355–371.

Harwood, S.A., & Lee, S.S. (2015). Immigrant friendly community plans: Rustbelt efforts to attract and retain immigrants. In M. Burayidi (Ed.), *Cities and the politics of difference: Multiculturalism and diversity in urban planning* (pp. 236–264). Toronto: University of Toronto Press.

Hayden, D. (2009). *Building suburbia: Green fields and urban growth, 1820–2000.* New York: Vintage Books.

Haynes, B.D. (2001). *Red lines, black spaces: The politics of race and space in a black middle-class suburb.* New Have, CT: Yale University Press.

Heiman, R. (2015). *Driving after class: Anxious times in an American suburb.* Berkeley: University of California Press.

Helling, A., & Sawicki, D.S. (2003). Race and residential accessibility to shopping and services. *Housing Policy Debate, 14*(1–2), 69–101.

Henricks, M. (2012, October 3). Go west, young entrepreneur [Blog post]. Retrieved from https://www.americanexpress.com/us/small-business/openforum/articles/go-west-young-entrepreneur/

Herzog, L. (2014). *Global suburbs: Urban sprawl from the Rio Grande to Rio de Janeiro.* New York: Routledge.

Hester, R.T. (1984). *Planning neighborhood space with people.* New York: Van Nostrand Reinhold.

Hester, R.T. (2006). *Design for ecological democracy.* Cambridge, MA: MIT Press.

Hinshaw, M.L. (2002). Monster houses? No! *Planning, 68,* 25–27.

Hirsch, A.R. (1983). *Making the second ghetto: Race and housing in Chicago, 1940–1960.* Cambridge, MA: Cambridge University Press.

Hirsch, A.R. (2006). Less than Plessy: The inner city, suburbs, and state-sanctioned residential segregation in the age of Brown. In T.J. Sugrue & K.M. Kruse (Eds.), *The new suburban history* (pp. 33–57). Chicago: University of Chicago Press.

Hise, G. (1997). *Magnetic Los Angeles: Planning the twentieth-century metropolis.* Baltimore: Johns Hopkins University Press.

Ho, E.S.Y., & Bedford, R.D. (2006). The Chinese in Auckland: Changing profiles in a more diverse society. In W. Li (Ed.), *From urban enclave to ethnic suburb: New Asian communities in Pacific Rim countries* (pp. 203–230). Honolulu: University of Hawai'i Press.

Holston, J. (1998). Space of insurgent citizenship. In L. Sandercock (Ed.), *Making the invisible visible: A multicultural planning history* (pp. 37–56). Berkeley: University of California Press.

Hopkins, K. (2011, September 27). In California, with high AP scores comes high pressure. *US News and World Report.*

Horton, J. (1995). *The politics of diversity: Immigration, resistance, and change in Monterey Park, California.* Philadelphia: Temple University Press.

HoSang, D. (2010). *Racial propositions: Ballot initiatives and the making of postwar California.* Berkeley: University of California Press.

Hossfield, K. (1988). *Division of labor, division of lives.* Unpublished PhD dissertation, University of California, Santa Cruz.

Hou, J. (Ed.). (2013). *Transcultural cities: Border-crossing and placemaking.* New York: Routledge.

Hughes, L. (1951/1990). *Montage to a dream deferred.* Reprinted in *Selected Poems of Langston Hughes.* New York: Vintage.

Hukill, T. (1999, September 16–22). Power plays: When unions attempt to organize Silicon Valley's growing Vietnamese workforce, they find custom, language and history stand in the way. *Metroactive.* Retrieved from http://www.metroactive .com/papers/metro/09.16.99/vietnamese-9937.html.

Hull, D. (1999, November 11). School boundary plan OK'd: Fremont Mission San Jose High attendance area will be left largely intact. *San Jose Mercury News.*

Hull, D. (2000a, March 2). Weibel might be split three ways: School boundaries stir public outrage. *San Jose Mercury News.*

Hull, D. (2000b, June 16). Debate widens over Fremont schools schism: Drive for district may divide the city. *San Jose Mercury News.*

Hull, D. (2000c, November 9). Three victors favor Irvington attendance area: Fremont vote solidifies school boundary changes. *San Jose Mercury News.*

Hull, D. (2001, February 25). Race becomes an unexpected issue in effort to split Fremont School District: A new segregation fight spinoff system proposed by parents would be widely affluent, mostly Asian. *San Jose Mercury News.*

Hum, T. (2004). Immigrant global neighborhoods in New York City. *Race and Ethnicity in New York City, 7,* 25–55.

Hwang, S. (2005, November 19). The new White flight: In Silicon Valley, two high schools with outstanding academic reputations are losing White students as Asian students move in. Why? *Wall Street Journal,* p. A1.

Hyra, D., & Prince, S. (Eds.). (2015). *Capital dilemma: Growth and inequality in Washington, D.C.* New York: Routledge.

Hyun, J. (2005). *Breaking the bamboo ceiling: Career strategies for Asians.* New York: Harper Business.

Imperial Investment and Development Company. (n.d.). The Globe: One destination . . . a world of discovery [Brochure]. Milpitas, CA.

International Socialists. (n.d.). Black workers on the move [Brochure], p. 5.

Jackson, J. B. (1984). *Discovering the vernacular landscape.* New Haven, CT: Yale University Press.

Jackson, K. T. (1985). *Crabgrass frontier: The suburbanization of the United States.* Oxford: Oxford University Press.

Jacobs, A. B. (1985). *Looking at cities.* Cambridge, MA: Harvard University Press.

Jick, T. D. (1979). Mixing qualitative and quantitative methods: Triangulation in action. In J. V. Maanen (Ed.), *Qualitative methodology* (pp. 135–148). Beverly Hills, CA: Sage.

Jiménez, T. R., & Horowitz, A. L. (2013). When White is just alright: How immigrants redefine achievement and reconfigure the ethnoracial hierarchy. *American Sociological Review 78*(5), 849–871.

Johnson, C. (2000, November 23). High-tech boom awakens Fremont; Mostly White bedroom community in multicultural Silicon Valley hub. *San Francisco Chronicle*, p. A28.

Joint Venture. (1997). *Joint Venture's index of Silicon Valley*. San Jose: Collaborative Economics. Retrieved from http://siliconvalleyindicators.org/pdf/index1997.pdf

Joint Venture. (2005). *Joint Venture's index of Silicon Valley*. San Jose: Collaborative Economics. Retrieved from http://siliconvalleyindicators.org/pdf/index2005.pdf

Jones, S. (2000, May 8). The future of Fremont schools; Splitting up the district would undercut its vision of excellence. *San Jose Mercury News*.

Jones-Correa, M. (2008). Race to the top? The politics of immigrant education in the suburbs. In D. S. Massey (Ed.), *New faces in new places: The changing geography of American immigration* (pp. 308–340). New York: Russell Sage Foundation.

Kalita, S. M. (2005). *Suburban sahibs: Three immigrant families and their passage from India to America*. New Brunswick, NJ: Rutgers University Press.

Kammer, J. (2015, October). *The Hart-Celler Immigration Act of 1965: Political figures and historic circumstances produced dramatic, unintended consequences*. Washington, DC: Center for Immigration Studies.

Kao, J. (2005, March 25). GATE barring academic success. *Smoke Signal, 40*(9), 5.

Kaplan, D. H., & Li, W. (2006). Introduction: The places of ethnic economies. In D. H. Kaplan & W. Li (Eds.), *Landscapes of the ethnic economy* (pp. 1–16). Lanham, MD: Rowman & Littlefield.

Katz, B., & Lang, R. E. (Eds.). (2004). *Redefining urban and suburban America: Evidence from Census 2000*. Washington, DC: Brookings Institution Press.

Keil, R. (Ed.). (2013). *Suburban constellations: Governance, land and infrastructure in the 21st century*. Berlin: JOVIS Publishers.

Kelly, B. M. (1993). *Expanding the American Dream: Building and rebuilding Levittown*. New York: SUNY Press.

Kendig, L. (2004). *Too big, boring, or ugly: Planning and design tools to combat monotony, the too-big house, and teardowns*. Washington, DC: American Planning Association.

Kiersz, A. (2015, January 6). New American homes are bigger today than they were during the housing bubble. Retrieved from http://www.businessinsider.com/house-size-chart-2015-1

Kim, C. J. (2004). Imagining race and nation in multiculturalist America. *Ethnic and Racial Studies, 27*(6), 987–1005.

Kim, E. S. H. (2011). *Mini-malls and memorials: Vietnamese and the re-shaping of American cities and suburbs*. Unpublished PhD dissertation, Harvard University, Cambridge, MA.

Kirp, D. L., Dwyer, J. P., & Rosenthal, L. A. (1997). *Our town: Race, housing, and the soul of suburbia*. New Brunswick, NJ: Rutgers University Press.

Knack, R. E. (1999). Cutting monster houses down to size. *Planning, 65*(10), 4.

Kneebone, E., & Berube, A. (2013). *Confronting suburban poverty in America*. Washington, DC: Brookings Institution Press.

Kneebone, E., & Garr, E. (2010). *The suburbanization of poverty: Trends in metropolitan America, 2000 to 2008.* Washington, DC: Brookings Institution Press.

Knox, P. L. (2008). *Metroburbia, USA.* New Brunswick, NJ: Rutgers University Press.

Kotkin, J., & Cox, W. (2015, March 18). The evolving geography of Asian America: Suburbs are new high-tech Chinatowns. *Forbes Magazine.* Retrieved from http://www.forbes.com/sites/joelkotkin/2015/03/18/the-evolving-geography-of-asian-america-suburbs-are-new-high-tech-chinatowns/2/

Kruse, K. M. (2005). *White flight: Atlanta and the making of modern conservatism.* Princeton, NJ: Princeton University Press.

Kruse, K. M., & Sugrue, T. J. (Eds.). (2006). *The new suburban history.* Chicago: University of Chicago Press.

Kuk, K. (2010, May 28). *New Asian destinations: A comparative study of traditional gateways and emerging immigrant destinations.* Unpublished master's thesis, Cornell University, Ithaca, NY.

Kushner, D. (2009). *Levittown: Two families, one tycoon, and the fight for civil rights in America's legendary suburb.* London: Bloomsbury.

Kvamme, E. F. (2000). Life in Silicon Valley: A first-hand view of the region's growth. In C.-M. Lee, W. F. Miller, M. G. Hancock, & H. S. Rowen (Eds.), *The Silicon Valley edge: A habitat for innovation and entrepreneurship* (pp. 59–80). Stanford, CA: Stanford University Press.

Kwate, N. O. A., Loh, J. M., White, K., & Saldana, N. (2013). Retail redlining in New York City: Racialized access to day-to-day retail resources. *Journal of Urban Health: Bulletin of the New York Academy of Medicine, 90*(4), 632–652.

Kwong, P. (1996). *The new Chinatown.* New York: Hill and Wang.

Laguerre, M. S. (1999). *Minoritized space: An inquiry into the spatial order of things.* Berkeley, CA: Institute of Governmental Studies Press, Institute of Urban and Regional Development.

Lai, C. D. (2009, July). *Chinatowns: From slums to tourist destinations* (Paper No. 89). Hong Kong: David C. Lam Institute for East-West Studies.

Lai, C. D., Vancouver Centre of Excellence for Research on Immigration and Integration in the Metropolis, & Shao You-Bao Overseas Chinese Documentation and Research Center. (2001). *A study of Asian-themed malls in the Aberdeen District of city of Richmond, British Columbia.* Vancouver: Vancouver Centre for Excellence for RIIM.

Lai, D. C. (2000). The impact of new immigration policies on the development of New Chinatown and new Chinese shopping plazas in Canada. *Asian Profile, 28*(2), 99–116.

Lang, R. E., & Danielsen, K. A. (2002). Monster houses? Yes! No! *Planning, 68*(5).

Lang, R. E., & LeFurgy, J. B. (2007). *Boomburbs: The rise of America's accidental cities.* Washington, DC: Brookings Institution Press.

Lasner, M. (2014, October). Swingsites for singles. *Places Journal.* Retrieved from https://placesjournal.org/article/swingsites-for-singles/#0

Lasner, M. G. (2015). The complex: Social difference and the suburban apartment in postwar America. In J. Archer, P. J. P. Sandul, & K. Solomonson (Eds.), *Making suburbia: New histories of everyday America* (pp. 343–363). Minneapolis: University of Minnesota Press.

Lassiter, M. D. (2006). *The silent majority: Suburban politics in the Sunbelt South.* Princeton, NJ: Princeton University Press.

Lawrence-Zúñiga, D. (2015). Residential design guidelines, aesthetic governmentality, and contested notions of southern California suburban places. *Economic Anthropology, 2*(1), 120–144.

Lee, J., & Zhou, M. (2015). *The Asian American achievement paradox.* New York: Russell Sage Foundation.

Lee, J. K.-J. (2004). *Urban triage: Race and the fictions of multiculturalism.* Minneapolis: University of Minnesota Press.

Leeman, J., & Modan, G. (2010). Selling the city: Language, ethnicity and commodified space. In E. Shohamy, E. Ben Rafael, & M. Barni (Eds.), *Linguistic landscape in the city* (pp. 182–198). Bristol, UK: Multilingual Matters.

Lefebvre, H. (1974/1991). *The production of space.* (D. Nicholson-Smith, Trans.). Cambridge, MA: Blackwell.

Lewis, R. (2004). Industry in the suburbs. In R. Lewis (Ed.), *Manufacturing suburbs: Building work and home on the metropolitan fringe* (pp. 1–15). Philadelphia: Temple University Press.

Ley, D. (1995). Between Europe and Asia: The case of the missing sequoias. *Cultural Geographies, 2*(2), 185–210.

Ley, D. (2010). *Millionaire migrants: Trans-Pacific life lines.* West Sussex, UK: Wiley Blackwell.

Ley, D., & Murphy, P. (2001). Immigration in gateway cities: Sydney and Vancouver in comparative perspective. *Progress in Planning, 55*(3), 119–194.

Li, P. S. (1992). Ethnic enterprise in transition: Chinese business in Richmond, B.C., 1980–1990. *Canadian Ethnic Studies, 24*(1), 120–138.

Li, W. (1998). Anatomy of a new ethnic settlement: The Chinese ethnoburb in Los Angeles. *Urban Studies, 35*(3), 479–501.

Li, W. (2006). Spatial transformation of an urban ethnic community: From China-town to ethnoburb in L.A. In W. Li (Ed.), *From urban enclave to ethnic suburb: New Asian communities in Pacific Rim countries* (pp. 74–94). Honolulu: University of Hawai'i Press.

Li, W. (2009). *Ethnoburb: The new ethnic community in urban America.* Honolulu: University of Hawai'i Press.

Li, W., & Lo, L. (2009). *Highly-skilled Indian migrations in Canada and the US: The tale of two immigration systems* (International Migration and Diaspora Studies Working Paper Series 4–6). New Delhi, India: Jawaharlal Nehru University.

Li, W., & Lo, L. (2012). New geographies of migration? A Canada-U.S. comparison of highly skilled Chinese and Indian migration. *Journal of Asian American Studies, 15*(1), 1–34.

Lin, J., & Kao, C. (2002). Saving face: Voices suppressed by culture. *Smoke Signal, 37*(8), 11.

Lipsitz, G. (2006). *The possessive investment in whiteness: How White people profit from identity politics.* Philadelphia: Temple University Press.

Lipsitz, G. (2007). The racialization of space and the spatialization of race: Theorizing the hidden architecture of landscape. *Landscape Journal, 26*(1), 10–23.

Lo, L. (2006). Suburban housing and indoor shopping: The production of the contemporary Chinese landscape in Toronto. In W. Li (Ed.), *From urban enclave to ethnic suburb: New American communities in Pacific Rim countries* (pp. 119–133). Honolulu: University of Hawai'i Press.

Lo, L., Preston, V., Anisef, P., Basu, R., & Wang, S. (2015). *Social infrastructure and vulnerability in the suburbs.* Toronto: University of Toronto Press.

Logan, J. R. (2003). Ethnic diversity grows, neighborhood integration lags. In A. Berube, B. Katz, & R. E. Lang (Eds.), *Redefining urban and suburban America: Evidence from Census 2000* (pp. 211–234). Washington, DC: Brookings Institution Press.

Logan, J. R., Zhang, W., & Alba, R. D. (2002). Immigrant enclaves and ethnic communities in New York and Los Angeles. *American Sociological Review, 67*(2), 299–322.

Louie, V. (2001). Parents' aspirations and investment: The role of social class in the educational experiences of 1.5- and second-generation Chinese Americans. *Harvard Educational Review, 71*(3), 438–475.

Loukaitou-Sideris, A. (1996). Cracks in the city: Addressing the constraints and potentials of urban design. *Journal of Urban Design, 1*(1), 91–103.

Loukaitou-Sideris, A. (2012). Addressing the challenges of urban landscapes: Normative goals for urban design. *Journal of Urban Design, 17*(4), 467–484.

Low, S. (2004). *Behind the gates: Life, security, and the pursuit of happiness in fortress America.* New York: Routledge.

Lowe, L. (1996). *Immigrant acts: On Asian American cultural politics.* Durham, NC: Duke University Press.

Lowell, B. L. (2000). *H-1B temporary workers: Estimating the population* (Working Paper). Washington, DC: Georgetown University Center for Comparative Immigration Studies.

Loyd, J., Toxey, A., Farrell, R., Yee, E. & Cohen, P. (2000, Fall). Mission San Jose District. A geographic profile of Fremont, California. Prepared for Department of Geography, University of California, Berkeley. Retrieved on November 1, 2011, from http://oldweb.geog.berkeley.edu/ProjectsResources/CommunityProfiles/FremontProject/WebPages/MissionSanJose.html

Lucy, W. H., & Phillips, D. L. (2000). *Confronting suburban decline: Strategic planning for metropolitan renewal.* Washington, DC: Island Press.

Lukes, T. J., & Okihiro, G. Y. (1985). *Japanese legacy: Farming and community life in California's Santa Clara Valley.* Cupertino: California History Center & Foundation.

Lung-Amam, W. (2013a). "Dumb White kids" and "Asian nerds": Race and ethnic relations in Silicon Valley suburban schools. In J. Hou (Ed.), *Transcultural cities: Border-crossing and placemaking* (pp. 117–190). London: Routledge.

Lung-Amam, W. (2013b). That "monster house" is my home: The social and cultural politics of design reviews and regulations. *Journal of Urban Design, 18*(2), 220–241.

Lung-Amam, W. (2015). Malls of meaning: Building Asian America in Silicon Valley suburbia. *Journal of American Ethnic History, 34*(2), 18–53.

Lydon, M., & Garcia, A. (2015). *Tactical urbanism: Short-term action for long-term change.* Washington, DC: Island Press.

Lyons, C. (1996, November 21). Milpitas Square draws 10,000 for grand opening under rainy skies. *Milpitas Post.*

Ma, A. (2013). The changing face of the San Francisco Japantown: A western addition story. *Clio's Scroll: The Berkeley Undergraduate History Journal, 15*(1), 44–57.

Ma, E. A. (2014). *Hometown Chinatown: A history of Oakland's Chinese community, 1852–1995.* New York: Routledge.

Maeda, D. J. (2005). Black panthers, red guards, and Chinamen: Constructing Asian American identity through performing blackness, 1969–1972. *American Quarterly, 57*(4), 1079–1103.

Mahler, S. J. (1995). *Salvadorans in suburbia: symbiosis and conflict.* Boston: Allyn and Bacon.

Majury, N. (1994). Signs of the times: Kerrisdale, a neighborhood in transition. *Canadian Geographer, 38*(3), 265–269.

Malone, M. S. (1985). *The big score: The billion dollar story of Silicon Valley.* New York: Doubleday.

Marcuse, P. (2009). Spatial justice: Derivative but causal of social injustice. *Spatial Justice, 1*(4), 1–6.

Marech, R. (2002, May 17). Little Asia: Fremont community largely made up of immigrants with means. *San Francisco Chronicle.*

Massey, D. S. (Ed.). (2008). *New faces in new places: The changing geography of American immigration.* New York: Russell Sage Foundation.

Massey, D. S., & Denton, N. A. (1993). *American apartheid: Segregation and the making of the underclass.* Cambridge, MA: Harvard University Press.

Matloff, N. (2003). On the need for reform of the H-1B non-immigrant work visa in computer-related occupations. *University of Michigan Journal of Law Reform, 36,* 815.

Matthews, G. (2003). *Silicon Valley, women, and the California dream: Gender, class, and opportunity in the twentieth century.* Stanford, CA: Stanford University Press.

Mayorga-Gallo, S. (2014). *Behind the white picket fence: Power and privilege in a multiethnic neighborhood.* Chapel Hill: University of North Carolina Press.

McCloud, J. (1987, October 26–November 8). Fremont chases upscale retail. *Northern California Retail Journal,* p. 9.

McKenzie, E. (1994). *Privatopia: Homeowner associations and the rise of residential private government.* New Haven, CT: Yale University Press.

McKibben, C. (2011). *Racial beachhead: Diversity and democracy in a military town.* Stanford, CA: Stanford University Press.

McManus, R., & Ethington, P. J. (2007). Suburbs in transition: New approaches to suburban history. *Urban History, 34*(2), 317–337.

McMillen, D. P. (2006). Teardowns: Costs, benefits, and public policy. *Land Lines, 18*(3), 1–5.

Mercer, J. (1988). New faces on the block: Asian Canadians. *Canadian Geographer, 32,* 360–362.

Mitchell, D. (2000). *Cultural geography: A critical introduction.* Malden, MA: Blackwell.

Mitchell, D. (2003). *The right to the city: Social justice and the fight for public space.* New York: Guilford.

Mitchell, K. (1997). Conflicting geographies of democracy and the public sphere in Vancouver BC. *Transactions of the Institute of British Geographers, 22*(2), 162–179.

Mitchell, K. (1998). Fast capital, race, modernity, and the monster house. In R. M. George (Ed.), *Burning down the house: Recycling domesticity* (pp. 187–214). Boulder, CO: Westview.

Mozingo, L. A. (2011). *Pastoral capitalism: A history of suburban corporate landscapes.* Cambridge, MA: MIT Press.

Nahm, H. Y. (n.d.). Great Asian shopping centers & supermarkets. *Goldsea Asian American Parenting.* Retrieved on November 1, 2011 from http://www.goldsea .com/Parenting/Malls/malls.html

Nasar, J. L., Evans-Cowley, J. S., & Mantero, V. (2007). McMansions: The extent and regulation of super-sized houses. *Journal of Urban Design, 12*(3), 339–358.

Nasar, J. L., & Stamps, A. E., III. (2009). Infill McMansions: Style and the psychophysics of size. *Journal of Environmental Psychology, 29*(1), 110–123.

Nassauer, J. I. (1995). Messy ecosystems, orderly frames. *Landscape Journal, 14*(2), 161–170.

National Trust for Historic Preservation. (2008, March). Advocacy for alternatives to teardowns. *Teardowns Resources Guide.* Retrieved from www.Preservation Nation.org/teardowns/

Naz8 Cinemas. (2009, March 29). Retrieved from http://naz8.com/

Newman, K. S. (1993). *Declining fortunes: The withering of the American Dream.* New York: Basic Books.

Ng, J. C., Lee, S. S., & Pak, Y. K. (2007). Contesting the model minority and perpetual foreigner stereotypes: A critical review of literature on Asian Americans in education. *Review of Research in Education, 31*(1), 95–130.

Ngai, M. M. (2014). *Impossible subjects: Illegal aliens and the making of modern America.* Princeton, NJ: Princeton University Press.

Nguyen, B. (2007, May 16). *Anderson Cooper 360 Degrees.* CNN. Retrieved on April 23, 2012 from http://transcripts.cnn.com/TRANSCRIPTS/0705/16/acd.02.html

Nicolaides, B. M. (2002). *My blue heaven: Life and politics in the working-class suburbs of Los Angeles, 1920–1965.* Chicago: University of Chicago Press.

Nicolaides, B. M. (2006). How hell moved from the city to the suburbs: Urban scholars and changing perceptions of authentic community. In T. J. Sugrue &

K. M. Kruse (Eds.), *The new suburban history* (pp. 80–98). Chicago: University of Chicago Press.

Nicolaides, B. M., & Wiese, A. (2006). *The suburb reader*. New York: Routledge.

Nicolaides, B. M., & Wiese, A. (2016). *The suburb reader* (2nd Ed.). New York: Routledge.

Nicolaides, B. M., & Zarsadiaz, J. (2015, November 5). Design assimilation in suburbia Asian Americans, built landscapes, and suburban advantage in Los Angeles's San Gabriel Valley since 1970. *Journal of Urban History*. doi:10.1177/0096144215610773

Niedt, C. (Ed.). (2013). *Social justice in diverse suburbs: History, politics, and prospects*. Philadelphia: Temple University Press.

Noguchi, S. (2009, January 4). High grades, high stress for Asian-American students in bay area. *San Jose Mercury News*.

Nusser, S. P., & Anacker, K. B. (2013). What sexuality is this place? Building a framework for evaluating sexualized space: The case of Kansas City, Missouri. *Journal of Urban Affairs, 35*(2), 173–193.

Ochoa, G. L. (2013). *Academic profiling: Latinos, Asian Americans, and the achievement gap*. Minneapolis: University of Minnesota Press.

Ogbar, J. O. G. (2001). Yellow power: The formation of Asian-American nationalism in the age of black power, 1966–1975. *Souls, 3*(3), 29–38.

Oliver, M. L., & Shapiro, T. M. (2006). *Black wealth, white wealth: A new perspective on racial inequality*. New York: Taylor & Francis.

O'Mara, M. P. (2005). *Cities of knowledge: Cold War science and the search for the next Silicon Valley*. Princeton, NJ: Princeton University Press.

O'Mara, M. P. (2006). Uncover the city in the suburb: Cold War politics, scientific elites, and high-tech spaces. In T. J. Sugrue & K. M. Kruse (Eds.), *The new suburban history* (pp. 57–79). Chicago: University of Chicago Press.

Ong, A. (1999). *Flexible citizenship: The cultural logics of transnationality*. Durham, NC: Duke University Press.

Ong, A. (2003). Techno migrants in the network economy. In U. Beck, N. Sznaider, & R. Winter (Eds.), *Global America? The cultural consequences of globalization* (pp. 153–173). Liverpool: Liverpool University Press.

Oral History Associates, & Mission Peak Heritage Foundation. (1989). *City Of Fremont: The first thirty years, history of growth*. Fremont, CA: Mission Peak Heritage Foundation.

Orfield, G. (2001). *Schools more separate: Consequences of a decade of resegregation*. Cambridge, MA: Civil Rights Project, Harvard University.

Orfield, M. (1997). *Metropolitics: A regional agenda for community and stability*. Washington, DC: Brookings Institution Press.

Orfield, M., & Luce, T. F. (2013). America's racially diverse suburbs: Opportunities and challenges. *Housing Policy Debate, 23*(2), 395–430.

Park, E. J. (1993). *Asian Americans in Silicon Valley: Race and ethnicity in the postindustrial economy*. Unpublished PhD dissertation, University of California, Berkeley.

Park, E. J., & Li, W. (2006). Asian Americans in Silicon Valley: High-technology industry development and community transformation. In W. Li (Ed.), *From urban enclave to ethnic suburb: New Asian communities in Pacific Rim countries* (pp. 74–94). Honolulu: University of Hawai'i Press.

Park, J. J., & Liu, A. (2014). Interest convergence or divergence? A critical race analysis of Asian Americans, meritocracy, and critical mass in the affirmative action debate. *Journal of Higher Education, 85*(1), 36–64.

Pastor, M. J. (2001). Geography and opportunity. In N. J. Smelser, W. J. Wilson, & F. Mitchell (Eds.), *America becoming: Racial trends and their consequences* (Vol. 1, pp. 435–468). Washington, DC: National Academies Press.

Patrick L. (2006, December 4). Review of 99 Ranch Market. Posted to and retrieved from http://www.yelp.com/biz/99-ranch-market-richmond

Pattillo-McCoy, M. (2013). *Black picket fences: Privilege and peril among the Black middle class.* Chicago: University of Chicago Press.

Pearce, R. R. (2006). Effects of cultural and social structural factors on the achievement of White and Chinese American students at school transition points. *American Educational Research Journal, 43*(1), 75–101.

Pellow, D. N., & Park, L. S.-H. (2002). *The Silicon Valley of dreams: Environmental injustice, immigrant workers, and the high-tech global economy.* New York: New York University Press.

Peri, G., Shih, K., & Sparber, C. (2014). Foreign scientists and engineers and economic growth. *Cato Papers on Public Policy, 3*, 107–184.

Pew Research Center. (2013). *The rise of Asian Americans.* Washington, DC: Pew Research Center.

Pitti, S. J. (2003). *The devil in Silicon Valley: Northern California, race, and Mexican Americans.* Princeton, NJ: Princeton University Press.

Powell, J. (1999). Race, poverty, and urban sprawl: Access to opportunities through regional strategies. *Forum for Social Economics, 28*(2), 1–20.

Preserve Mission Ranch (2007, February 23). Home page. Retrieved on July 15, 2011, from http://home.comcast.net/~missionranch/

Preston, V., & Lo, L. (2000). "Asian theme" malls in suburban Toronto: Land use conflict in Richmond Hill. *Canadian Geographer, 44*(2), 182–190.

Qadeer, M. A. (1997). Pluralistic planning for multicultural cities: The Canadian practice. *Journal of the American Planning Association, 63*(4), 481–494.

Qadeer, M. A. (1998). *Ethnic malls and plazas: Chinese commercial developments in Scarborough, Ontario.* Toronto: Joint Centre of Excellence for Research on Immigration and Settlement.

Ray, B. K., Halseth, G., & Johnson, B. (1997). The changing "face" of the suburbs: Issues of ethnicity and residential change in suburban Vancouver. *International Journal of Urban and Regional Research, 21*(1), 75–99.

Reang, P., & Akizuki, D. (2000, February 25). Changes rock district: Parents to fight school ruling. *San Jose Mercury News.*

Retzloff, T. (2015). Gay organizing in the "desert of suburbia" of metropolitan Detroit. In J. Archer, P. J. P. Sandul, & K. Solomonson (Eds.), *Making suburbia:*

New histories of everyday America (pp. 51–62). Minneapolis: University of Minnesota Press.

Rhomberg, C. (2004). *No there there: Race, class, and political community in Oakland.* Los Angeles: University of California Press.

Richards, S. (2000). *Silicon Valley: Sand dreams & silicon orchards.* Carlsbad, CA: Heritage Media Corp.

Robles, R. (2013). *Asian Americans and the shifting politics of race: The dismantling of affirmative action at an elite public high school.* New York: Routledge.

Rockstroh, D. (1999, January 17). Imbalance in Fremont Schools; Panel's advice: Boundary changes, year round classes. *San Jose Mercury News.*

Rogers, E. M., & Larsen, J. K. (1986). *Silicon Valley fever: Growth of high-technology culture.* New York: Basic Books.

Rojas, J. (2003). The enacted environment: Examining the streets and yards of East Los Angeles. In C. Wilson & P. E. Groth (Eds.), *Everyday America: Cultural landscape studies after J. B. Jackson* (pp. 255–275). Berkeley: University of California Press.

Rose, J. (2001). Contexts of interpretation: Assessing immigrant reception in Richmond, Canada. *Canadian Geographer, 45*(4), 474–493.

Rosen, H. (1978). The typical club is typical of Mission. *Smoke Signal, 12*(7), 1.

Roth, B. J., & Allard, S. W. (2015). The response of the nonprofit safety net to rising suburban poverty. In K. B. Anacker (Ed.), *The new American suburb: Poverty, race and the economic crisis* (pp. 247–284). Farnham, UK: Ashgate.

Ruffin, H. G. (2009). Sunnyhills race and working class politics in postwar Silicon Valley, 1945–1968. *Journal of the West, 48*(4), 113–123.

Ruffin, H. G. (2014). *Uninvited neighbors: African Americans in Silicon Valley, 1769–1990.* Norman: University of Oklahoma Press.

Saito, L. T. (1998). *Race and politics: Asian Americans, Latinos, and Whites in a Los Angeles suburb.* Urbana: University of Illinois Press.

Sanchez, C. (2004a, November 3). Children of immigrants seek to define their identity. Radio broadcast, National Public Radio, Morning Edition.

Sanchez, C. (2004b, November 29). Immigrants weigh splitting from California school system. Radio broadcast, National Public Radio, Morning Edition.

Sánchez, G. J. (2004). "What's good for Boyle Heights is good for the Jews": Creating multiracialism on the eastside during the 1950s. *American Quarterly, 56*(3), 633–661.

Sandercock, L. (2000). When strangers become neighbours: Managing cities of difference. *Planning Theory & Practice, 1*(1), 13–30.

Sandercock, L. (2003). *Cosmopolis II: Mongrel cities of the 21st century.* London: Continuum.

Saxenian, A. (1985). Silicon Valley and Route 128: Regional prototypes or historic exceptions. In M. Castells (Ed.), *High technology, space, and society* (Vol. 28, Urban Affairs Annual Reviews, pp. 81–105). Beverly Hills, CA: Sage.

Saxenian, A. (1994). *Regional advantage: Culture and competition in Silicon Valley and Route 128.* Cambridge, MA: Harvard University Press.

Saxenian, A. (1999). *Silicon Valley's skilled immigrants: Generating jobs and wealth for California* (No. 21). San Francisco: Public Policy Institute of California.

Saxenian, A. (2006). *The new argonauts: Regional advantage in a global economy.* Cambridge, MA: Harvard University Press.

Saxenian, A., Motoyama, Y., & Quan, X. (2002). *Local and global networks of immigrant professionals in Silicon Valley.* San Francisco: Public Policy Institute of California.

Schafran, A. (2009). Outside endopolis: Notes from Contra Costa County. *Critical Planning, 16*(1), 10–33.

Schafran, A. (2012, June). Urban field notes: Exploring the cities of the Carquinez. *The Urbanist,* (514).

Schein, R. H. (2006). *Landscape and race in the United States.* New York: Routledge.

Seaton, C. T. (2014). *Hippie homesteaders: Arts, crafts, music and living on the land in West Virginia.* Morgantown: West Virginia University Press.

Segall, E. (2011, June 3). The Globe Mall in Fremont is ready for new start. *Silicon Valley Business Journal.*

Self, R. O. (2003). *American Babylon: Race and the struggle for postwar Oakland.* Princeton, NJ: Princeton University Press.

Self, R. O. (2006). Prelude to the tax revolt: The politics of the "tax dollar" in postwar California. In T. J. Sugrue & K. M. Kruse (Eds.), *The new suburban history* (pp. 145–160). Chicago: University of Chicago Press.

Shankar, S. (2008). *Desi land: Teen culture, class, and success in Silicon Valley.* Durham, NC: Duke University Press.

Shaw, S. J. (2011). Marketing ethnoscapes as spaces of consumption: 'Banglatown—London's Curry Capital.' *Journal of Town and City Management, 1*(4), 381–395.

Short, J. R., Hanlon, B., & Vicino, T. J. (2007). The decline of inner suburbs: The new suburban gothic in the United States. *Geography Compass, 1*(3), 641–656.

Sies, M. C. (1997). Paradise retained: An analysis of persistence in planned, exclusive suburbs, 1880–1980. *Planning Perspectives, 12*(2), 165–191.

Singer, A. (2004). The rise of new immigrant gateways. In A. Berube, B. Katz, & R. E. Lang (Eds.), *Redefining urban and suburban America: Evidence from Census 2000* (pp. 155–180). Washington, DC: Brookings Institution Press.

Singer, A., Hardwick, S. W., & Brettell, C. B. (2009). *Twenty-first century gateways: Immigrant incorporation in suburban America.* Washington, DC: Brookings Institution Press.

Skop, E. (2002). *Saffron suburbs: Indian immigrant community formation in metropolitan Phoenix.* Unpublished PhD dissertation, University of Arizona, Department of Geography, Tucson.

Skop, E. (2012). *The immigration and settlement of Asian Indians in Phoenix: Ethnic pride vs. racial discrimination in the suburbs.* Lewiston, NY: Edwin Mellen.

Skop, E., & Li, W. (2005). Asians in America's suburbs: Patterns and consequences of settlement. *Geographical Review, 95*(2), 167–188.

Smith, C., & Logan, J. (2006). Flushing 2000: Geographic explorations in Asian New York. In W. Li (Ed.), *From urban enclave to ethnic suburb: New Asian communities in Pacific Rim countries*. Honolulu: University of Hawai'i Press.

Smith, R. (2010). *The prince of Silicon Valley: Frank Quattrone and the dot-com bubble*. New York: St. Martin's.

Smith, S. (1959). The rural-urban fringe problem: Common characteristic of areas of rural-urban transitions is disorganization of economic, political, and social processes. *California Agriculture, 13*(2), 2–2.

Smith, T., Sonnenfeld, D. A., & Pellow, D. N. (2006). *Challenging the chip: Labor rights and environmental justice in the global electronics industry*. Philadelphia: Temple University Press.

Soja, E. W. (1989). *Postmodern geographies: The reassertion of space in critical social theory*. London: Verso.

Soja, E. W. (2000). *Postmetropolis critical studies of cities and regions*. Oxford, UK: Blackwell.

Soja, E. W. (2010). *Seeking spatial justice*. Minneapolis: University of Minnesota Press.

Somashekhar, S. (2003, September 6). Mission San Jose kicks off its football resurrection: 2002 varsity season cancelled because of lack of size, experience. *TriValley Herald*.

South Bay Chinese Club. (n.d.). Retrieved August 30, 2016, from http://www.southbaychineseclub.org/

Southworth, M. (2003). New Urbanism and the American metropolis. *Built Environment, 29*(3), 210–226.

Squires, G. D., & Kubrin, C. E. (2005). Privileged places: Race, uneven development and the geography of opportunity in urban America. *Urban Studies, 42*(1), 47–68.

Staff Report. (2000, September 14). Board rejects Fremont schools' split. *San Francisco Chronicle*.

Staff Writers. (1974). Mission grades get average test scores. *Smoke Signal, 21*(7), 1.

Stocking, B. (1999, April 15). Cupertino adjusts to influence of immigrants: Reconciliation of old, new still emotional debate. *San Jose Mercury News*, p. A1.

Straus, E. E. (2014). *Death of a suburban dream: Race and schools in Compton, California*. Philadelphia: University of Pennsylvania Press.

Sue, D. W., Bucceri, J., Lin, A. I., Nadal, K. L., & Torino, G. C. (2007). Racial microaggressions and the Asian American experience. *Cultural Diversity & Ethnic Minority Psychology, 13*(1), 72–81.

Sugrue, T. J. (1996). *The origins of the urban crisis: Race and inequality in postwar Detroit*. Princeton, NJ: Princeton University Press.

Szold, T. S. (2005). Mansionization and its discontents: Planners and the challenge of regulating monster homes. *Journal of the American Planning Association, 71*(2), 189–202.

Tachieva, G. (2010). *Sprawl repair manual*. Washington, DC: Island Press.

Takaki, R. (2012). *Strangers from a different shore: A history of Asian Americans*. New York: First Back Bay.

Talen, E. (2008). *Design for diversity: Exploring socially mixed neighborhoods.* Oxford, UK: Elsevier.

Thomas, J. (1989). City profile: Fremont. *Northern California Real Estate Journal, 3*(21), 11.

Tobias, M. (1985). *Deep ecology.* San Francisco: Pfeiffer.

Trounstine, P. J., & Christensen, T. (1982). *Movers and shakers: The study of community power.* New York: St. Martin's.

Vallejo, J. (2012). *Barrios to burbs: The making of the Mexican American middle class.* Stanford, CA: Stanford University Press.

Vance, J. E. (1964). *Geography and urban evolution in the San Francisco Bay Area.* Berkeley: Institute of Governmental Studies, University of California.

Vergara, B. (2008). *Pinoy capital: The Filipino nation in Daly City.* Philadelphia: Temple University Press.

Vicino, T. (2008). *Transforming race and class in suburbia: Decline in metropolitan Baltimore.* New York: Palgrave Macmillan.

Vicino, T. J. (2012). *Suburban crossroads: The fight for local control of immigration policy.* Lanham, MD: Lexington Books.

Viloria, T. (1996, February 16). County sues Fremont developer over creek cleanup. *San Jose Mercury News,* p. 1b.

Wadhwa, V. (2009). Tapping talent in a global economy: A reverse brain drain. *Issues in Science and Technology, 25*(3), 45–52.

Wadhwa, V., Saxenian, A., Rissing, B. A., & Gereffi, G. (2007). *America's new immigrant entrepreneurs: Part I.* Durham, NC, and Berkeley: Duke University, Master of Engineering Management Program, and University of California, Berkeley, School of Information.

Waldie, D. J. (2005). *Holy land: A suburban memoir.* New York: Norton.

Walker, R., & Lewis, R. D. (2001). Beyond the crabgrass frontier: Industry and the spread of North American cities, 1850–1950. *Journal of Historical Geography, 27*(1), 3–19.

Wallace, D. (2013, November 29). Triangle's Little India. *Triangle Business Journal.*

Walter, J. (1987, May 14). Colleges: The Smoke Signal looks at the college scene at Mission. *Smoke Signal, 21*(7), 1.

Wang, S. (1999). Chinese commercial activity in the Toronto CMA: New development patterns and impacts. *Canadian Geographer, 43*(1), 19–35.

Waters, J. L. (2005). Transnational family strategies and education in the contemporary Chinese diaspora. *Global Networks, 5*(4), 359–377.

Waters, J. L. (2006). Emergent geographies of international education and social exclusion. *Antipode, 38*(5), 1046–1068.

Watson, S. (2006). *City publics: The (dis)enchantments of urban encounters.* New York: Routledge.

Weinberg, P. J. (2001). Monster homes: How big a house is too much? *Zoning and Planning Law Report, 24*(17), 17–21.

Weiss, M. A. (2002). *The rise of the community builders: The American real estate industry and urban land planning.* Frederick, MD: Beard Books.

Wells, A. S., & Crain, R. L. (1997). *Stepping over the color line: African-American students in White suburban schools.* New Haven, CT: Yale University Press.

Wiese, A. (2004). *Places of their own: African American suburbanization in the twentieth century.* Chicago: University of Chicago Press.

Williams, J. C. (1998). Frederick E. Terman and the rise of Silicon Valley. *International Journal of Technology Management, 16*(8), 751–760.

Williamson, J. (2013). *Designing suburban futures: New models from build a better burb.* Washington, DC: Island Press.

Wilson, J. H., & Singer, A. (2011). *Immigrants in 2010 metropolitan America: A decade of change* (Report paper). Washington, DC: Brookings Institution Press.

Wilson, W. J. (1987). *The truly disadvantaged: The inner city, the underclass, and public policy.* Chicago: University of Chicago Press.

Wong, B. P. (1998). *Ethnicity and entrepreneurship: The new Chinese immigrants in the San Francisco Bay area.* Upper Saddle River, NJ: Allyn and Bacon.

Wong, B. P. (2005). *The Chinese in Silicon Valley: Globalization, social networks, and ethnic identity.* Lanham, MD: Rowman & Littlefield.

Wong, C. (n.d.). New mall puts Milpitas on the map: APA developer offers one-stop shopping. *Bay News.*

Wong, L., & Netting, N. (1992). Business immigration to Canada: Social impact and racism. In V. Satzewich (Ed.), *Deconstructing a nation: Immigration, multiculturalism and racism in '90s Canada* (pp. 93–121). Halifax, Nova Scotia: Fernwood.

Wood, J. (2006). Making America at Eden Center. In W. Li (Ed.), *From urban enclave to ethnic suburb: New Asian communities in Pacific Rim countries* (pp. 23–40). Honolulu: University of Hawai'i Press.

Yibada. (n.d.). Retrieved on October 10, 2010, from http://www.en.yibada.com

Young, I. M. (1990). *Justice and the politics of difference.* Princeton, NJ: Princeton University Press.

Youngdahl, J. (2009, March 18). A round of applause for Fremont, USA; A new documentary details the hard but admirable work of getting along. *East Bay Express.*

Zhang, L. (2010). *In search of paradise: Middle-class living in a Chinese metropolis.* Ithaca, NY: Cornell University Press.

Zhou, M. (1992). *Chinatown: The socioeconomic potential of an urban enclave.* Philadelphia: Temple University Press.

Zhou, M. (2000). Social capital in Chinatown: The role of community-based organizations and families in the adaptation of the younger generation. In M. Zhou & J. V. Gatewood (Eds.), *Contemporary Asian America: A multidisciplinary reader* (315–335). New York: New York University Press.

Zhou, M. (2004). Are Asian Americans becoming "White?" *Contexts, 3*(1), 29–37.

Zhou, M. (2008). The ethnic system of supplementary education: Non-profit and for-profit institutions in Los Angeles' Chinese immigrant community. In M. Shinn & H. Yoshikawa (Eds.), *Toward positive youth development: Transforming schools and community programs* (pp. 229–251). Oxford: Oxford University Press.

Zhou, M. (2009). *Contemporary Chinese America: Immigration, ethnicity, and community transformation.* Philadelphia: Temple University Press.

Zhou, M., & Kim, S. (2006). Community forces, social capital, and educational achievement: The case of supplementary education in the Chinese and Korean immigrant communities. *Harvard Educational Review, 76*(1), 1–29.

Zhou, M., & Li, X.-Y. (2003). Ethnic language schools and the development of supplementary education in the immigrant Chinese community in the United States. *New Directions for Youth Development, 2003*(100), 57–73.

Zhou, M., & Logan, J. R. (1991). In and out of Chinatown: Residential mobility and segregation of New York City's Chinese. *Social Forces, 70*(2), 387–407.

Zillow (n.d.). Retrieved June 15, 2016 from Zillow.com

Zukin, S. (1996). *The cultures of cities.* Cambridge, MA: Wiley-Blackwell.

INDEX

Asian malls *(continued)*
109; covenants, codes, and restrictions
(CC&Rs), 118–19, 120; criticism of, 114;
as cultural and community meeting
grounds, 109–12; definition of, 99;
design and development control of, 123;
desirable retail and, 123–24; developers
on Asian malls, 121–22, 126–27, 128;
diversity and, 130, 131; "double-
consciousness," 107; *East 38*, 106; ethnic
orientation of the anchor store, 107–8;
familial bonds and, 111; "fear" of,
122–23; Feng, Tommy, on, 122; Fong,
Joe, on, 113; food, 108–9, 110; form,
location, and management of, 100–101;
*Fremont Market Analysis and Retail
Strategy*, 117, 127, 129, 134; Fremont
Times Square, 104, 119, 119*fig.*; hours
and management, 102–3; importance of,
134–35; introduction to, 98–100; Little
Taipei, 46, 98, 99*fig.*; Lo, Tony, on, 101;
Luk, John, on, 103, 111; Marina Foods,
120; Milpitas Square shopping center,
101, 102, 104, 110, 111–12; multicultural
ideologies, 114–15; multicultural
rhetoric, 115; Nahm, H. Y., on, 110, 111;
99 Ranch, 1, 101, 107, 108*fig.*, 110, 202n4;
Ong, Aiwah, on, 112, 113; Pacific East
Mall, 102; Pacific Mall, 102; as places
both special and mundane, 103–5;
political participation and, 104; as
problem spaces, 100, 115–123; public
scrutiny and regulation of, 100; race
and, 124; as racialized space, 136; as
racially exclusionary, 116; retail
condominiums, 101–2, 116–18, 122;
retail condominiums, new regulations
concerning, 118–19, 120; review
process for, 118; rhetoric of
multiculturalism, 129; San Gabriel
Square, 101, 112; Schwob, Jeff, on, 120,
122, 131; signage, 116; significance of,
99–100; social geographies and, 99; as
spaces of comfort and acceptance,
105–7; as spaces of hybridity and
experimentation, 107–9; special
occasions and, 104–5; Su, Philip, on,
101, 106–7, 109, 112; subdivision of

space, 102; Thomas Consultants on, 116;
vs. traditional American suburban
shopping centers, 135–36; translocal and
transnational connections, 112–14;
Tri-City Beat on, 115; Tsui, Angela, on,
117, 125; Walker, Mary, on, 111; Wang,
Charles, on, 102, 103, 104, 120–21; Wei,
Denise, 110; youth magazines, 113; Zeng,
Debbie, 109–10. *See also* Globe Mall
Asian overflow, 85–87; from Fremont, 85;
intraracial divides between native-born
Asian Americans and Asian
immigrants, 85–86; Livermore, 85;
Pleasanton, 85; racial segregation, 85,
200n68; Tindo, Natalie, on, 85–86;
Xu, Maureen, on, 86
*Assessment of Asian-Themed Retail: City of
Fremont*, 116, 120, 129, 130
Avalon gated community, 46, 47*fig.*,
206n27

Baker, George, 151
"bamboo ceiling," 51
"barbell economy," 37
Barnett, Susan, 88
Berkeley Bowl, 128
Blackwell, Roger, 109, 111
Briggs, Xavier de Sousa, 18
Brooks, Charlotte, 31
Bruegmann, Robert, 139

Cai, Walter, 110–11
California's five highest-ranking public
schools, 53, 198n2
Chadbourne elementary school, 144
chain migrations, 66
Chan, Dan, 113
Chan, Dan and Elaine, 56
Chan, Suzanne, 130, 133, 168
Chang, Shenglin, 107, 110, 158
change as an inescapable urban
condition, 182
Chans, David, 20, 21
Chans, David and Elaine, 19–20
Chen, Paul, 138, 148–49
Cheng, Wendy, on Asian Americans in
San Gabriel Valley, 96
Chinese Americans, 50

identities, 76; for African American and Latino students, 74–75; Chinese versus Taiwanese, 74; Cho, Ellie, on, 78; class divides, 77; Farr, Anamarie, on, 75–76; Frank, Maxine, on, 76; income and academic achievement, 77; Indian Americans, 74; Jones, Paula, on, 77; Kao, Jennifer, on, 75; label for immigrants, 74; Mitchell, Alice, on, 76; Park, Sally, on, 76–77; Phillips, Sam, on, 77–78; race, class, and academic performance, intersection between, 76–77; racial and ethnic divisions, 74–75; racial and ethnic identity, 74; racial divide, 75–76; reverse racism, 75–76; *Smoke Signal* survey on ethnicity, 74; student stereotypes, 75, 78; Walker, Mary, on, 74

ethnoburbs, 5, 198n110

euphemisms for racial segregation, 173

exam systems in Asia, 65

exclusionary zoning, 11, 30, 144

Facebook, 186

Fair Housing Act (1968), 30, 195n40

Farr, Anamarie, 75–76

"fear" of Asian malls, 122–23

fences, 166

Feng, Tommy, 122

feng shui, 158

Filipino Americans, 38

Filipinos, 37, 38, 196n61

Fong, Joe, 113

Fong, Melony, 72

Forbes magazine on Mission San Jose, 59

Forest Park Elementary, 57

form-based codes, 179

Foucault, Michel, 9

Frank, Maxine, 76

Fred E. Weibel Elementary School, 87–88

Fremont: academic culture and practices in, 16–17; advantages to locating in, 39; Ardenwood neighborhood, 57; Asian American community and cultural infrastructure, 41; Asian American income, 46; Asian immigrants and, 40; Asian malls, use of, 124; Asian overflow, 85; *Assessment of Asian-Themed Retail: City of Fremont*, 116, 120, 129, 130; Avalon neighborhood, 46, 47*fig.*, 206n27; Berkeley Bowl, 128; Central Business District, 129–130; Chan, Suzanne, on, 130; Cho, Steve, on, 131; city officials on Asian malls, 122–23; class picture from the Irvington Grammar School's eighth-grade class, 25; comparison of Fremont's racial composition, foreign-born population, and median household income to the San Francisco-Oakland-San Jose Metropolitan Statistical Area between 1960 and 2010, 37*table*; "cosmoburb," 46; diversity and, 128–29, 130, 131; *Downtown Community Plan and Design Guidelines*, 130; Dutra, Dominic, on, 131; education, 56; elders practicing tai chi, 2*fig.*; faith institutions, 34; "fear" of Asian malls, 122–23; Feng, Tommy, on, 122; Fremont Economic Development Department, 116; *Fremont Market Analysis and Retail Strategy*, 117, 127, 129, 134; Fremont School Board and the politics of school boundaries, 87; Fujiwara, Yoshio, 34; General Motors (GM), 29–30, 195n38; General Motors (GM) auto plant, 29*fig.*; General Plan of, 124–25; Glenmoor Gardens, 30, 143–44, 147, 164; "greenfield McMansionization," 146, 206n29; Gurdwara Sahib, 3; Hendricks, Mark, on, 47; high-tech businesses in, 39; Hu, Timothy, on, 45–46; immigrant succession, importance of, 45; immigration and racial integration, 176; incorporation, 27; Indian Americans, 40–41; Irvington neighborhood, 2; Jones, Paula, on, 28; Lake Elizabeth, 2; Lang, Robert, on, 46; LeFurgy, Jennifer, on, 46; Li, Andrew, 32; Li, David, on, 32–34; Li, Diana, on, 126; as "Little Taipei" and "Little India," 46; location of, 1; Luk, John, on, 126, 127; map of, xii; McMansions, 138, 139, 172; Mission Ranch, 30, 143–44, 146–47, 147*fig.*, 164; Morrison, Mayor Gus, on, 39; Natarajan, Anu, on, 131–32; Niles